PROFESSIONAL SERVICES MARKETING

HOW THE BEST FIRMS
BUILD PREMIER BRANDS,
THRIVING LEAD GENERATION ENGINES,
AND CULTURES OF
BUSINESS DEVELOPMENT SUCCESS

MIKE SCHULTZ
JOHN E. DOERR

WILEY

John Wiley & Sons, Inc.

Published by John Wiley & Sons, Inc., Hoboken, New Jersey.

Published simultaneously in Canada.

For general information on our other products and services or for technical support, please contact our Customer Care Department within the United States at (800) 762-2974, outside the United States at (317) 572-3993 or fax (317) 572-4002.

Wiley also publishes its books in a variety of electronic formats. Some content that appears in print may not be available in electronic books. For more information about Wiley products, visit our web site at www.wiley.com.

Library of Congress Cataloging-in-Publication Data:

Schultz, Mike, 1974–
    Professional services marketing : how the best firms build premiere brands, thriving lead generation engines, and cultures of business development success / Mike Schultz & John Doerr.
        p. cm.
    Includes bibliographical references and index.
    ISBN 978-0-470-43899-2 (cloth : acid-free paper)
    1. Service industries–Marketing. 2. Branding (Marketing) 3. Marketing. I. Doerr, John. II. Title.
    HD9980.5.S38 2009
    658.8–dc22   2009007398

Printed in the United States of America

10 9 8 7 6 5 4 3 2 1

To my dad, Stan Schultz, the father every son wants.

—MES

To the memory of my dad, Joseph Doerr. His time was too short, but it sure was full.

—JED

Contents

Acknowledgments   *vii*

Introduction   *xv*

1 What Marketing Can Do for a Firm   1

2 Marketing Planning   17

3 Keys to Building a Terrible Marketing Strategy   33

4 The Seven Levers of Lead Generation and Marketing Planning   39

5 How to Think about Fees and Pricing   53

6 Don't Worry about Your Competition
(Let Them Worry about You)   69

7 The "Get It Done" Culture   79

8 Brand—What It Is; Why Bother   93

9 Three Elements of Well-Crafted Brand Messaging   105

10 Uncovering Your Key Brand Attributes   121

11 Your Firm, Your Brand   139

12 RAMP Up Your Brand   153

13 On Being Unique and Other Bad Marketing Advice   163

14 Building Brand and Marketing Messages   177

15 On Becoming a Thought Leader   195

16 Marketing Communications and Lead Generation Tactics   211

17 Introduction to Lead Generation   249

18 Value and Offers in Lead Generation   257

19 The Case for Sustained Lead Generation and Relationship
Nurturing   265

20 Targeting   279

21 RAIN Selling   289

22 Networking, Relationships, Trust, and Value   301

23 Selling with Hustle, Passion, and Intensity   313

About Wellesley Hills Group   321

About RainToday.com   323

About the Authors   325

Index   327

Acknowledgments

We'd first like to acknowledge our colleagues at the Wellesley Hills Group and RainToday.com who kept the train running while we took the time to write this book: Rachel Hayes, Bob Croston, Mark Fortune, Bob Van Emburgh, Patrick Cahill, Sandy O'Dell, Erica Stritch, Mary Flaherty, Laurie Stafinski, Aaron Joslow, Kelly Kerr, Karina Duran, Terese Riordan, Jae-ann Rock, and Sue Brisson, all of whom work with hustle, passion, and intensity (HPI). Thanks as well to our extended team who worked with us on the research we've cited in the book and on the book itself: Mark Eisner, Andrea Rosal, and Scott Whipple. We'd also like to thank Michael Sheehan, Michael May, Edmond Russ, Paul Dunay, and Kevin McMurdo, who generously gave their time to lend their thoughts and experiences to the content of the book.

To our valued clients, we thank you for the privilege of working with you and accepting us as members of your team. To the contributors, members, and readers of RainToday.com, we appreciate your support, content, questions, and interactions with us through the years.

We'd like to thank leading bloggers, thinkers, and writers who, over the past several years, have influenced our thoughts about marketing, sales, and business, including the following bloggers:

Tom Asacker	A Clear Eye	www.acleareye.com
John Hill	A Daily Dose of Architecture	archidose.blogspot.com
Bruce MacEwen	Adam Smith Esq.	bmacewen.com/blog
Adrants	Adrants	adrants.com
Chris Crain	Advertising Age	adage.com/index.php

David Wolfe	Ageless Marketing	agelessmarketing.typepad.com
Al Nye	Al Nye The Lawyer Guy	www.alnyethelawyerguy.com
Gerry Riskin	Amazing Firms, Amazing Practices	gerryriskin.com
Amy Campbell	Amy Campbell's Web Log	blogs.law.harvard.edu/amy
Chad Horenfeldt	Anything Goes Marketing	anythinggoesmarketing.blogspot.com/index.html
Brian Carroll	B2B Lead Generation Blog	blog.startwithalead.com
Tom Varjan	Bald Dog Barking Board	bald_dog.blogspot.com
Barbara Walters Price	Barbara Walter's Price's Marketing U	bwprice.blogs.com/marketingu
Bob Bly	Bob Bly Copywriter	bly.com/blog
John Moore	Brand Autopsy	brandautopsy.typepad.com
Chris Brown	Branding & Marketing	brandandmarket.com
Derrick Daye	Branding Strategy Insider	www.brandingstrategyinsider.com
Brian Solis	Brian Solis	briansolis.com
Richard Carufel	Bulldog Reporter's Daily Dog	bulldogreporter.com/dailydog
Paul Dunay	Buzz Marketing for Technology	buzzmarketingfortech.blogspot.com
Chris Brogan	Chris Brogan	chrisbrogan.com
Ben McConnell & Jackie Huba	Church of the Customer	www.churchofthecustomer.com
Scott Howard	Collective Wisdom	scloho.net
Valeria Maltoni	Conversation Agent	conversationagent.com
CopyBlogger	CopyBlogger	copyblogger.com
Stephen Seckler	Counsel to Counsel	www.counseltocounsel.com/blog.html
Rick Telberg	CPA Trendlines	cpatrendlines.com
Sam Decker	Decker Marketing	decker.typepad.com
Drew McLellan	Drew's Marketing Minute	drewsmarketingminute.com

John Jantsch	Duct Tape Marketing	ducttapemarketing.com/weblog.php
Karen Axelton	Entrepreneur.com Daily Dose	entrepreneur.com/blog
Karen E. Klein	Financially InKleined	kareneklein.blogspot.com
Stephen D.Levitt & Stephen J. Dubner	Freakonomics	freakonomics.com/blog
Michelle Golden	Golden Practices	goldenmarketing.typepad.com
Michael McLaughlin	Guerrilla Consulting	guerrillaconsulting.typepad.com
Guy Kawasaki	How to Change the World	blog.guykawasaki.com
Patrick Lamb	In Search of Perfect Client Service	patrickjlamb.com
Rohit Bhargava	Influential Marketing Blog	rohitbhargava.typepad.com
Julie Power	Internet Marketing Report Online	eimr.blogspot.com
Joseph Jaffe	Jaffe Juice	www.jaffejuice.com
Jim Calloway	Jim Calloway's Law Practice	jimcalloway.typepad.com
Johnnie Moore	Johnnie Moore	johnniemoore.com
Ed Poll	Law Biz Blog	lawbizblog.com
Larry Bodine	LawMarketing Blog	blog.larrybodine.com
Joshua Fruchter	LawyerCasting	lawyercasting.com
Jim Hassett	Legal Business Development	adverselling.typepad.com
Allison Shields	Legal Ease Blog	legalease.blogs.com
Phil Gerbyshak	Make It Great	philgerbyshak.com
Danny Flamberg	Manhattan Marketing Maven	manhattanmarketingmaven.blogs.com
Alain Thys & Stefan Kolle	Marketing & Strategy Innovation	blog.futurelab.net
Ardath Albee	Marketing Interactions	marketinginteractions.typepad.com
Ilise Benun & Peleg Top	Marketing Mentor	marketingmixblog.com
Andy Beal	Marketing Pilgrim	marketingpilgrim.com
Angela Natividad	Marketing Vox	marketingvox.com

Michael Daehn	Marketinggenius Blog	marketingenious.com
Jon Miller	Modern B2B Marketing	blog.marketo.com
Carolyn Elefant	MyShingle	myshingle.com
Keith Ferrazzi	Never Eat Alone	nevereatalone.typepad.com
Jim Horton	Online PR	online-pr.blogspot.com
Phil Gomes	Phil Gomes	philgomes.com/blog
Rita Keller	Possibilties for CPA Firm Leaders	cpamanagement.blogspot.com
Todd Defren	PR Squared	pr-squared.com
Robyn Levin	R. Levin Marketing Group	robynlevin.com
Francine McKenna	re: The Auditors	retheauditors.com
Robert Ambrogi	Robert Ambrogi's LawSites	legaline.com/lawsites.html
Bob Sullivan	Sales & Marketing Effectiveness	infogrow.typepad.com/sales_ marketing_effective
James Obermayer	Sales Lead Management Association	blog.salesleadmgmtassn.com
KoMarketing Associates	Search Engine Marketing Blog	komarketingassociates.com/ blog
Jill Konrath	Selling to Big Companies	sellingtobigcompanies.blogs .com
Seth Godin	Seth Godin's Blog	sethgodin.typepad.com
Steve Rucinski	Small Business CEO	smbceo.com
Anita Campbell	Small Business Trends	smallbiztrends.com
Jay Lipe	Smart Marketing	jaylipe.typepad.com
Jeff Moore	Solo Accountant Reporter	jemoore.typepad.com
Matt Dickman	Techno Marketer	technomarketer.typepad.com
Robert Millard	The Adventure of Strategy	www.robmillard.com
Suzanne Lowe	The Expertise Marketplace	expertisemarketing.typepad .com
Enrico Schaefer	The Greatest American Lawyer	greatestamericanlawyer.typepad .com
Steve Gershik	The Innovative Marketer	theinnovativemarketer.blogs .com

Thomas E. Kane	The Legal Marketing Blog	legalmarketingblog.com
Bruce Marcus	The Marcus Letter	marcusletter.com
Marcia Yudkin	The Marketing Minute	yudkin.com/marksynd.htm
David Bilinsky	Thoughtful Legal Management	thoughtfullaw.com
Tom Peters	Tom Peters!	tompeters.com
Charlie Green	Trust Matters	trustedadvisor.com/trustmatters
Steve Miller	Two Hat Marketing	www.twohatmarketing.com
Ed Kless	Verasage Community Section	verasage.com/index.php/ community
David Meerman Scott	Web Ink Now	www.webinknow.com
Dave Crouch	Website Solutions Blog	ten24web.com/header/ website-solutions-blog
B.L. Ochman	What's Next Blog	whatsnextblog.com
Ashby Jones	WSJ Law Blog	blogs.wsj.com/law

We'd like to acknowledge the RainToday.com authors, who help us bring the best marketing and sales advice to the professional services world, including:

Contributing editors: Charles H. Green*, C.J. Hayden, Jill Konrath*, Bruce W. Marcus*, Michael W. McLaughlin*, Vickie K. Sullivan, and Alan Weiss.

Authors: Tim Adams, Felipe Aguiar, Jason Alba, Ardath Albee, Dave Alexander, Paige Arnof-Fenn, Ron Baker, Elise Bauer, Robbie Baxter, Ilise Benun*, Barbara Bix, Catherine Blake, Bob Bly*, Larry Bodine*, Annette Boyle, Laurie Brown, Scott Buresh, Mark Burton, Marcie Callan, George Calys, Jim Camp, Joan Capelin, Brian Carroll*, Ken Carson, Jim Cathcart, Michelangelo Celli, Lyn Chamberlin, Paul Cherry, Scottie Claiborne, Michelle Class, Cynthia Coldren, Paul Collins, Karen Compton, Charlie Cook, Mike Cook, Kimberly Cooley, Stephanie Craft, Gale Crosley, Michael Cucka, Fiona Czerniawska, Virginia Daffron, Doug Davidoff, Mark Dembo, Kevin Dervin, ArLyne Diamond, Brian Dietmeyer, Hugh Duffy, Jill Eastman, Kevin Eikenberry, Jonathan Farrington, Brad Farris, Neil Fauerbach, Keith Ferrazzi*, Erin Ferree, Colleen Francis, Robert Galford, Amy Gesenhues,

Scott Ginsberg, Paul Gladen, Sally Glick, Mitchell Gooze, Rebecca Gould, Pamela Gordon, Don Gray, Jim Grigsby, Keri Hammond, Ford Harding, Cal Harrison, Todd Hendries, Elizabeth Henry, Greg Heydel, Casey Hibbard, Dr. Reed K. Holden, Sara Holtz, Bob Howard, Dianna Huff, Dick Jacques, Jay Jaffe, Dave Jakielo, Linda Jenkins, Catherine Jewell, Ron Karr, Kimberly Kayler, Ashley Kizzire, Ed Kless*, Jonathan Kranz, Sheryl Kravitz, Art Kuesel, Susan Wylie Lanfray, Terri Langhans, Brent Larlee, David A. Lax, Marsha Leest, Mel Lester, Mark Levy, Don Linder, Jay Lipe*, Ken Lizotte, Pam Lontos, Phil Lotane, Richard Lozano, Sharon Machrone, Eliot Madow, Barry Maher, David Maister, Kathy Maixner, Larry Mandelberg, Steve Markman, Bob Martel, Nancy Martinez, Harry Max, Matthew May, Paul McCord, Patrick McEvoy, Patrick McKenna, Maureen McNamara, Nilofer Merchant, Todd Miechiels, Robert Millard*, Nicholas Miller, Barry Moltz, Robert Moment, Gwen Moran, Tiffany Mura, Glenn Murray, Harriet Nezer, Ernest Nicastro, Lyne Noella, Tim Noworyta, James Oberymayer*, Julia O'Connor, Sandy O'Dell, Erica Olsen, Lisa Ordell, Abhay Padgaonkar, Michelle Palmer, Roger Parker, Roger C. Parker, Chris Perrino, Barnes Dennig, Promise Phelon, Tom Pick, Dick Pirrozollo, Michael Platt, Ed Poll*, Michael Port, Elge Premeau, Janet Ellen Raasch, Sridhar Ramanathan, Lydia Ramsey, Carey Ransom, Lauren Rikleen, Kelley Robertson, Andrea Rosal, Alan Rosenspan, Dan Safford, Mark Satterfield, Anne Scarlett, James Schakenbach, Ilene Schwartz, David Meerman Scott*, Jeff Scurry, Stephen Seckler*, Randy Shattuck, Alan Sharpe, E. Michael Shays, Idora Silver, Rick Sloboda, Ron Smith, Tom Snyder, Andrew Sobel, Michael Stelzner, Doug Stern, Ruth P. Stevens, Jeff Thull, Nick Usborne, Mike Van Horn, Tom Varjan*, Michelle Wacek, Steve Walmsley, Wendy Ward, Steve Waterhouse, Michael Webb, Wendy Weiss, Richard Weylman, Richard White, Ruth Winett, Eva Wisnik, Jeff Wolf, and Mark Zweig. (NOTE: Authors with an asterisk after their names are also noted previously in the list of bloggers.)

We are also grateful to Matt Holt, Executive Editor at John Wiley & Sons, who shared our vision for this book from the outset. Our thanks also go to Daniel Ambrosio and Jessica Campilango, who helped us keep on target through the editing process, and to everyone else at Wiley who helped see this book to its final form.

—Mike Schultz and John Doerr

The task of writing a book is more than just the act of writing. The true work goes on behind the scenes as you draw upon your family, friends, and colleagues to support, encourage, and often put up with you as you drive to the finish line. To Chris Mirabile, my wife, my best friend, and my guide through this journey called life, thank you for always believing in me and my dreams. To my sons, John Michael and Andrew, just because you are who you are. To my mom, Gloria Doerr, who has always been my inspiration for staying young by working hard, even when you have done so for 82 years. To my siblings, Jean, Judi, Jennifer, Jodi, and Jim (and *all* their children and grandchildren), thank you for defining family, caring in a very special way, and selecting wonderful people to bring into our family. And, of course, to Mike, co-author and friend, who continues to energize me. I couldn't have done my part without you all.

—John Doerr

Thank you, John, my co-author, partner, and friend. Dan Cohen, thank you for your teaching and support and for being the model of selling with hustle, passion, intensity, and integrity. Steve Lisauskas and Dean Ierardi, for everything you both do and give. Tony Bettencourt for cooking everything up. Nancy Harris, for the love you give and happiness you spread. To my sister Allyson for giving me the front seat at least once or twice a year. Toby, my constant companion.

And to my wife and best friend, Erica Schultz.

—Mike Schultz

Introduction

One of the great things about professional services marketing, and one of the most challenging, is that *everyone* has an opinion. The conflicting advice covers just about every aspect of marketing from big-picture strategy to the most detailed of tactics. Amid all the contradictory advice, all the must-do tactics, all the marketing maxims, and all the horror stories of marketing gone bad are the decisions you have to make about what to do to grow *your* firm. Then, after you have finally sorted through your decisions, you have to make sure you do a good job getting it all done (and avoiding the pitfalls that can trip you up) so marketing can impact the firm's growth like it should. Sorting out what's what is no easy task.

As consultants to professional services firms and researchers in the field, we've spoken with literally thousands of professional service firm leaders over the past few decades. Different as their situations and firms might be, the challenges are similar. We often hear comments such as:

- "We argue about what we're going to do with marketing all the time . . . and then do nothing."
- "Some people believe in marketing and business development, and some people don't. This wreaks havoc on our ability to get on the same page about what we've got to do to grow."
- "It seems like everyone here is a decision maker. This hamstrings our ability to move forward on almost anything worthwhile."
- "Crafting and then establishing a brand message has got to be the most painful and elusive thing we've ever tried to do. Even after all this

time, people don't even agree on what a brand is, never mind what we stand for."

- "We get a lot of advice about how to build a marketing plan, but it doesn't seem to make sense for us. We spend a lot of time on fruitless activities, and then don't know what we're missing and where we have gone wrong."
- "We've put together marketing plans, and we think we've done a good job. But we don't know if they are really good, because, while we always start with a lot of energy, implementation wanes. We just don't get them done."
- "If our senior people could just get more at bats—more cracks at new deals—we would win them; it's just so hard to get in front of the right buyers."
- "Everyone talks a good game like they're going to sell more, but then they don't."
- "We've hired marketing firms to help us, and it just never turns out as well as we hoped it might."
- "I'd never say it publicly, but it's hard to differentiate. So many firms *look* just like us and can *say* the same things we say, even if, in reality, we are quite different."
- "When we're busy, we don't market, because we have no time. Then we come off of projects and wonder where the next project is going to come from. This revenue roller coaster is not a fun ride."
- "We're just too small; we don't have the resources and budget to either generate leads or become well-known in the market."
- "Clients view our work as a commodity and pressure us on fees all the time."
- "We've tried [select tactic]: cold calling, webinars, seminars, podcasts, white papers, primary research, conference exhibiting, sponsorships, direct mail, speaking, referral programs, hiring big-gun business developers, marketing partnerships, branding, advertising, public relations, articles, books, e-mail marketing, search engine marketing, skywriting, telepathy, and so on. And none of them worked."

However, we also hear stories of how firms both large and small have dominated their particular space because of their marketing and branding efforts. They have become thought leaders, implemented lead generation campaigns that filled the pipeline and yielded a flood of business, and built systems and processes to ensure that their success can build on itself.

Success rarely comes easily, though. The professional services firms that succeed with marketing and selling typically have at least one thing in common: They've had failures, usually some whoppers, on their way to becoming the marketing and selling machines that they are.

Our aim in *Professional Services Marketing: How the Best Firms Build Premier Brands, Thriving Lead Generation Engines, and Cultures of Business Development Success* is to help you sort out what's what in both the strategy and the tactics of marketing so you can make the best decisions on what to do and to help you avoid some of the mistakes so common to professional service firm marketing.

Good managers can be described as seeing the forest through the trees. One of our goals in writing this book is to help you manage the entire marketing process. From building marketing strategies and plans to crafting brand and marketing messages, to implementing an ongoing lead generation engine, to supporting the firm's sales efforts—good day-to-day management and decision making mean the difference between marketing success and failure.

If good managers can see the forest through the trees, good leaders are the ones who stand up and shout, "Wrong forest!" when they need to. Firms need to make the right decisions about what to do, what to spend, and how to place key people in the right roles to harness their time and energy. Yet, despite the best of intentions, the alligators sometimes get them. Firms of all shapes and sizes fall into ruts, creating unproductive processes and unproductive internal conversations. Perhaps most important of all, what firms (and the people inside the hallowed firm walls) did *last year* to make them successful isn't necessarily what they need to do *this year*. These are the challenges of leadership.

It's our sincere hope that *Professional Services Marketing* will lend insight that can help you manage *and* lead your marketing and growth efforts.

Before you get started on the journey, here are a few things to keep in mind:

- The first rule of services marketing—a key to revenue and profitability growth—is getting your service right. The more value you deliver, the more satisfied your clients will be. The more satisfied they are, the more likely it is they will stay loyal to your firm and refer other clients to you. This has been well established in research such as *The Service Profit Chain*[1] and *How Clients Buy.*[2] It also makes obvious sense. Get your service right, because the better your firm is able to deliver value to clients, the more marketing will make an impact. You may be saying to yourself, "We're striving all the time to serve our clients at a higher level. Yet, given how good we are right now—today—what should we do to market and sell?" If this is you, you're reading the right book.

- Along with our client work with numerous professional services firms and our experience as services marketing practitioners, this book draws on the primary research we've conducted through our own firm, the Wellesley Hills Group, and our publishing arm, RainToday .com. Our research studies include *How Clients Buy: The Benchmark Report on Professional Services Marketing and Selling from the Client Perspective* (2009), *Benchmark Report on Fees and Pricing in Professional Services* (2008), *What's Working in Lead Generation* (2007), *The Business Impact of Publishing a Book* (2006), and several others. For more information and background on this research, visit www.raintoday.com.

- This book is written for professional services firms of all sizes. Which concepts from the book you use and how you apply them are questions of calibration. Throughout the book we provide examples

---

1. James L. Heskett, Thomas O. Jones, Gary Loveman, W. Earl Sasser, and Leonard A. Schlesinger, "Putting the Service-Profit Chain to Work," *Harvard Business Review*, 72 (March–April 1994): 164–174.
2. Mike Schultz and John Doerr, *How Clients Buy: 2009 Benchmark Report on Professional Services Marketing & Selling from the Client Perspective* (Framingham, MA: RainToday. com, 2009), Figure 3.1, 22, http://www.raintoday.com/howclientsbuy.cfm

from and analysis of firms both large and small. You'll find quotes, case studies, and stories throughout. Specifically for the purposes of this book, we spoke with (and thank) a number of firm leaders, including:

- Mike May, professor at Babson College, former Partner and Co-Vice Chairman at KPMG and former Global Managing Partner of the strategy business at Accenture.
- Kevin McMurdo, Chief Marketing Officer, Perkins Coie.
- Paul Dunay, Global Director of Integrated Marketing, BearingPoint.
- Mike Sheehan, CEO, Hill Holliday.
- Edmond Russ, Chief Marketing Officer, Grant Thornton.

In his book *Blink*,[3] Malcolm Gladwell popularized the concept of "thin slicing." You can think of thin slicing as the ability to discern what's really important about something quickly, often without a lot of information. Who can thin slice? Typically people with years of experience, and many different experiences. Much as some might like a step-by-step primer on how to create and lead a major league marketing and sales engine, there is no substitute for experience, talent, skill, and passion. Many of the components of professional services marketing—from strategy development to crafting marketing messages to connecting with clients and earning their trust—require the right kind of thinking *and* the right kind of experience.

Whether you're the firm leader, marketing leader, sales leader, or individual contributor on the team, with the right thinking plus the right experience you'll be able to make the best decisions as quickly as you should, discern the paths of success from the paths of danger, and be able to reap maximum benefits from your toil. (Whether good thinking plus experience yields the ability to thin slice or just plain competence, who is to say?) While we provide concrete, specific advice and examples throughout the book, our hope in *Professional Services Marketing* is that we influence your thinking. The experience (and hustle, passion, and intensity), you'll have to provide yourself.

---

3. Malcolm Gladwell, *Blink* (New York: Little, Brown, 2005).

We all know that professional services firms used to rely solely on repeat business and referrals to fuel growth. Long as they might for the old days when all the marketing they had to do was hang out a shingle and all the selling they had to do was answer the phone when it rang, those days are gone. The ship has sailed. The parade's gone by. The cheese has moved.

And with this change comes opportunity. All you need to do is take advantage of it.

—Mike Schultz and John Doerr

1

What Marketing Can Do for a Firm

There is no doubt that if marketing were done perfectly, selling, in the actual sense of the word, would be unnecessary.

—Peter Drucker

Question: How does a CEO fix his company's technology problems?
Answer: He yells louder at his information technology manager.

This is an old joke with the tech folks, now gaining popularity in marketing. When new business isn't coming in like it's supposed to, the managing partner (or president or COO) doesn't offer much insight on what to do, but turns up the volume on this one-note message: *Do some marketing!* This can be funny if you aren't (1) the target of the message and the rant that typically accompanies it, (2) desperate for revenue, and (3) frustrated because you know that, no matter how loud the yell, it won't do much to stampede new clients through the door.

Before we "do some marketing," let's explore what it can do for a professional services firm. Effective marketing at a professional services firm produces essentially four measurable outcomes:[1]

---

[1] There are other positive outcomes of marketing, such as increased financial value of the firm for a liquidity event. Depending on the situation, other outcomes may be extremely important and in the spotlight. For the purposes of this book, we'll focus specifically on the first three major outcomes of marketing noted.

1. Conversations with potential buyers.
2. Better odds of winning client engagements.
3. Higher revenue per engagement and client, and higher fees for services.
4. Increased affinity with the actual and potential workforce.

Service firm marketers sometimes bellyache that they don't get the respect they deserve from firm leaders and billable professionals. More often than you might think, it's because they don't deserve the budgets they have and don't produce the business impact that warrants esteem from company leadership. Marketers: Do a better job producing these business outcomes, and you'll find respect, admiration, and robust budgets as you merrily go along. Firm leaders (or you, if you're the leader and the marketer): Demand these outcomes. Get behind initiatives that produce these outcomes. And if you are pitched a course of action that doesn't serve these masters, it's a strong candidate for the cutting-room floor.

Firm leaders and marketers make the best marketing decisions, and implement the best marketing programs, when they keep their eyes on the first three prizes. Throughout the course of this book, we will explore in depth *how* firms employ marketing and selling to achieve these outcomes. Before we do this, it's important to explore *what* marketing can do for firms.

Generate New Conversations with Potential Buyers

Call it lead generation, call it business development, call it the first step in selling, or call it any other name; firms need to create conversations with potential clients before they can make a sale. That might sound basic— because it is. Still, the concept of creating an external conversation, one that can produce a new client and new revenue, too often doesn't find its way into the internal marketing conversations at the firm.

Why? Because for many firms, repeat business and referrals used to be sufficient by themselves to attract new clients and grow revenue. While repeat business and referrals are still *necessary* for firms and are often still the major way service firms fill the front end of the business development pipeline, they are often no longer *sufficient* to sustain current revenue levels or grow the firm.

During the halcyon days of flowing referrals, less competition, and simpler industry dynamics, many professional services firms operated less like businesses and more like country clubs. Answering the phone was pretty much all the lead generation they did. Times certainly have changed.

To examine just how much times had changed, the Wellesley Hills Group and RainToday.com surveyed 231 buyers of professional services across a number of professional services categories. Together, these buyers represented over $1.7 billion of services purchased in the previous year.

In this survey we asked buyers questions in two principal areas:

1. How do you identify and engage discussions with providers of professional services?
2. During your decision-making process, what factors influence your decision to engage (or not engage) a particular provider of professional services?

The results, published in *How Clients Buy: 2009 Benchmark Report on Professional Services Marketing and Selling from the Client Perspective,*[2] included data on the methods buyers use to find potential service providers. (See Figure 1.1.)

Based on our research, we can see that referrals are still the top methods buyers use. Regardless of changing industry dynamics, service businesses remain relationship businesses built on foundations of trust. Service buyers seek referrals from colleagues and other service providers, even when they know they can find providers themselves, because they want to know who their trusted friends and advisors trust. When buyers receive a name from someone they trust, the service provider is the beneficiary of *transferred trust* from the referrer to them.

---

[2] Mike Schultz and John Doerr, *How Clients Buy: 2009 Benchmark Report on Professional Services Marketing & Selling from the Client Perspective* (Framingham, MA: RainToday. com, 2009), Figure 3.1, 22, http://www.raintoday.com/howclientsbuy.cfm

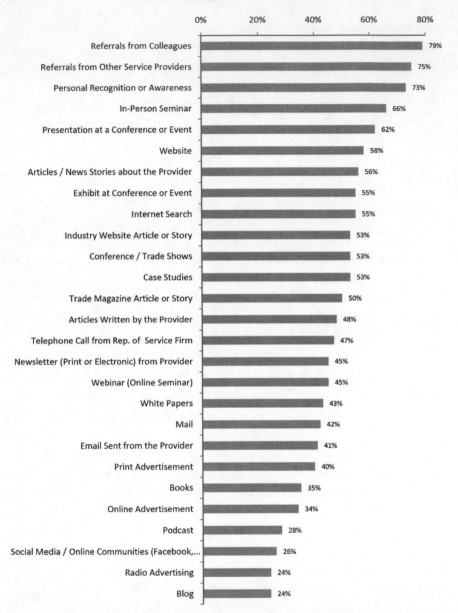

Figure 1.1   Methods Buyers Are Very/Somewhat Likely to Use to Initially Identify and Learn More about Professional Service Providers

For example, let's say Jim is the president of a midsize manufacturing company and he's talking to Mary, his chief operating officer (COO).

Jim: Mary, we've got to get a handle on why we're losing market share to other domestic providers.

Mary: When I was at ManuCorp, Jim, we ran into the same problem. We used Steve Smith and his team at Arch Consulting, and it turned out we were losing share based on three factors, two of which we never even considered. Once we knew what we were dealing with and implemented the turnaround plans we conceived with Steve and his team, we shot back up to number one in 18 months. I can give him a call and see if he can come in to talk to us about it.

Assuming Jim trusts Mary, Steve Smith and Arch Consulting now have a significant advantage in winning an analysis and strategy engagement because of the trust that Mary has *transferred* to Jim through the referral. Transferred trust is the power of the referral and why it's so much easier and quicker for service providers to win business from referrals than with any other method.

Ranking third in our findings—the only other method besides referrals that scored greater than 70 percent—was "personal recognition or awareness" of the provider. This has numerous implications for how firms can use marketing to generate new conversations. In the world of marketing, we have a word for recognition and awareness: *brand*. As a concept, brand is often misunderstood, misapplied, and argued about in professional services firms. That brand is a major factor in your ability to grow a firm is indisputable. (*How* to establish a brand [as well as how one should think about brand at a professional services firm] is the subject of Chapters 8 through 14.)

As we mentioned earlier, referrals and brand are not enough to satisfy most firms' growth desires. The next most popular methods buyers use to find service providers are conference and seminar presentations. This is true for a number of reasons (we cover this in some detail in Chapter 16); but for now, suffice it to say that public speaking can be a very powerful component of generating conversations in the marketplace.

When it comes to speaking engagements, perhaps the greatest challenges are getting them and getting good ones. Who does get them? People with a reputation (aka brand) for being great speakers, who are thought leaders in particular areas, or who are known to be an attendance draw (again, they have a brand). How can one develop said brand aside from leaving it to luck and hope? The best way is smart, focused marketing over an extended period of time.

Even as we move down the list of methods buyers use to identify potential service providers, the methods are still used quite frequently by buyers. Five or six out of every 10 buyers are using providers' web sites and Internet searches, reading news stories both online or in print, visiting conference exhibits, meeting people at conferences, and reading case studies.

Even those methods seemingly lost in the middle or relegated to the bottom of the list, such as "telephone call from rep of service firm" (47 percent very or somewhat likely to use), "mail" (42 percent), and "e-mail sent from provider" (41 percent), can be extremely useful for generating conversations if employed correctly.

"You can't long for the good old days."

—Mike Sheehan, CEO, Hill Holliday

MARKETING'S FOUR MEASURABLE OUTCOMES

Marketing can deliver:

1. New conversations with potential buyers.
2. Better odds of winning client engagements.
3. Higher revenue per engagement and per client, and higher fees for your services.
4. Increased affinity with the actual and potential workforce.

If marketing is not delivering some subset of these outcomes, it's not good marketing.

At first, because so many methods come before those toward the bottom of the list, you might be tempted to dismiss the latter as not worth notice. As a part of the *How Clients Buy* research, we also asked buyers who were likely to attend conference presentations and seminars (two of the top tactics after referral and brand) how they found out about these events. Mail, e-mail, and telephone were among the top ways, with mail still far outpacing the other tactics. In other words, the best ways to get people to your speeches are those tactics that appear at first blush to be less effective, tactics that many professional services industry watchers have for years panned as not worthwhile.

The methods buyers use to find you shown in Figure 1.1 only scratch the surface of how you can use marketing tactics to connect with potential new buyers. Throughout the book, we explore in detail how all firms can and must move beyond referrals, employing specific marketing tactics to reach the many untapped opportunities for creating new conversations.

Improve the Odds of Winning New Client Engagements

Jim is a senior vice president for a supply chain consulting firm. He has 20 years of experience in the industry and is widely regarded by those who know him as a top expert and practitioner in his field. On Monday, his assistant told him that his business development team had set up two prospect meetings (new conversations) for him for the week, one on Tuesday and one on Wednesday.

Jim's meeting on Tuesday was with Joyce, the vice president of operations at a large commercial shipping company, and was set up by Audrey, one of his company's top business developers. Here's how the meeting went:

Jim: Nice to meet you, Joyce. I'm glad to be here.
Joyce: Nice to have you here. Over the past several months it's been great getting to know about you and your firm. I've read your white paper on emerging supply chain management technologies as well as listened to you deliver a webinar on strategies for global sourcing in my industry.

Jim: That's great to hear. I hope you enjoyed the presentation. Might I ask how you heard about the webinar?

Joyce: Well, I have been meaning to come to one of your events for a long time, ever since Audrey called me back 11 months ago to introduce you all. She mentioned that she'd put me on your company communication list.

For one reason or another either the events weren't the right timing or they didn't fit my schedule. But I've been getting the event invitations and brochures in the mail along with the research briefings you send out with them. Oh, and your newsletters. So I've followed along.

Now that dealing with supply chain technology is square on the middle of my plate, when Audrey sent me the e-mail to view your on-demand presentation on your capabilities in the area, I put it on my to-do list to call her. Of course, she called me first, so I was more than happy to set up this conversation. I'm ready to dive in with you to see how you might help. . . .

Compare this beginning to Jim's next meeting, on Wednesday with Eric, the vice president of operations at a large steel company set up by Sarah, another business developer at his firm. The meeting kicked off a bit differently:

Jim: Nice to meet you, Eric. I'm glad to be here.

Eric: Good to have you here as well. Now, Sarah's done a good job over the past few years of trying to get in touch with me, so I figured I'd let her persistence pay off and we could, at her request, get together to meet. Supply chain technology is, after all, on my plate these days.

Jim: Great. I'm glad Sarah's done such a good job keeping you up-to-date. I'm assuming you know about our firm and what we do since Sarah must have sent you our newsletter and event invitations. Have you ever attended one of our webinars or seminars?

Eric: Actually, Jim, I don't know anything about you or your firm. You have newsletters and webinars? I'll be sure to check them out in the future. Meanwhile, can you tell me a bit about you, your firm, and your areas of focus?

Jim: Ah, sure. Let's start there, then.

Of course, we'd all rather have the conversations that go like the one with Joyce than the one with Eric. The difference? Company marketing reached Joyce but didn't reach Eric.

"We help our lawyers identify market opportunities, then help them craft and deliver messages that lead them to be recognized as thought leaders, market leaders. In our marketing department, everything we do is designed to create opportunities for meaningful face time between our lawyers and clients or prospects. Legal services buyers make their decisions based on a combination of experience and trust. Face time helps our lawyers pass that chemistry test of trust most clients impose before they hire. We want our prospects to leave those meetings thinking, 'I like these people. I trust these people. I think these lawyers know what they're talking about. If their references turn out to be genuine and honest, let's hire them.' Helping lawyers to prepare for quality face time that leads to relationships and work—that's essential for professional services marketing, in my opinion."

—Kevin McMurdo, Chief Marketing Officer, Perkins Coie

Because Joyce received the company's marketing, she:

- Knew about the company.
- Could articulate how the company helped people like her solve problems like hers.
- Remembered the company during her time of need and planned to call in.
- Felt affinity and preference for the company before ever interacting with an individual from the company personally due to the education she received from company marketing efforts.

To that last point, it's likely that even though Joyce didn't have any history working with the company, she built up a level of affinity for it and

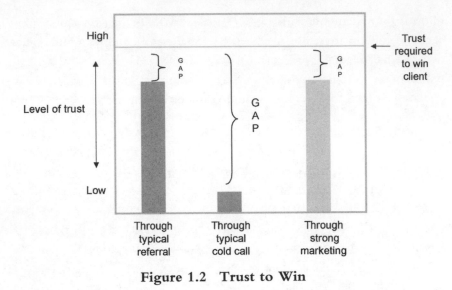

Figure 1.2   Trust to Win

initial trust in it. This is similar to what happens with a referral: trust transferred from the referral giver to the service provider.

Marketing, when done right, can create a similar trust effect. (See Figure 1.2.) Instead of receiving the transferred trust that comes from the referral source, the company builds up the trust itself over time through its marketing activities. Is it the same kind of trust that comes after having worked with a company and having gone through thick and thin for several years? Of course not, but it's enough trust and affinity to make the sales process kick off that much more strongly, go that much more smoothly, and have that much more chance of success.

In our consulting work at Wellesley Hills Group, we consistently hear stories that support this argument. Time and time again, clients report that a white paper download, a newsletter, and a speech they made at a conference have all contributed to their ability to connect more quickly or more deeply with their prospective new clients.

Research supports the argument as well. According to the 2003 CIMS Business Influencer Study, there are 49.7 million technology influencers in the United States alone. Some 3.3 million reside in the management information systems/information technology (MIS/IT) department (7 percent), 11 million are senior management (23 percent), and 34.5 million are departmental heads (70 percent). Of these IT decision makers, 43.8 percent will strongly consider purchasing from a company with high brand recognition. Only 18.6 percent would consider buying from a brand they never heard of.

Higher Revenue and Higher Fees

It can be just as difficult to sell a $5,000 engagement as it is to sell a $50,000 engagement as it is to sell a $500,000 engagement. While the nitty-gritty of that leap might be just a bit off, the essence of the statement is true.

You can grow your firm by adding new clients, or you can increase the size of your deals. What is the average revenue you generate with your clients? Say it is $50,000 per year in revenue to the firm. What can you do to increase that by 20 percent, 80 percent, or even 100 percent?

Marketing plays a role in increasing this average in a number of ways.

Packaging the Services

Marketing your services as a package can increase differentiation, perception of the value of the service, and a client's trust that the service firm will deliver on the promise of the service. Indeed, service packaging can make a significant impact on the average size of client engagements.

At Wellesley Hills Group we have offered marketing planning, marketing message development and implementation, and telephone business development for years. Yet, when we packaged and marketed these services together as Services in Demand^{SM}, the marketplace took that much more notice of the value and distinction of our approach to lead generation, and our own practice picked up substantially. The outcomes for our own firm were higher average client engagement revenue *and* higher client satisfaction (which went hand in hand).

Communicating a Strong Value Proposition

It is marketing's role to highlight the value of a firm or a particular service. Consider a service like "profitability analysis and consulting." You could position its value by stating, for example, "We can analyze the profitability of your divisions by product and service lines and geographic divisions, and give you a report detailing where you can improve your revenue and profit," a reasonably attractive approach.

Or you could position the same service by saying, "We help our clients in manufacturing save hundreds of thousands of dollars. We have accomplished these results for dozens of companies such as Companies A, B, and C through our profitability consulting work," a much stronger and compelling value for potential clients.

Cross-Selling the Entire Firm

Cross-selling is usually a vastly untapped area of opportunity for firms. In our research for Wellesley Hills Group clients, we've asked clients of our clients, "If ABC Consulting (our client) were to offer this service, do you think you might find that valuable?" Time and time again we hear that not only would they find it valuable, but they have already engaged similar services with another firm. In fact, in many cases our client would have been the preferable choice. In just as many cases, our client *already offers the service* but failed to communicate in its marketing efforts to its own clients and to prospects alike that the service already existed.

Establishing and Strengthening Brand

The saying used to be that nobody ever got fired for buying IBM, the point being that the stronger the brand, the less fear, uncertainty, and doubt (FUD) come along with it. The more FUD a buyer has in a company, the less willing it is to take large risks and to spend large dollar amounts on that company. Marketing has the ability to communicate with buyers that its firm (1) exists and (2) can be trusted enough as a service provider that the risk is like buying from IBM.

Marketing can also affect the strength of the fees you can get for your services revenue. In 2008 the Wellesley Hills Group and RainToday.com published a series of *Fees and Pricing Benchmark Reports*[3] for the following industries:

- Consulting
- Marketing, advertising, and public relations (PR)
- Architecture, engineering, and construction
- Law
- Accounting and financial services

Among the findings were nuggets about brand leader firms and the fees they command in, for example, the consulting industry. Brand leaders:

- Priced their services at a higher level than their competitors in the market (42 percent of brand leaders were considered premium-priced versus 28 percent of lesser-known firms).
- Realized higher *actual* hourly rates compared to the lesser-known firms in all categories of professionals. (See Figures 1.3 and 1.4.)

While brand leaders and their "best-kept secret" firm brethren both reported that, on average, their standard or published fees for top-level professionals were $300 per hour (Figure 1.3), the brand leaders reported *realizing* $300 in actual fees at this level (Figure 1.4). In contrast, lesser-known firms reported realizing $250, or 20 percent less than the leading firms. Data across the other professional services industries were largely similar to the consulting industry data.

---

[3] Mike Schultz and John Doerr, *Fees and Pricing Benchmark Report: Consulting Industry 2008* (Framingham, MA: RainToday.com, 2008), http://www.raintoday.com/ feesandpricingreport.cfm

Figure 1.3   Median Hourly Billable Rates for Consulting Industry—Standard/Published, by Brand Reputation

When we ask leaders of strategy consulting firms what companies they consider to be their competition, we hear comments like, "We compete with firms like McKinsey, Bain, Boston Consulting Group, and other major firms, and we charge fees similar to theirs." Of course, the firms mentioned are extremely well-known and respected.

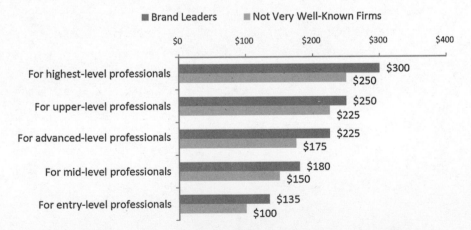

Figure 1.4   Median Hourly Billable Rates for Consulting Industry—Actual/Realized, by Brand Reputation

Upon further investigation, we discover that while this is sometimes true, more often than not the lesser-known firm in reality charges less in fees per hour than the better-known firm and is willing to discount engagements more often than brand leaders to win deals. If given the choice, would they *want* to discount or charge lower fees? No. But they do, largely because if they proposed similar fees, many clients would opt to give the business to the better-known firm—the power of FUD in evidence once again.

We are not so sure we would completely agree with Peter Drucker that marketing can make selling entirely unnecessary. But it surely can make selling easier and the outcomes more successful.

As you continue reading, remember that marketing can deliver four core measurable outcomes:

1. New conversations with potential buyers.
2. Better odds of winning client engagements.
3. Higher revenue per client and per engagement, and higher fees for your services.
4. Increased affinity with the actual and potential workforce.

If marketing is not delivering some subset of these outcomes, it's not good marketing.

2 | Marketing Planning

Plans are nothing; planning is everything.

—Dwight D. Eisenhower

Regulation play in the 1925 U.S. Open ended in a tie between Willie Macfarlane and golf legend Bobby Jones. Their first playoff round also ended in a tie. Jones then lost the Open by one stroke to Macfarlane in the second playoff round.

In the first round of the tournament, on the eleventh hole, Jones's approach shot had slid off the front of the green into the high rough. As his practice swing swept through the grass near his ball, Jones saw the ball had moved. Nobody else saw it. Still, Jones informed his playing partner, Walter Hagen, that the ball had indeed moved, and he assessed himself a penalty stroke.

After the round, folks lauded Jones for adhering to the rules. His response: "You'd as well praise me for not breaking into banks."

Business, like golf, doesn't always go according to plan. When setbacks happen at professional services firms, strong leaders do not look the other way or let themselves off the hook. When profitability flags in a division or practice area, these leaders hold themselves and the team accountable.

Less often, however, do leaders assess themselves penalty strokes when the firm fails to craft or execute a marketing and business development plan

17

that will help the company succeed. Year after year, business leaders at the vast majority of service firms dedicate much blood, sweat, and tears to the delivery of strong client work, recruitment of great people, and investment in technology for the company. Marketing and business development, however, remain the redheaded stepchildren.

We are not saying that service firm leaders should focus any less on client delivery and the strength of their internal teams. After all, the backbone, and the essence, of any service firm is the quality of its people and assets. (See "Competencies and Assets" section in Chapter 11.)

Still, creating and improving the overall concept of the service, communicating the firm's value to the market, and doing it in a way that displays excellence in the strategy and tactics of marketing rarely get the attention they deserve.

It is no longer debatable that strong marketing and business development can have a major impact on the success of the professional service firm (although we still see firms argue long and hard about this very topic). Even in firms that agree that marketing is needed, a chasm lies somewhere between that knowledge and strong marketing plan development and execution. Firms that rarely fail to deliver to clients fail to deliver the best marketing plans that (1) can get implemented and (2) when implemented will make the most positive difference for the firm. This failure is avoidable.

MARKETING PLANS BEFORE BUSINESS PLANS?

A RainToday.com member once posed this question to us:

Many midsize and even larger professional services firms have no business plan. I've had to use the marketing plan to back into a business plan or general direction for the year. I find this is the case more often than not. Do you see this as well? It's almost impossible to get deal makers at all levels (managing partner on down) to take the time and, more important, make the decision on building a business plan, which should then facilitate the marketing strategy.

First things first. Many professional services businesses don't have a formal strategic plan because they don't need one. Why don't they need one? you ask.

Strategy at professional services firms is different from strategy at other types of companies. At many (but certainly not all) professional services firms, strategy boils down to selecting a set of industries to target, services (practice areas) to offer, and geographies to serve. Sometimes you'll also find the requisite smattering of "Let's focus on high-growth markets" or "Let's suspend services that are slowing down or becoming commodities." Brilliant!

Revenue projections are based on arbitrary measures such as the leaders' or owners' desire to make a certain amount of money, percent of delivery capacity (i.e., we have this many people who can bill this much, so we'll make this much money), or simply picked-out-of-the-air percentage growth targets.

General direction for the year, depending on the firm's stage of growth, consists of strengthening the quality of services delivered, improving operational efficiencies, adding the right amount of staff to match historical growth pace, improving marketplace visibility, per-haps offering new services, and here and there something more strategic, like acquiring another business or entering new markets. (And, of course, most firms state the obligatory "we're focusing on our people" strategy messages internally.)

Because these strategies don't always change from year to year, the firms' leaders don't feel compelled to produce written business plans. And if they do, it's in a PowerPoint deck—a short one (or a long one that, if the gods of mercy had smiled upon us, would have been a short one)—and an Excel spreadsheet with projected revenue and costs.

Not having a business plan in a formal sense is neither bad nor good. What's not good is when firms get lazy about trying to be better or more competitive, and about delivering the value they say they deliver to the market, aren't serious about focusing on their people, and retain people who aren't giving their all to the firm's mission and clients.

Business plans do become important if you're looking to raise capital because you need investors, or if you are actually trying something new and bold. Without the need for capital (or the need to satisfy another stakeholder like a board of directors), many services firms don't need formal business plans.

Regardless of whether a business plan exists, marketing can still be the impetus for something interesting or strategic to happen at the company.

Marketing can:

- Be the key to unlocking growth in particular industry segments.
- Change radically your overall ability to generate leads and win new business.
- Create new service packaging and pricing such that revenue, margin, and repeat business increase.
- Force the firm to study its own messages and value propositions, thus creating a stronger shared understanding of the purpose and strengths of the firm.
- Uncover services or industry segments that are stronger prospects for revenue and margin growth than others, and focus firm efforts on these better opportunities.

Even if you don't have a formal business plan, you should have a clear idea before you develop a marketing plan as to where the company expects to or wants to head. Or you can take your best guess and make some assumptions. Either way, your tactical marketing plan must be driven by overall revenue targets and long-term firm growth goals. Set your company's goals, and you can start the marketing plan toward reaching these goals.

With goals in sight, you need to begin with some assumptions for what it will take to hit those goals. It's common for firms to throw down the gauntlet with a big, hairy, audacious goal (BHAG) for revenue growth. But while they might have the eyes for growth, in the end many don't have the stomach. Serious growth usually requires serious investment in both marketing budget and time. Even with proper investment, growth does not happen overnight. The truth about marketing for professional services firms is that success requires patience and persistence to give the investment time to pan out.

A Marketing Planning Process for Services Firms

As you build your marketing plan, address each of the seven planning phases shown in Figure 2.1. This process will help you gain buy-in from each of the necessary stakeholders by involving them in the process and by producing a plan that makes the most sense for your firm.

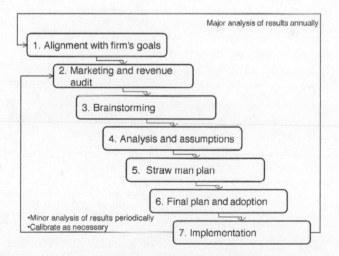

Figure 2.1   Service Firm Marketing Planning Process

© Wellesley Hills Group.

Phase 1: Alignment with Firm's Goals

If you know where the firm is going, you can build a marketing and sales plan to reach that goal. Many a marketing plan has failed to get adopted (or got adopted but didn't get funded when push came to shove) because the marketers wanted to "change the face of marketing" and ramp up activities, only to be told by management, "Thanks for the aggressive plan, but now let's get back to reality." However, many a firm has not reached its growth goal because it did not build a marketing plan that could plausibly build a strong-enough brand and deliver enough leads and new clients to reach the revenue goal.

When considering your growth goals, get all stakeholders together— marketers, leadership, management—and agree on growth goals that are aligned with your overall firm strategy and goals.

The one big question to ask is: What are our revenue and growth goals?

GETTING EVERYONE ON THE SAME PAGE

In our consulting work with services firms, we often see firm leaders who have misaligned goals and don't even know it. As a result, the marketing planning discussions don't progress. How can they, when one partner wants to grow 50 percent and the other is hoping to ease his way into retirement in three years? We have found that asking people to state their goals in terms of revenue and growth percentages tells only half the story. So we ask client leaders to write a complete story about what will happen to the firm over the next two years. If you think you are not on the same page at your firm, conduct the following visioning exercise to find what future everyone sees for the firm.

Ask each person to write a brief newspaper story about how the firm looks two years into the future. Make sure they write their goals as a story with emotion and image, not as a management report. If it helps, as a template you can point them to the *Wall Street Journal* articles that appear in full columns on the front page. To help people get started, you can suggest an opening like this:

Two years after implementing its new marketing and growth plan, [*Your Firm*] had hit all its growth goals. "I remember the first discussions around the plan," [*Your Name*] recounted. "We knew if we wanted to . . . "

Be specific:

- What were those goals?
- How has the firm culture around marketing and business development changed?
- What new clients have you gained?
- What were the obstacles you had to overcome?
- What was your role in this success story?
- Where are you now?

Have each person share his or her story with the leadership team. Are your goals in alignment? Where are you at odds? Use these stories as the backdrop as you go through your marketing planning process.

Phase 2: Marketing and Revenue Audit

Before you can decide how marketing is going to support your growth goals, you need to know the current state of your marketing efforts. You need to know where your clients and revenue came from in previous years so you can plan where it can and will come from in the next year.

Marketing audits can be simple or complex, depending on your situation. A multi-office firm may break the audit down by regions and/or practice areas. A smaller firm can usually put all its information into one audit. In any event, what you need to know is the same no matter your firm's size or complexity.

Menu of questions to ask:

Revenue Audit

1. Where did our revenue come from last year? What divisions? What practices? What services?
2. Did new clients usually begin with one particular service and then migrate elsewhere into the firm?
3. Do different market segments buy different services from us? Which ones? Where are the overlaps and opportunities for cross-selling and marketing?
4. What was the volume of repeat business versus new business?
5. Where did our new business come from (lead sources)?
6. Why did we lose the clients we lost? (And can we be brutally honest with ourselves about this?)
7. Why did we lose the new business opportunities we lost? (Get everyone in the habit of finding out the real answers.)
8. Given the company's growth goals, where will the revenue come from next year? (No one knows this answer for certain. Don't be afraid to take a guess.)

Marketing Audit

1. What is the status of our database?
2. How well are we known in our target markets? How strong is our brand?
3. Does our messaging currently serve us well? Will it serve us well for the areas in which we want to grow?
4. Are we better known for certain offerings, specialties, geographies, or industries than others? Are they what we want to be known for?
5. How have we segmented our markets? How have we performed in the various segments?
6. How well do we sustain our lead generation and marketing efforts?
7. What worked and what didn't last year in our lead generation campaigns? Do we have something that worked well? (Do more.) That didn't work at all? (Stop doing it.) That the jury

is still out about? (Have patience, but know what you are measuring.)

8. Have our target markets shifted in buying patterns or preferences?
9. Has the nature of our competition changed? If so, how?
10. Is our value proposition resonating overall? In specific target areas?
11. Do we have any special marketing assets (white papers, thought pieces, presentations) we can begin to leverage, continue to leverage, or get more out of?
12. Did any specific service launches or initiatives work well or not work as well as they could have? Why? Why not?
13. Do we have any external market data or internal research that will affect how we approach our service offerings, growth potential, or marketing tactics going forward?
14. Is market share important to us? If so, where do we stand? (Note: Market share isn't usually important for service firms. See Maxim 5 in Chapter 13.)
15. What other marketing efforts worked? What didn't work? Did we implement well?

Phase 3: Brainstorming

You should include all stakeholders in any brainstorming process; but in services firms filled with smart people, all of whom will have an opinion on marketing, it is even more critical. At the end of the process you want people to be on board with the plan.

The menu of questions to ask depends on your situation but can include virtually any of the other questions outlined in this chapter. The purpose is to generate ideas and leave no stone unturned that could be a difference maker.

"With professional services firms, investment in marketing seems like a good idea in the beginning of the year. Then, as bonus time approaches, they cut back because the investment comes out of the leaders' pockets. By July they're doing nothing because the senior partners aren't fully bought into the long-term investment in marketing."

—Mike Sheehan, CEO, Hill Holliday

Phase 4: Analysis and Assumptions

After brainstorming, identify where the opportunities truly lie. You have your business objectives. You have ideas. Now generate scenarios of different marketing strategies and paths. Evaluate the pluses and minuses of each path.

Ask yourself what will happen if it works and what won't happen if it doesn't work. Then look at the strategies in aggregate, asking how they will work together (or not) to produce the results you need. Employ heuristics: Switch scenarios around, add and remove budgets and resources, add and remove tactics.

Menu of questions to ask:

1. What is the potential for improvement in our current marketing and sales processes? Why do we think that's the case? What are the details here?
2. If we employed [*insert marketing tactic here*], what effect would that have on our success?
3. If we didn't employ [*insert marketing tactic here*], what wouldn't happen that we want to happen?
4. What would happen if we employed [*insert marketing tactic here*] that works for other firms?
5. What radical, outside-the-norm ideas do we have?
6. Where are the best opportunities we can take advantage of?
7. What opportunities look good but, in the end, aren't likely to work because we just won't get them done?
8. What are the most successful firms in our field doing? Should we do something similar? Should we do something different? What aren't they doing that we can do?

9. What are the most successful companies outside of our field doing? Can we apply what they do and thus be innovative in our field?

10. Are our marketing and sales (or business development or rainmaking) processes working together to produce the best results?

11. How long might it take for results to materialize? Based on what assumptions?

12. How will we know if it's working? What do we need to measure? What will be difficult to measure but we still believe is essential?

13. Is there any low-hanging fruit that we can immediately address to either fix glaring problems or get fast results?

> "Not everything that can be counted counts, and not everything that counts can be counted."
>
> —Albert Einstein

Phase 5: Straw Man Plan

Put together the highlights of a plan, including all parts relevant to your business—growth goals, tactics, budget, competitive analysis, responsibilities, expected outcomes, time frames, and so on. It could be one page, or it could be thirty. This will depend on your need for detail; complexity of the organization (i.e., number of service lines, geographies, industry specialties, nature of competition, etc.); and organizational expectations. Take care, however, to be able to summarize it all in a page or two, or on a slide or two. You must have something to look at so you can say, "All together, this is what we're up to. Everything else is just the detail of how we'll get it all done."

Your straw man plan should include an analysis of the budget and expectations of outcomes. From here, you can make adjustments, see what happens with different scenarios, and get feedback from important stakeholders.

DON'T SPARE THE STRAW MAN

A straw man is an argument (or person or document) that serves as a stand-in to be picked at, knocked down, and eventually replaced by a final version. As you put forth your straw man plan, give explicit instructions to your colleagues to poke holes in it. The final plan will be that much stronger for it; and when you roll out the final plan, your ability to defend it will be stronger as well.

Phase 6: Final Plan and Adoption

Put forth a final plan, and gain commitments you need for budget and resources. Roll the plan out to important stakeholders within the company and communicate with all who will have a role in the plan implementation.

Menu of questions to ask:

1. Are we prepared to implement this plan?
2. Are we prepared to implement it well?
3. Finally, and possibly most important, does everyone agree that we want to press on to reach our revenue goal (even though we might have stated it earlier), and do we have commitment (not just compliance or lip-service agreement) from the leadership and our team to do whatever they can to help us get there?

REAL COMMITMENT OR JUST GOOD INTENTIONS?

One law firm invites us to their office annually to help them get marketing moving at the firm. Each year, they agree, "This is the year we make it happen!" The partners get excited. The team rallies around going to market more aggressively. Then, each year, the managing partner states at the eleventh hour, "I don't believe in marketing. Let's get started slowly. How about a letter to a few dozen companies we'd like to work with?" Three years later that letter is yet to be mailed. We keep talking to them out of curiosity, waiting to see if something changes. So far, it hasn't happened.

Phase 7: Implementation

As you implement, make sure you are constantly looking to evaluate better alternatives, to alter the plan to chase successes and discontinue fruitless efforts, and to take advantage of opportunities that may arise during the year.

The entire planning process often takes two weeks to three months, depending on any number of factors. It can take longer if your firm is very large and you're constantly building and refining marketing plans; but it shouldn't take longer because of organizational barriers, indecisiveness, or lack of energy and effort. Try to keep it as contained as possible.

Keep in mind that these seven phases are not always mutually exclusive. For example, you may get a revenue goal from the company (phase 1), devise a revenue growth scenario (phase 5), and then go back to phase 2 and move forward from there. Your company may not announce a revenue goal until December 15 (or it may never announce one), but you might need to assume one in November so you can build the plan and recalibrate it when the actual number comes out.

It's also quite possible that marketing plans can drive the revenue goal. Perhaps through your brainstorming and planning, you build a plausible scenario that can add significantly to revenue. The possibilities for this are more available than most firms think.

If you have multiple divisions and practice areas, you should consider bottom-up budgeting and planning. Let the strategic business unit (SBU) or practice heads build a plan they can believe in, and then calibrate with them as all plans come in. If you do this, take care to standardize budget and other planning templates so you can easily roll them up.

Two Helpful Tools

We've created two tools to help readers of *Professional Services Marketing* build their marketing plans.

The Budget Planning Tool is a simple Excel spreadsheet built to help you:

- Lay out your marketing tactics so you can see your overall mix.
- Visualize when during the year your firm will employ each marketing tactic.
- Visualize the budget for each tactic.

The Marketing and Sales Funnel Analysis Tool is an Excel spreadsheet built to help you make assumptions with the seven levers described in Chapter 4. With it you can determine how many leads you need to generate and how many you need to close to reach your overall growth goals. The tool allows you to take your current lead generation metrics and see how changes, such as adding more leads, closing more deals from those leads, and changing your client retention rate, will make a difference in revenue generation from year to year.

The tool calculates the five-year revenue implications of increasing your leads, close rates, retention rates, and referral rates. The data are presented in seven helpful charts and graphs.

This tool will help you to:

- Plan your revenue.
- Justify your lead generation budget and efforts.
- Determine where you need to invest your marketing dollars (whether it be sales training, lead generation, customer referral programs, or somewhere else).

- Calculate the lifetime revenue of your customers.
- Establish your metrics (average revenue per customer, close ratios, client loyalty, etc.).
- Forecast return on investment (ROI) for both individual marketing campaigns and your overall marketing plan.
- Create real and meaningful new client-generation goals.

To download these tools, visit www.whillsgroup.com/booktools

3 | Keys to Building a Terrible Marketing Strategy

Man, how can a guy miss what's been right in front of him all this time?

—Bizarro

Over the years we've worked with many professional service firm leaders to build marketing plans that will work well for them. There must, however, be a secret primer out there on how to build terrible marketing strategies for professional services firms. During the past two decades we've come across so many marketing strategies that have failed for similar reasons that we figure everyone must be in the know and we have simply been left out of the loop.

After much research to find the source, the secret codex still eludes us. So, we feel compelled to seize this moment for posterity and codify the process of building terrible marketing strategies.

Here goes:

Build the Strategy from the Top Down

> *Question:* In a ham and eggs breakfast, what's the difference between the
>   pig and the chicken?
> *Answer:* The chicken was compliant, but the pig was committed.

Nothing turns off partners, division leaders, and other leadership types more than being handed a strategy and told to "Make it happen." Force-feed the strategies from on high, and you're likely to get compliance, but rarely commitment. Practice leaders may take the strategy and run with it, perhaps even put a bit of effort and sweat into it, yet they can and frequently do walk away at the first sign of trouble.

Without going through the process of crafting the strategies and tactics themselves—brainstorming possibilities, performing what-if analyses, researching best practices, and backtracking when suggested actions don't seem likely to work—the team's dedication to implementation will be weak.

Once the tactics feel burdensome to implement, or at the first sign that senior management isn't going to hold the team's feet to the fire, implementation grinds to a standstill. Nothing makes a terrible strategy more terrible than one doomed to be ignored or, at best, tolerated by the team members responsible for making it a success.

Don't Consult with Expert Tacticians

Just as devastating as a top-down strategy is a strategy built without input from experts deeply knowledgeable about the underlying marketing and business development tactics. When you identify your specific tactics—even if the tactics are largely decent choices for a successful marketing strategy—without talking with people who have serious, relevant experience, the actual outcome will probably differ from the one you envision.

For example, you might conduct a seminar or webinar and want to fill the room with decision makers, but in reality you generate little or no attendance. Or you manage to generate some attendance, but then you do a poor job of delivering content that will help you connect with potential clients. (Try a hard-sell approach; most decision makers really despise that.) Then you can ruin your follow-up by not doing it, doing it too late, or doing it poorly.

Maybe you set out to support lead generation and client communication with a web site; but you end up with a web site that no one can find, no one can use, is hard on the eyes, provides no value, is not client focused, and generally reflects poorly on your company. You might then employ direct mail for lead generation and generate no response—with no idea why it didn't work, and no way to find out!

Leave out the tactical expertise, and the terrible marketing outcomes you can achieve are endless.

Look Only at Your Own Industry and Competition

If you want your marketing strategy to never reach beyond average, make sure you look only at your own industry and competition.

Let's say your company is an accounting firm. Make sure you look only at what other accounting firms are doing for growth. Ignore law, management consulting, technology, and consumer products companies. This is a great way to miss out on all the newest marketing trends, technologies, and possibilities. Plus, if you look only at your own industry for inspiration, you'll never be a leader. Being late to the game is a great component to a terrible marketing strategy.

Make sure that, when you're studying the competition to see what they're doing, you look only at your direct competitors. Following the accounting example, let's say you're in a 50-person accounting firm outside of New York City. Focus only on other midsize accounting firms. Don't even think about considering what KPMG LLP or PricewaterhouseCoopers are doing, and don't worry much about what the 200-person firm might be up to. They're too big for you to care about, and you don't want to get too much inspiration from companies that have grown well or are larger than you.

Don't Create an Environment of Fervent Execution

Even if you allow your leaders to craft the company and practice area growth plans and if you have the tactical expertise to get things done, by fostering a culture where marketing and business development are second fiddle, you will stay in the land of terrible marketing. A great way to get started here is to set action steps and goals and not hold people accountable to them. Professional services cultures are often good at making nice and not wanting to stir things up when someone isn't pulling their marketing and business development weight.

You might think this is a tactical versus strategic issue. It's not. Company strategists and leaders must make sure the environmental factors that support performance are not in place: Don't set clear expectations or give feedback, don't make tools and resources available, and don't put incentives and consequences in place to guide people's behavior. (Or, dear CIA disinformation operative in training, set incentives that will guide the wrong behaviors. See what that does.)

To end up with the terrible strategy, it's also contingent upon leadership to ensure that the people tasked with executing do not have the skills and knowledge, are not motivated to perform, and are not, indeed, the right people for the job.

Execution must not be made a strategic priority by leadership—if it's not a priority, your marketing strategy has a chance to be not only terrible, but tragic. It's a fantastically terrible and devious marketing strategy that has everything in place that could allow it to succeed, and then fails because no one gets it done. These kinds of good intentions gone bad warm the little black hearts of many a terrible marketing strategist. Brilliant times two!

Don't Plan for Behavioral or Organizational Change

Professional services firms are products of the collective behaviors of the people within them. That's a mouthful; but, in essence, it simply means we are what we do. Marketing strategies are most powerful when they are bold, venture into uncharted territory, are creative and new, and require lots of energy and enthusiasm to be implemented well.

Thus, almost without exception, a marketing strategy's success is contingent on some level of change, be it evolutionary or revolutionary.

Regardless of what you set forth in your plan, if the strategists and leaders aren't bent on making behavioral and organizational change happen, you'll end up with the same thing you had last year and the year before. Doing nothing different than what you have done in the past is sometimes, all by itself, a terrible marketing strategy.

Form a Marketing Committee, Then Take Them to Abilene

A family in Coleman, Texas, was having a nice afternoon playing dominoes outside, when the father-in-law suggested, "Let's take a trip to Abilene for dinner." No one really wanted to go, but they didn't want to seem disagreeable; so they hopped in the non-air-conditioned car and made the two-hour trip to Abilene.

Five hours later the family returned, tired, sticky, cramped from the drive, and recovering from the underwhelming cafeteria meal they had in Abilene. "Wasn't that a great trip," one of them remarked, thinking that everyone else had a good time but her. The mother-in-law then said, "Actually, I didn't really want to go but you all seemed to. I didn't want to spoil everyone's fun, so I didn't say anything." It turned out no one wanted to go, even the father-in-law who suggested the trip, but they all hopped in the car and went to Abilene anyway.[1]

Service firms tend to employ smart people, most of whom like to involve themselves and weigh in on important decisions, such as marketing strategy. Marketing committees form. When these lovely decision-making bodies get nice and big, two things happen.

---

[1] Inspired by Jerry Harvey, *The Abilene Paradox and Other Meditations on Management* (San Francisco: Jossey-Bass, 1988).

First, innovative and interesting ideas get squashed before they can gain momentum. With anything new or visionary, it's difficult to get everyone to agree, and it's easy for people to say no and poke holes in ideas. The tired, less exciting ideas remain on the table.

It's kind of like getting 20 people to agree on the same dinner to eat. So many interesting possibilities get excluded for this reason or that. Everyone ends up with macaroni and cheese and a wedge of iceberg lettuce posing as a salad.

Second, people begin to agree with watered-down and uninspiring ideas because they think other smart people agree with them so they must be okay, they're sick of the ongoing committee discussion, and actions eventually need to be taken. They also know better ideas won't make it very far, so they publicly swallow the pill and declare, "I agree. Let's go!" Privately they think, "This is a terrible idea, but I guess it's where everyone wants to go."

In other words, the committee decides to take the firm to Abilene and doesn't look back, sometimes until they've spent a year and a half on the trip.

What you're hoping for here, if you want your terrible marketing strategy to come out in full force, is to encourage pluralistic ignorance, the phenomenon that occurs when several people in a group disagree with the norm of the group but don't say anything because they think everyone else agrees. Since no one says anything even when they disagree, even if everyone has second thoughts, the room stays silent and the trips to Abilene get spot numero uno on the priority list.

Even marketing strategies that could be good can become terrible marketing strategies if you set your mind to making them so. If you're willing to do what you must to keep innovative ideas off the table, let other companies exploit opportunities in the market faster than you do, and structure your organization to stifle frank discussion, commitment, and execution, you'll be able to come up with the best terrible marketing strategies on the block.

4 | The Seven Levers of Lead Generation and Marketing Planning

Concentrate all your thoughts upon the work at hand. The sun's rays do not burn until brought to a focus.

—Alexander Graham Bell

Over the past several years we've seen a shift in thinking about how marketing dollars are spent at professional services firms. No longer is the quarterly ad spend or the "we have done it every year" trade show getting automatic sign-off. The question asked more and more, and one you should ask about all of your spending on marketing and lead generation, is: "If I spend X on this marketing tactic, what should I expect in return?"

Unfortunately, too much of marketing spending—in both dollars and time—is still wasted in professional services firms. In the same vein as "Who Was the Ad Wizard?" in Chapter 12, if you were to open up your local business journal, without a doubt you would see advertisements for professional services firms (some well-designed, some not so much) aiming to

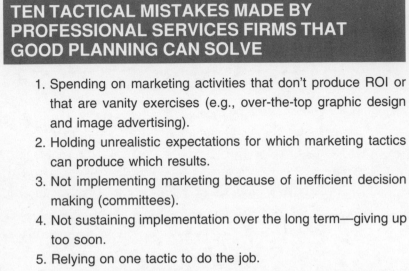

TEN TACTICAL MISTAKES MADE BY PROFESSIONAL SERVICES FIRMS THAT GOOD PLANNING CAN SOLVE

1. Spending on marketing activities that don't produce ROI or that are vanity exercises (e.g., over-the-top graphic design and image advertising).
2. Holding unrealistic expectations for which marketing tactics can produce which results.
3. Not implementing marketing because of inefficient decision making (committees).
4. Not sustaining implementation over the long term—giving up too soon.
5. Relying on one tactic to do the job.
6. Poor implementation (e.g., poorly written marketing copy, poorly designed web sites, or poorly targeted campaigns).
7. Dropping leads and failing to nurture leads.
8. Not communicating value in your marketing.
9. Not integrating the various marketing tactics.
10. Planning poorly for lead generation—all the steps in the process.

"generate awareness." While there is nothing wrong with using marketing to generate awareness or brand, these organizations are generating awareness among tens of thousands of readers who are not likely to be the best targets for their services. The funds to create such an ad and to run it week after week would surely be much better spent on reaching out to the smaller, more targeted pool of, say, 1,600 prospects the firm would actually like as clients. For the most part, spending on ads like this is a waste, as are so many ill-conceived marketing endeavors. Ill-conceived advertising campaigns are, of course, just one example of waste that sneaks into marketing plans and campaigns. It's easy to waste a lot of money in web site development, direct marketing, thought leadership development, business development, public relations, and virtually any other tactic you can think of.

How does any company get rid of this kind of waste, whether it be in marketing or in other parts of the business?

The company focuses on it with keen eyes and manages its business as processes with inputs and outputs. Your marketing and lead generation efforts should be no different.

Make Outcomes Assumptions

You can plan the desired outputs of your efforts using calculations based on what you know about your firm's typical pipeline success. For an example, consider the "Metrics of Services in Demand" chart we use with Wellesley Hills Group clients.

Assume that:

- Your targeting activities yield 2,000 prospective clients with whom you'd like to work.
- Over the course of a year, you implement a lead generation program (this means multiple outreach efforts and campaigns, not just a single effort) that yields 160 leads, or 8 percent of 2,000.
- Of those leads, 30 percent, or 48 prospects, are qualified (i.e., they're the right company and the right person, they have needs, they have the financial ability to buy, etc.).[1]

You close 30 percent of the qualified leads, yielding 14 new clients. Therefore, 9 percent of your initial leads close for this example.[2]

---

[1] In our research, respondents reported that 25 percent of leads were qualified, 25 percent were bad fits, and 50 percent were long-term. From *What's Working in Lead Generation: A Benchmark Report on How to Spend Your Time, Energy, and Money for the Best Marketing ROI in B2B Professional Services* (RainToday.com, 2007).

[2] Note that the numbers in the chart are purely fictional and are not meant to be indicative of typical ratios for business-to-business professional services. Metrics for each industry, company, and service line vary tremendously.

METRICS OF SERVICES IN DEMAND—EXAMPLE 1

| | | | Outputs | |
| | | 8% | 30% | 30% |
Activity	Prospects	Leads	Qualified Opportunities	Clients
Targeting	2,000			
Lead Generation		160		
Business Development and Nurturing			48	
Close				14

Client Data

Average revenue per client per year: $150,000.

Retention of revenue from year to year: 60 percent.

Growth rate[3] per retained client: 5 percent.

> ## YOUR REVENUE RETENTION IS UNIQUE TO YOUR FIRM
>
> What should the revenue retention from current clients be for a professional services firm? That all depends on the nature and type of your service. You might think for an accounting firm that anything less than 90 percent retention would be bad; whereas for a firm that has a turnaround or workout practice, any client retention over zero percent would indicate trouble. As a law firm, you may retain

---

[3] Growth rate per retained client year example: You have a client that spends $100,000 with you in the first year. If you sell on average $120,000 to that client in the second year, regardless of why (e.g., client grows, you sell more services to them, etc.), your growth rate per client per year is 20%.

a client from one year to the next, but revenue might be $100,000 one year when the client company buys another business, and $15,000 another year when all it needs is your review of a few contracts. While your industry may have averages or rules of thumb, your revenue retention target should be unique to your firm.

Given these assumptions, here's what your returns look like:

REVENUE RETURN OVER TIME BASED ON EXAMPLE 1

	Year 1	Year 2	Year 3	Year 4	Total
New revenue	$ 2,100,000				$ 2,100,000
Retained revenue		$ 1,260,000	$ 793,800	$ 500,094	$ 2,553,894
Growth per retained customer		$ 63,000	$ 39,690	$ 25,005	$ 127,695
Revenue added per year	**$2,100,000**	**$1,323,000**	**$833,490**	**$525,099**	**$4,781,589**

It doesn't matter if your budget is $60,000, $1.6 million, $10.6 million, or more. Spending on advertising and marketing with no clear expectations of adding leads to a pipeline (such as outlined earlier) is inefficient at best, and more often just crazy.

Still, it happens. Spending gets a green light all the time because of the wrong reasons:

- Your competitors have big spreads in the trade magazines and business journals: "We need to triple our advertising budget to keep up!"
- Your competitors got mentioned in the *Wall Street Journal* again: "We need a PR retainer fast!"
- You need more leads: "Let's hire a cold caller . . . let's hire a big-gun business developer . . . let's buy search engine ads . . . let's sponsor

the big conference and send everyone to network and bring home some bacon!"

- Your firm finally agrees you need to get serious about marketing: "Let's start with a new tagline, a new logo, new data sheets, and a new web site!"

What does all of this spending get you? Well, it definitely gets you spending. And maybe you get other benefits, too, but probably not what you could be getting if you approach building a marketing, lead generation, and business development engine that will work for you in the right way.

Playing with the Assumptions

Back to our example. Now you have an initial set of overall goals you expect to achieve though your marketing and business development activities. What would happen, though, if you could make incremental improvements to your conversion rates?

Suppose, for example:

- Your target-to-lead ratio moves from 8 percent to 10 percent.
- Your ratio of leads to qualified opportunities moves from 30 percent to 35 percent.
- Your ratio of qualified opportunities to client wins moves from 30 percent to 33 percent.

Your client revenue retention moves from 60 percent to 65 percent. Therefore, 12 percent of your initial leads close for this example.

Client Data
Average revenue per client per year: $150,000.
Retention of revenue from year to year: 65 percent.
Growth rate per retained client: 5 percent.

METRICS OF SERVICES IN DEMAND—EXAMPLE 2

| | | | Outputs | |
| | | 10% | 35% | 33% |
Activity	Prospects	Leads	Qualified Opportunities	Clients
Targeting	2,000			
Lead Generation		200		
Business Development and Nurturing			70	
Close				23

Here's what happens:

- You win 23 clients instead of 14.
- Revenue in the first year is now just under $3.5 million, or about $1.4 million higher than in Example 1.
- The four-year revenue stream from one year of lead generation activities is now $8.5 million, or $3.7 million higher than before.

REVENUE RETURN OVER TIME BASED ON EXAMPLE 2

	Year 1	Year 2	Year 3	Year 4	Total
New revenue	$3,450,000				$3,450,000
Retained revenue		$2,242,500	$1,530,506	$1,044,571	$4,817,577
Growth per retained customer		$112,125	$76,525	$52,229	$240,879
Revenue added per year	**$3,450,000**	**$2,354,625**	**$1,607,031**	**$1,096,800**	**$8,508,456**

First Year	Four-Year Revenue Gain
Was $2.1 million	Was $4.8 million
Now $3.5 million	Now $8.5 million
Grew $1.4 million	Grew $3.7 million

Results have moved up quite a bit as a result of proactive choices you've made to improve how many leads you generate, how many of those leads become qualified opportunities, how often you close new business that's in your pipeline, and how well you do getting those clients to come back for more year after year.

"The marketing department should help local offices understand and identify the importance of targeted marketing. Our offices are located in large metropolitan areas—the population is often in the millions. Yet, our target markets—our collective network of groups and individuals—may only be a few hundred individuals. What people think of as "public" visibility isn't necessarily what we need to achieve in professional services. Creating high visibility among our targets requires a different set of tactics."

—Kevin McMurdo, Chief Marketing Officer, Perkins Coie

You also could have increased:

- Your overall target pool, which, assuming the targets are the same quality as the original set, would have yielded you more leads to move into the pipeline.
- The average size of your deals.
- The annual revenue growth rate per retained client.

Note as well that if you typically get referrals from current clients, every new client you win increases your referral base. From the perspective of the model, this is something you should keep in mind as you factor in how many leads you plan to generate.

Only Seven Levers Matter

Boil it down, and only seven levers matter to increase your revenue:

1. Number and/or quality of targets.
2. Number of overall leads.
3. Number of qualified leads.
4. Number of pipeline opportunities converted to clients.
5. Revenue per client.
6. Revenue retention.
7. Growth rate per client.

Everything you could possibly do in marketing should be viewed through the lens of these levers. You shouldn't pursue any tactic in marketing and business development that doesn't move one of these levers up, or keep one of these levers from falling.

Here are just a few paths you could pursue to move the levers in the right direction. Note that each successive point builds on previous points.

1. Increase the Number and/or Quality of Targets

Preparation
- Create a universal definition of what a good target client is for your company overall, for specific geographies, industries, or functional specialties within your firm (see Chapter 20 on targeting).
- Research the overall universe of good targets for your firm. (Are there 200 of them, 2,000 of them, 200,000? Who are they? Where are they?)

Strategy
- Launch new services to existing clients or existing services to new industries, geographies, or functional areas.
- Launch or package existing services for targets outside of your current target definition (i.e., package services for smaller or larger companies).

Database Population

- Identify companies and people through available list-building sources, such as data compilers, associations, and third-party list sources.
- Identify target companies one by one.
- Identify decision makers, influencers, and referral sources one by one.
- Increase house list with:

  - Stepping-stone service offers and stepping-stone marketing tactics.[4]
  - Conversion of offers through direct outreach (mail, e-mail, telephone); semidirect outreach (speeches, seminars, teleseminars, trade shows); and broad outreach (search engine optimization, search engine advertising, traditional advertising, public relations, social media marketing).

2. Increase the Number of Overall Leads

- Increase your frequency of touches to targets.
- Increase the effectiveness of touches to targets through. You can choose all or a mix of efforts such as:

  - Improve Brand RAMP (recognize, articulate, memorize, prefer; see Chapter 12).
  - Improve message resonance, differentiation, and substantiation in value proposition (see Chapter 9).
  - Increase referrals.
  - Improve lead generation tactic choice, mix, and quality.
  - Test and improve lead generation tactics.
  - Increase lead qualification and conversion through web site and other lead capture mechanisms (e.g., trade shows).

---

[4]Your marketing efforts can be your stepping-stones to building trust with potential clients. For example, a webinar or live seminar can provide value while allowing the prospect to sample what you have to offer. In the same way, a stepping-stone or entry service allows new clients to try you out before they commit to larger engagements.

- Increase and improve use of stepping-stone service offers and marketing-based offers.

- Increase culture of business development and effectiveness of team members in generating leads (see Chapter 7).

3. Increase the Number of Qualified Leads

Preparation
- Create universal definition of qualified lead (see Chapter 20.)

  - Budget/ability to spend.
  - Authority—who?
  - Need—what?
  - Time frame—when?
  - Fit—how?

Improvement
- Improve targeting to generate more qualified versus unqualified leads.
- Improve message resonance, differentiation, and substantiation in your value proposition.
- Improve sales skills to uncover a complete need set, establish relationship and fit, and create urgency (see Chapter 21 on RAIN selling).
- Improve consideration of your firm when a client establishes a short-term time frame to buy through Brand RAMP, lead nurturing, and relationship development.

4. Increase the Number of Qualified Leads Converted to Clients

- Improve message resonance, differentiation, and substantiation in value proposition.
- Improve sales skills to uncover complete need set, establish relationship and fit, create urgency, craft and communicate solutions, negotiate to win engagements, gain commitment, and close deals.

- Improve preference for working with your firm versus other options (brand preference, personal relationships).

5. Increase Revenue per Client

- Improve cross-selling.
- Improve service packaging.
- Improve pricing model.
- Increase ability to generate higher hourly or project fees.
- Improve communication and substantiation of value and impact of engagements.
- Improve deal negotiation.
- Reduce focus on lower-revenue-generating clients (or jettison them completely).

6. Increase Revenue Retention

- Improve perception of service quality.
- Strengthen perception of value of work, team, and company.
- Improve relationships with the right people, right structures, and right processes.
- Increase defense against competitor inroads.

7. Improve Growth Rate per Retained Client

This lever is a combination of levers 5 and 6.

* * *

Each one of the objectives listed for the seven levers could be a part of your path to growing your revenue. But it's a long list, and you can't do everything all at once. Deciding which of the seven levers you need to move and which paths you will take to move those levers aren't easy decisions. And the "how" questions remain.

- How do I increase defenses against competitive inroads?
- How do I segment and target my market?
- How do I improve the effectiveness of my lead generation campaigns?
- How do I engage pretty much anything mentioned in the previous several pages? Where should I start?

These questions and more trip up many a service firm. Consider these questions in the light of resources that you have or that you can garner, the realities of your budget, how long it will take for your efforts to bear fruit, and the opportunity cost of doing one thing versus another. We'll do our best to help you approach answering them throughout the rest of this book.

One final thought for you to consider: Not only do you have to make decisions on where and how to grow revenue, but you also have to know which revenue you don't want. Some markets may have poor growth potential. You don't want to serve industries or deliver services in which you can't produce the highest-quality outputs or that will distract you from your core business model. Not all revenue is profitable; for the most part you don't want to bring in a dollar of revenue that will cost you a dollar and two cents to deliver.

5 | How to Think about Fees and Pricing

Time is but the stream I go a-fishing in.

—Henry David Thoreau

Service providers are faced with two questions when it comes to fees and pricing:

1. What pricing structure should we use?
2. How do we maximize our fees?

How you approach your marketing and brand positioning can and will have a strong influence on how you answer each of these questions.

The Basic Landscape of Pricing Structure

Before we can begin a discussion around marketing and its relationship to your fees, we must first lay out before you the variety of pricing options.

Ultimately, there are three ways in which professional services firms charge clients for their services:

1. Time-based fees, such as hourly, daily, or monthly fees.
2. Fixed fees.
3. Contingent fees, where some or all fees are at risk until certain milestones are reached or goals are achieved.

Just the mention of these three pricing constructs engenders emotional reactions and debate from service providers.

- "I never charge by the hour."
- "I'd never leave any of my fees contingent on any possible outcome."
- "As much as some in my industry say the billable hour is dead, it's what we use most of the time. It doesn't seem dead to me."[1]

PRICING AND PROFIT MAXIMIZATION

Professional services firms are almost always, from a microeconomic perspective, profit-maximizing firms. Their goal, then, is to determine the price and output levels that will maximize profit. Stated a different way, the goal is *not* to grab market share or pursue other objectives at the expense of profit. You might think profit maximizing is a given for any company in any industry, but there are a number of alternative objectives a firm could base its pricing approach on, such as initial market entry, market share maximization, or competitor restriction. This is important as a warning to the profit-maximizing service firm: Many pricing strategies touted for business in general don't support the profit maximization model that service firms need to pay attention to. If you pursue those strategies, do so with your eyes wide open.

---

[1] Direct quotes are from survey participants in our most recent Fees and Pricing Benchmark Report.

In determining prices or fees, your goal is to help the firm reach overall financial goals (assuming, once again, that maximum profit is firmly planted in mind). To do this, the fee and pricing structures need to fit the positioning of the firm and must be set at a level that enough clients will purchase the services so that the firm reaches its goals.

Whereas some of these reactions are based on the rigors of business analysis, many others are pure emotion. Perhaps the firm has had a bad experience as a buyer or a seller because of a particular pricing structure; maybe it offered a contingent fee and did what it was supposed to do but the client didn't, and as a result that big contingent fee never appeared. When something like this happens, emotions can be raw for a long time.

By and large, most firms are clear as to what pricing model to use for their particular situation. From our research on fees and pricing in various segments of professional services firms, we discovered that few find a huge challenge as to which model to use.

Firms that find uncertainty about which pricing model to use extremely or very challenging include:

- Consulting: 34 percent
- Law: 15 percent
- Architecture, engineering, and construction: 14 percent
- Marketing: 13 percent
- Accounting: 12 percent

It is worth noting that consulting firms are at the top of the list. Is it any wonder prospects look askance at fee structures so often? Over one-third of consultants aren't certain about how to set their fees. Are you one of them?

Hourly and Daily Fees

The concept of hourly and daily fees is much maligned across professional services. There's a particular amount of fuss these days about the so-called death of the billable hour. Some consultants to the professional market tout the concept with missionary zeal. Because of its absoluteness, that zeal is largely misplaced. While many professionals could generate more business and profit using other pricing models, there's nothing inherently wrong with the billable hour. In some situations, hourly is likely the best, and sometimes the only, option.

Sorry to rain on the billable hour death parade, but reports of the demise of the billable hour have been greatly exaggerated.

According to our research on fees and pricing, a majority of professional services firms are just as likely to use hourly and daily fees as they are a fixed-fee arrangement. Of course, the rate of usage does vary widely based on the type of professional service.

Percentages of firms that use hourly and/or daily fees "most of the time" or "sometimes":

- Architecture, engineering, and construction: 82 percent
- Law: 76 percent
- Accounting: 59 percent
- Consulting: 55 percent
- Marketing: 51 percent

Percentages of firms that use fixed fees "most of the time" or "sometimes":

- Consulting: 85 percent
- Architecture, engineering, and construction: 75 percent
- Accounting: 73 percent
- Marketing: 68 percent
- Law: 59 percent

"I don't think the billable hour is dead. It's too prevalent. But, I do think that we need to have a strategy for each client. What fee arrangement is best for the client? Earlier this year while attending a conference, I listened to an in-house lawyer describe a remarkable relationship with his law firm.

He confessed that he 'paid a little more' for the services of this particular firm, and they worked under a number of fee arrangements—hourly, fixed, blended, retainer. After eight months on an annual retainer, the firm approached him suggesting they reduce the retainer amount, based on actual use. Now, all of his work is with his trusted firm. In the end, the fee structure itself matters less than the demonstration of caring, an awareness of the client's situation, and a willingness to act in the best interest of the client, even if it's against the short-term financial interests of the firm. Caring is the strategy that converts clients from satisfied to loyal."

—Kevin McMurdo, Chief Marketing Officer, Perkins Coie

PROS AND CONS OF HOURLY OR DAILY FEES

Pros	Cons
Easy and straightforward to understand.	Moves discussion away from the value of the outcome to the cost of time.
Easy to build firm business models based on expected rates and expected utilization of people.	Requires strict accounting for time internally and invites scrutiny of individual units of time by clients who otherwise might not be so price sensitive.
Less risky to firm profitability—if a project takes more time, you bill for more time.	Creates easier comparison with other firms by clients, often creating increased fee pressures.
Keeps scope creep issues at bay.	Higher fees and margin can often be achieved through fixed-fee and contingent pricing.
May be the only pricing model a buyer will accept, particularly for larger buyers and larger deals.*	Invites inefficiency, redundancy, and the temptation to focus on time and not output of work.

(*Continued*)

*There are often, but not always, ways around this, including sole sourcing.

Sets straightforward parameters for staff accountability, and focuses efforts.

Establishes a path forward for loosely defined projects.

Eliminates the need for constant rescoping if projects come in regular or rapid succession.

Allows for simple project scoping and adjustments as engagements change over time.

Reduces energy and creativity in solving problems faster and becoming more efficient.

Fixed Fees

Fixed fees—charging an overall fee for an engagement—is the most commonly used pricing construct across most professional services specialties.

PROS AND CONS OF FIXED-FEE PRICING

Pros	Cons
Straightforward for buyer to understand.	Makes scoping more difficult for complex engagements or those with difficult-to-define outcomes, staff needs, or end points.
Shifts expectations from pay for time to pay for outcomes.	If project outcomes, stages, or work needs are amorphous, requires the setting of service-level agreements (SLAs); SLAs can be difficult to set and manage.
For buyers, investment is fixed—no need to worry about cost overruns.	Increases the difficulty and time needed to sell consecutive engagements if each requires complex scoping and proposal approval.

No constant buyer evaluation of "How much time will that take?"

Allows service provider to focus 100 percent on the solution rather than on fulfilling expectations of spending time.

Promotes efficiency at seller organizations.

Demonstrates return on investment (ROI) more clearly for clients.

Maximizes the value of assets and intellectual capital.

Increases the risk of scope creep.

Buyers may require hourly/daily fees or fee breakdowns as a condition of awarding the engagement.

VALUE-BASED PRICING DOES NOT EQUAL FIXED-FEE PRICING

We often hear the words *value-based pricing* as a surrogate for *fixed-fee pricing*. Let us be clear: They are not the same thing. A top attorney at a business law firm might command $750 an hour. At a different firm the top attorney might command $500 an hour, or $225 an hour, or $125 an hour. Different clients will pay the different amounts based on their perception of the value of a particular attorney and his or her ability to get the job done for them. Indeed, the client who hires the $750-an-hour attorney probably wouldn't entertain the idea of using the $125-an-hour attorney for the same services, even if both attorneys stated that they had the same capabilities.

A technology consultant may be able to command $175 per hour where the going rate for that service might be $125. We have seen many service providers succeed with the argument that they get more done and have a higher success rate than the run-of-the-mill person in their field.

> Clients regularly pay more for what is arguably the same service someone else offers. Value is a function of the perceived fairness of price or return on investment in the mind of the buyer. The pricing model you choose is a tool to help you maximize profit while also creating value in the mind of the buyer. But that value price can come in the form of hourly and daily fees as well as fixed-fee or contingency arrangements.
>
> So what is value-based pricing? Mention value-based pricing to 10 different people (we have), and you'll get many different reactions and definitions of what it is. Our definition: Value-based pricing is a strategy that sets selling prices by the perceived value to the client, rather than on the actual cost of the service, the market price, competitors' prices, or the historical price.

Contingent Fees

Discussions of service firm pricing models often don't include contingent or incentive fees. These are fees garnered by service firms for reaching project milestones or achieving goals.

PROS AND CONS OF CONTINGENT OR INCENTIVE FEE PRICING

Pros	Cons
Service provider and client share the risk and the reward and can feel responsible to each other for reaching desired outcomes.	Requires a high level of trust between service provider and client for success.
Clients often enjoy reduced risk by only paying for outcomes.	Requires shared reaching of goals by service provider and client.
Increased risk borne by the service provider can be offset by increased reward for production.	Demands added levels of accounting and record keeping that are not always factored into the scope.

Creates competitive advantage if one firm determines how to win with contingent pricing while other firms in the same space haven't done so.	Creates service provider feast or famine (often, just famine) if not managed properly.
Is often the expected and accepted mode of pricing for a particular industry (e.g., plaintiff's attorneys, executive recruiters, M&A consulting, etc.).	Incents service providers to chase low-hanging fruit or easy wins for one client at the expense of energy and effort for another.

The three pricing models—hourly, fixed, and contingent—are not mutually exclusive. Many firms employ all three methods, and sometimes methods are mixed inside the same engagement (e.g., a $50,000 overall project fee with service-level agreements of a $5,000 bonus if X, Y, and Z milestones are hit and $175 per hour if additional D, E, and F are needed).

Making the decision to employ one pricing model versus another takes serious analysis and research; understanding of your markets, buyers, and competition; and sometimes vision for doing something new or different. Whatever models you choose, marketing and selling will influence the actual fees you can realize from your efforts.

Getting the Fees You Deserve

In professional services firms, pricing takes on all shapes, colors, and sizes. If we assume that the firm is in business to maximize value in the firm (versus, say, a lifestyle business), one thing is true: It wants to get the right fees for service to maximize growth, profits, and repeat business. A great way to do that, as we mentioned at the beginning of this chapter, is to maximize fees.

While there are lots of ways to skin the fee maximization cat, the firms that generate the highest fees have a number of characteristics in common.

Brand Reach and Reputation

It's clear (see the "Median Hourly Billing Rates" table) the firms that are well-known in their target markets receive higher fees than firms that are not as well-known in their target markets. This applies not only to getting higher fees, but also to getting more new client opportunities. In the Wellesley Hills Group and RainToday.com research report *What's Working in Lead Generation*,[2] well-known (branded) firms reported having a much easier time of generating leads.

MEDIAN HOURLY BILLING RATES REALIZED FOR THE HIGHEST-LEVEL PROFESSIONALS

Industry	Non–Brand Leaders	Brand Leaders	Percent Difference
Consulting	$250	$300	20%
Marketing, Advertising, and Public Relations	$150	$200	33%
Architecture, Engineering, and Construction	$160	$172	8%
Accounting and Financial Services	$200	$298	49%
Law Firms and Legal Services	$300	$450	50%

It's also true that thought leaders[3] and firms with excellent reputations generate higher fees. There's less perceived risk in working with known and well-regarded entities. The more important challenges are to clients, the less they're willing to risk on failure and the more they'll pay for firms they perceive will come through for them and succeed.

---

[2] *What's Working in Lead Generation* (RainToday.com, 2007), p. 26. www.raintoday.com/leadgenreport.cfm

[3] See Chapter 15 for data points on the effect of thought leadership on fee strength.

Lead Generation Engine

Firms rarely have just the right amount of work. Either there is not enough work to go around and it's all hands on deck to generate new business, or the firm is flush with work and everyone is busy delivering and not selling. Firms with anemic pipelines are often tempted to take new business at lower fees. If you're looking at a dry pipeline, it's easy to see why you might be tempted to price a deal or to accept a deal at a lower rate than you'd like. If you don't take the deal, you won't know where your lunch money will come from next month! If the pipeline is full and yielding business regularly, you'd have an easier time saying no to work beneath your typical fee structure.

A firm with an established lead generation engine doesn't have to worry about where the next sale is going to come from. It has a strong pipeline and therefore is not willing to do anything to win the business.

Value in Selling

We asked 231 buyers of professional services, "Thinking of the last few times you selected a provider, which of the following problems did you encounter during the process?" Service providers fancy themselves to be good listeners, responsive with client service, and experts on their clients' industries and needs. Yet the problems encountered most by buyers were:

- Did not listen to me: 38 percent
- Did not respond to my requests in a timely manner: 30 percent
- Did not understand my needs: 30 percent

Perhaps you deliver excellent service, can solve problems better than the competition, and are, indeed, the best option for a client. But if he can't tell that during his buying process, *he* won't know this and won't be inclined to pay a premium for you.[4] Each individual selling moment

---

[4] See Chapter 21 for a process to solve these problems.

can be an inflection point determining your ability to garner premium fees. How you position your value, deliver proposals, respond to questions and objections . . . these factors and a litany of others can be the key in generating the fees you deserve. If you're a solo practitioner, every time you sell you have the ability to improve your fee. If you're a large firm with hundreds or thousands of professionals and business developers, this inflection point is occurring perhaps dozens or hundreds of times a day across your firm.

Delivery Excellence

The more focused a firm is on the delivery of particular services, (1) the more focused it can be on delivering that service *particularly well* and thus delivering more value, and (2) the easier it is for the marketing and business development team to bring that strong service to market in terms of segmentation, targeting, messaging and differentiation, and tactical marketing outreach.

In addition, the more the firm can deliver a service well, the more satisfied clients will be, which in turn means more repeat business, referrals, and marketing success. Satisfied clients are much less likely to consider switching to a new service provider. (See Figure 5.1.)

If clients are not considering switching to new providers, firms will encounter less pressure from competitors and clients alike.

In other words, do what you do best, and you will have more satisfied clients, more repeat business, higher fees, and less price pressure.

Right Focus on Competition

When thinking about the competition, firms need to be more concerned about delivering more value than the competition and less concerned about the competition's actual pricing structure. This is not to say that knowing competitor pricing isn't valuable (it is). Indeed, 39 percent of firms engage

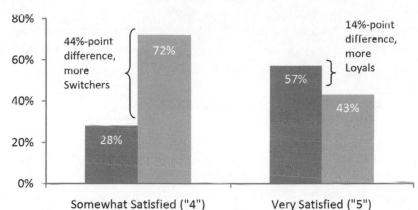

Figure 5.1 Difference in Loyalty between Satisfaction Levels: Somewhat Satisfied versus Very Satisfied

Source: How Clients Buy: 2009 Benchmark Report on Marketing and Selling Professional Services from the Buyer Perspective (RainToday.com, 2009).

AVOID DISCLOSING UNDERLYING FEE STRUCTURES, RETAINERS DETAILS, AND FIXED-FEE ENGAGEMENTS

According to our fee and pricing research, premium-price firms are less likely to break down the prices of retainers and fixed-fee engagements to their component parts, such as hourly rates, and share this information with clients. It's natural for clients to ask, "How did you come up with the fee?" or "What are the hourly or daily rates of the team involved?" Premium-price firms are less likely to share the nitty-gritty details.

These firms have largely figured out how to set service-level agreements that specify what will happen during the retainer period. Firms that do this have both the forethought to figure out the right service package and retainer structure and the fortitude to disengage from or pass on clients that push back on the underlying hourly structure. With both fixed-fee engagements and retainers, the more the conversation focuses on the underlying components of the price and price structure, the less it focuses on value, quality, and outcomes.

in research to identify their competitors' pricing and fees. This is, however, only a start.

The question the firm should ask is: "Given competitor pricing, what they do, and how they go about it, how can we offer more value than they offer and, thus, receive higher fees?" Premium-price firms concern themselves more with whether the firm can deliver superior value versus other providers and less with known or suspected pricing of competitors.

Employment of Value-Based Pricing

Service provider reactions to the concept of value-based pricing range across a wide spectrum—even to the point of concern about gouging clients by charging more than a standard hourly or daily fee.

One fee and pricing research respondent said that when he himself buys on value versus effort, "Many times I later feel that I overpaid." However, we've observed service firms more often on the other end of the spectrum. Their internal consideration of value-based pricing leads to *discussion* about delivering more value to clients, *actions* focused on delivering more value to clients, and, ultimately, the *actual delivery* of more value to clients.

A firm considering using this strategy should answer these questions:

- Can we employ the strategy? (Selling to government and in regulated markets sometimes hinders a firm's ability to do this, but then again, in many cases it doesn't.)

- For which services do we deliver stronger value than the competition or stronger value than firms can get if they sourced the services internally?
- In what areas do we deliver strong value in the eyes of our clients?
- How can we deliver higher value, given what the clients truly need?

Once you have meaningful answers to these questions, you can then move forward in your investigation of employing value-based pricing as a strategy.

Top Challenges Focus on Value

It's worthwhile to note that the top challenges uncovered in our fee and pricing research for professional services firms focus on value when it comes to pricing:

- Uncertainty about what price a particular client will accept (*because you don't know how well you sold the value*).
- Pressure not to leave money on the table (*because you think you sold the value—but you're not sure—so you're second-guessing your own fees and worrying they are too low*).

When a firm is able to increase its perceived and real value to clients, it will find that:

- Clients will likely be willing to accept higher fees (though, granted, you may never know the exact fees each client will actually be willing to accept).
- The firm will be less concerned with leaving money on the table, because it will be more confident in the fees it is charging.
- Clients will pressure the firm less, because they will have confidence in that firm's ability to deliver additional value.

Focusing on the value provided for clients and strengthening the overall value proposition of the firm can decrease some of the major challenges found in pricing services.

Wellesley Hills Group began working with a small consulting firm selling to the insurance industry several years ago. Let's call the two main partners Bill and Sam. Both Bill and Sam had been with a successful national consulting firm. In their work there, they had regularly commanded fees of $5,000 per day. Unfortunately, these same people doing the same work but no longer under their well-regarded consulting firm umbrella rarely could get clients anywhere near those fee levels. Bill and Sam were experiencing firsthand the negative effectives of not having a brand.

Fast-forward to three years later. Since beginning to work with us, Bill and Sam have created a web site focused on the needs of their target market, packaged their services in a way that is compelling and clear, conducted annual research to create cachet to all that they say, and built a regular ongoing communications plan *to their target market* that has established them as the go-to people for the types of services they offer.

In other words, they have established a brand, which has established in the minds of their market that Bill and Sam provide value. As prospects were intrigued and focused on the value, the focus on fees faded into the background; and they're now garnering "well-branded firm" fees once again. Naturally, they provide great service and value. The marketing and brand work they have done over time has positioned them as the firm people are eager to do with business with. And remember, this is a two-person firm.

The moral of this story is that whichever pricing model you employ, marketing pays off in many ways—not the least of which is in getting the fees you know you deserve.

6

Don't Worry about Your Competition (Let Them Worry about You)

What, me worry?

—Alfred E. Newman

Who are your closest competitors? How are you going to beat your competition? What makes you better than your competition? What are the differentiating factors between you and your competition?

You probably get asked these types of questions all the time from your prospects, your clients, and your internal staff. Should you have answers? Yes. But don't overdo it.

Over the years we have spoken with numerous clients about their strategies, and the conversation inevitably turns to the competition. We often find that the people who run services firms waste an inordinate amount of time and effort worrying about, and angling against, other firms that provide services to their target market. Often it's just not worth the intense time and focus that firms give it.

These mistakes are understandable, but they're still mistakes. Since time is something we all have precious little of, we list the most common mistakes so you can spend more time on the marketing issues that will make a bigger difference.

Mistake #1: Over-the-Top Competitive Research

Some service firm business and marketing plans list and describe page after page of information about their competition. One plan we reviewed included: "Over the past three months, we were able to successfully locate 37 negotiation consulting firms. Detailed descriptions follow, along with our unique positioning against each one. . . ."

Reaction: Obsessing about the competition to this degree is simply a waste of time and money. Most people would laugh at an accountant who confidently stated, "I have discovered that there are 62 other accounting firms in the state and can confirm that 51 of them offer a number of services similar to ours." Yet somehow this information shows up in service firm marketing plan after marketing plan as if it were a necessary component.

Mistake #2: Market and Service Offering Reluctance

Many services firms are reluctant to offer a new service that complements their current services because a competitor already offers it. "You see, we can't launch an intellectual property law practice. At least five other firms offer that in our market, and I learned in business school that first movers have an advantage. If you're not number one or number two, you shouldn't launch into the market."

Reaction: Law firms, consulting firms, information technology (IT) firms, financial services firms, and other professional services firms are not Coke and Pepsi. The market dynamics for services firms just don't work like this. (See more about this mistake later.)

Mistake #3: Clichéd Competitive Differentiation

"We at [*name here*] Tax and Consulting Services are the number-one provider in our market. Our biggest differentiator is our people, who take a strategic look at our clients' businesses and blend people, process, and technology to create efficient and effective solutions for our clients' most pressing strategic needs. We're more than tax services; we're strategic business advisors with the experience you need to solve your real problems." (This is real copy, by the way, and can be found on dozens of accounting firm web sites.)

Reaction: Copy like this takes up a lot of space and doesn't say much.

Mistake #4: Unique Methodology

"We have a *unique* methodology that allows us to deliver projects more efficiently and with greater ongoing success. There are five major steps: discovery, design, development, implementation, and measurement."

Reaction: Sure, it's unique—there's just one process exactly like this—but, with some variances, it's employed by hundreds of firms.

Misconceptions about the uniqueness of the firm or services hinder service business growth and success because they limit the thinking of the people who run firms and practices. Leaders spend days, months, and even years trying to find the unique services they can offer while perfectly fine but not-so-unique services could produce a steady stream of revenue.[1] What, then, should firms keep in mind?

Forget General Marketing Advice

Your marketing textbooks and many marketing consultants will advise you to:

- Be the first mover in a market. You'll have an advantage over later entrants.

---

[1] See Chapter 13 on being unique and other marketing mistakes.

- Be number one or number two in a market. No one else can make enough profit.
- Establish your unique selling proposition that other firms can't easily duplicate.
- Be amazingly different from other firms in your space. Being unique is key to your success.[2]

Do you think people in a six-person law firm can't make big money? They can, and they can do it in a market in which there are 200-person law firms that deliver similar services to similar kinds of clients.

Don't Worry about Crowded Markets

We can't tell you how many Italian restaurants are in New York's Little Italy (though we have eaten at a good number of them) or how many steak houses there are in Chicago; there are simply too many to count. But we are pretty confident that there is not a booming row of authentic French bistros in Peru, Maine.

If you're a human resources consultant and there are a multitude of human resources consultants that do what you do in the market in which you practice, it simply means there's a market for your type of services. If you look for a unique space to create a market and be the first mover, there's a good chance nobody's there because nobody's buying.

In the microeconomic technical sense, the Coke-versus-Pepsi market dynamic is *oligopoly*, while service firm markets are *monopolistic competition*. In oligopoly, you have a few top players with all the clout, market share, and profits; and everyone else is struggling to survive. This doesn't happen in monopolistic competition. There are 88 pizza restaurants in the Yellow Pages in Miami, Florida. The 89th can make it, too, if the pizza's good, food and labor costs are in line, and the newcomer plays its marketing cards right.

---

[2]See Chapter 13 for stories.

CHARACTERISTICS OF MONOPOLISTIC COMPETITION

From a microeconomic perspective, there are four types of firm dynamics:

1. Monopoly
2. Oligopoly
3. Monopolistic competition
4. Perfect competition

Who cares? Much of the bad advice given to service firms that we highlight in this chapter and throughout the book (be first in a market, be number one or number two, own a word in your market) is good advice for oligopolies but bad advice for monopolistic competition (i.e., most service firms). Many business cases and strategies focus on oligopoly—Merck versus GlaxoSmithKline, HP versus Dell, and Toyota versus VW. These firms are oligopolies.

Monopolistic competition—the type of firm most service businesses fall under—are characterized by:

- Many producers (firms) and many consumers (buyers).
- Perception from the market that there are non-price differences between firms but that those differences vary in degree and are often termed as subtle.
- Typically small barriers to entry and exit (lots of firms in your field can and do hang out a shingle).
- A degree of control by producers over the price they can command, versus monopolies that can charge whatever they want versus perfect competition firms that can only charge the same price as anyone else.

With perfect competition, firms can only charge what everyone else is charging (i.e., price of pork bellies on the exchange, price of corn that wholesalers are paying farmers on a particular day). These firms don't have to care much at all about other firms. They care only what the market is bearing for price.

Oligopolies live and breathe by their ability to beat the other guy. It's a constant game of one-upmanship. Most service firms are somewhere in the middle.

Enter a crowded market where there's a lot of business to be had and there are lots of clients with needs, and (assuming your pizza's any good) there's a good chance you can thrive. Open a French bistro in Peru, Maine . . . good luck selling foie gras.

Change the Question from Competition to Clients

Let's say you're interviewing someone for a job at your firm. It's perfectly reasonable for the candidate to ask you, "What differentiates you from your competition?" The same thing goes with your clients and prospects. You may feel the need to answer—comparing yourself both categorically to your competition and then against a specific competitor. And on and on about your competition.

You don't want the conversation to linger on about competitors. The more you talk about them, the more you validate that your client, prospect, or staff member should be comparing you to them.

Instead, like a good salesperson, take control of the questioning and you will take control of the conversation. For example, you might answer, "Well, we have a very robust research division that keeps us on the cutting edge of the supply chain field and" to my knowledge, none of our competitors do. In fact, they quote our research to make their points; but at the end of the day, we're the source and the leaders.

"I don't know what they do with our research. I know what we do, however, and how it makes our clients' lives better. Here's a specific example from your industry. . . ."

Drop the Clichés

When you do answer the question, "What makes you different?" don't answer, "Our people, process, and technology are efficient and effective. We are the best; we are unique and cutting-edge; we push the envelope, go the extra mile, are client-centered, and so on."

If you do, you'll simply be helping people win their game of buzzword bingo. (You don't believe us? Google *buzzword bingo*, and see what comes up first.)

Leave the clichés at home, and say something worthwhile.[3]

Overcome Your Greatest Competitor—Client Indifference

Finally, and perhaps most important realize that for most product companies, the competition is another product company. For many service businesses, the stiffest competition is the indifference of your client to do anything at all or the desire of your client to "just do it with in-house resources."

In *How Clients Buy: 2009 Benchmark Report on Professional Services Marketing and Selling from the Client Perspective,*[4] 40 percent of 200 buyers of consulting and professional services encountered service providers that did not understand their needs; and 32 percent said that the service providers did not convince them of the value they would receive from the service provider.

You have to convince the buyer of the value your services will bring to the table, regardless of how you stack up with some competitor. So worry less about who your competitor is, and worry more about the value you offer to the client. You'll win more deals in the process and beat your competitors without even giving them a second thought.

---

[3] See Chapter 14 on crafting your marketing messages.

[4] Mike Schultz and John Doerr, *How Clients Buy: 2009 Benchmark Report on Professional Services Marketing and Selling from the Client Perspective* (Framingham, MA: RainToday. com, 2009), Figure 3.1, 22, http://www.raintoday.com/howclientsbuy.cfm

"The competitive scriptures almost systematically ignore the importance of hustle and energy. While they preach strategic planning, competitive strategy, and competitive advantage, they overlook the record of a surprisingly large number of very successful companies that vigorously practice a different religion. These companies don't have long-term strategic plans with an obsessive preoccupation on rivalry. They concentrate on operating details and doing things well. Hustle is their style and their strategy. They move fast and they get it right."

—Amar Bhide, "Hustle as Strategy," *Harvard Business Review*, September 1, 1986.

When Competition Is the Order of the Day

We hope you're saying to yourself, "You're right. We should focus on our value and our ability to position that value to the market versus spending so much time on the competition." However, we understand that some service firms often find themselves up against the same firms regularly. For example, the big four accounting firms find themselves in competitive shoot-outs with the other big four accounting firms (and perhaps a smattering of Grant Thornton, UHY Advisors, and other large accounting firms, depending on the situation).

When it comes to marketing against the competition, remember the first three outcomes we initially stated that marketing can deliver for you:

1. Help you create conversations with potential buyers when they have a need. Firms often say, "I can't believe they bought technology services from Firm X, and we were never even part of the conversation!" You don't want that to happen.
2. Ease winning of client engagements by affecting the prospect's perception of your firm.
3. Increase your revenue per engagement and client, and increase your ability to generate premium fees.

From a macro perspective, you need to know enough about the competition to be able to say (1) who they are and (2) what they're doing at their own firms to move any of these three objectives forward.

This may require some competitive research. Indeed, between 33 percent and 52 percent of professional service firms conduct formal research to find out what their competitors are doing and how their competitors are pricing their services.[5]

Still, the question becomes, "What are you going to *do* about it?" The answers may affect marketing and may affect overall business direction. However, as much as firms make mountains out of the competition molehill, from a strategy perspective, it's not much more complicated than finding out where they stand in the market, what clients perceive about them, and figuring out what to do about it.

---

[5]Law Firms & Legal Services, 52 percent; Architecture, Engineering & Construction Services, 40 percent; Consulting, 39 percent; Marketing, Advertising & PR, 39 percent; Accounting & Financial Services, 33 percent. Mike Schultz and John Doerr, *Fees and Pricing Benchmark Report: Consulting Industry 2008* (Framingham, MA: RainToday.com, 2008), http://www.raintoday.com/category/11_1best_sellers.cfm

7

The "Get It Done" Culture

There's a hole in the bucket, dear Liza, dear Liza.
A hole in the bucket, dear Liza, a hole.

—Harry Belafonte

Question: On a scale of 1 to 5, 1 being "always" and 5 being "never," how often do you stick to project schedules and keep commitments you make to clients?

I'm guessing that most of you would give yourself a 1 (or a 2). Of course, you make commitments and keep them. What kind of professional would you be if you didn't?

Next question: On a scale of 1 to 5, 1 being "not challenging at all" and 5 being "extremely challenging," how challenging is it for you to implement your marketing and lead generation plans that you put in place at your own company, assuming all of the stakeholders at the company agree on the plan?

At the Wellesley Hills Group and RainToday.com, we asked 731 marketers and leaders at professional services businesses the same question as a part of our research report, *What's Working in Lead Generation*. Of the respondents, 76 percent said they found implementing their own marketing and lead generation plans "somewhat challenging" to "extremely challenging," even when they agree internally on the plans. Since service businesses

79

fancy themselves as pretty good at delivering on commitments they make to clients, we believe service providers should be able to execute the marketing commitments they make to themselves. Yet when it comes to sustained marketing, lead generation, and business development, they consistently let themselves down.

This failure to meet these marketing and selling commitments is usually due to three factors: (1) lack of performance readiness, (2) disconnect with reality, (3) and lack of will.

Challenge 1: Lack of Performance Readiness

The 1,000-mile journey to developing a culture of marketing implementation and rainmaking starts with the first step. If you're looking to create this culture of passion, energy, enthusiasm, and skill, start by making sure the bucket doesn't have any holes before you start to fill it up—or it won't hold water.

We see firms doing a certain percentage of what they need to do to help the professionals in the firm market and develop business—but rarely 100 percent. If you're doing only 70 percent of what you need to do, you don't get 70 percent results; you get much less. Like patching a leak in the bottom of a bucket, if you don't patch it 100 percent, it still leaks.

If your firm is looking to create a culture of business development performance, make sure you address the gamut of management topics you need to address in order to give yourself a fighting chance of success. If you don't, you may find yourself expending 90 percent of the effort—almost there—but still falling short of your growth goals.

Building a Performance Culture

There are six areas you should address in order to build a rainmaking firm. (See Figure 7.1.) Three are controlled by the organization, and three are brought to the table by individuals (but can be influenced by the firm).

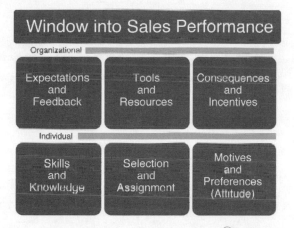

Figure 7.1   The Six Boxes®

Source: Binder Riha Associates. Used with permission.

Organizational Influences

    1. Expectations and Feedback

    2. Tools and Resources

    3. Consequences and Incentives

Individual Influences

    4. Skills and Knowledge

    5. Selection and Assignment

    6. Motives and Preferences (Attitude)

Expectations and feedback

According to Dr. Jim Harter, Gallup Consulting's Chief Scientist of Workplace Management and Well-Being, Gallup has asked over 12.5 million people: "Do I know what is expected of me at work?" By and large, just over half answer the question "strongly agree." In other words, just under half are not so sure of what's expected of them at work. Dr. Harter further told us, "Workplace performance suffers dramatically with those that answer below 'strongly agree.'"

When it comes to marketing and business development, in our experience, many professionals don't know what they're supposed to do at any given time, and they also don't know what they are supposed to produce. Some know they are "expected to network," "expected to make calls," "expected to 'build the brand,'" or "expected to spend 15 percent of their time on business development"; but rarely do they know what they need to do at 9 A.M., 11 A.M., or all day Tuesday.

> "Taking the leap from 'successful lawyer' to 'rainmaker' is more likely to be successful when the lawyer works with others. Marketing professionals, for example, help with the candid assessment of strengths and weaknesses, interpersonal skills, and networks that lead to new business."
>
> —Kevin McMurdo, Chief Marketing Officer, Perkins Coie

What happens without clear expectations and feedback? Inconsistency. (See Figure 7.2.)

- Inconsistent business development activities across all professionals with business development responsibilities.
- Inconsistent business development effort levels.
- Inconsistent persistence.
- Inconsistent improvement (due to lack of coaching).
- Inconsistent results.
- Inconsistent implementation of marketing tactical programs.
- Inconsistent implementation intensity.

Tools and resources

Marketers and rainmakers need the right resources to help them implement. Sometimes they need more time to do it, sometimes a budget for generating publicity, sometimes just an expense account. Perhaps they know that they're

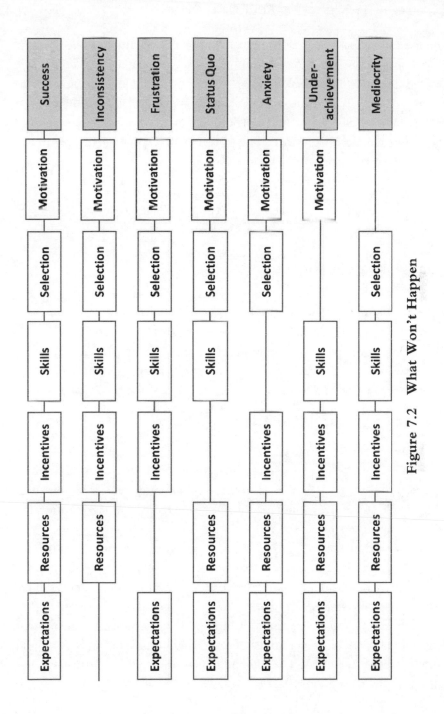

Figure 7.2   What Won't Happen

83

supposed to be marketing, but they don't have a good target profile or list of likely prospects.

It is possible a rainmaker doesn't have the right marketing or sales collateral materials to help them sell. And the marketer has no time, budget, or support to build them. A rainmaker may not need collateral but does need to bring a technical guru along to represent a specific expertise of the firm . . . but that technical guru can't afford to lose the billable time.

Whatever the need, rainmakers need the right level of resources in order to find and win new clients.

What happens without the right resource levels? Frustration.

- Ready to call, but doesn't have the names.
- Ready to present, but doesn't have materials.
- Ready to visit the client, but don't have the budget or time to go.
- Ready to implement a lead generation campaign, but can't get the firm to release the budget, or get a subject matter expert to review the campaign, or get a copywriter to make the words sing, or get a business developer or professional to follow up on inquiries.
- Ready to kick off a new Web project, but can't get final approval from various stakeholders to move forward.

Consequences and incentives

It's strange; some service firm leaders rush to add incentive compensation to inspire professionals to sell, while others vehemently resist compensation adjustments. Incentive compensation, built correctly, can significantly influence rainmakers to find more new clients.

However, incentive compensation, while necessary, is not sufficient. Even those service firm leaders that do institute incentive compensation plans rarely state (or if they do state, act on) any negative consequences of *not* hitting client development goals.

Lack of consequences and incentives is a particular challenge for professional services organizations because many don't see marketing and business development as a core component of their jobs. Client work and billable hours trump everything:

- "But I got billable and couldn't do that."
- "Well, I didn't make those calls [or write that article or attend that board meeting] because I got busy."
- "Sorry, I just didn't do that. On to other things."
- "Because I got caught up in all the leaders' requests for help with proposals, I didn't get the white paper project done."

If you want people to take your marketing and sales plans seriously, there have to be both incentives for taking action and consequences for not taking action.

People in organizations take on the behavioral traits of the leaders. If the leaders take anything, marketing included, seriously, then the rest of the team will follow suit. Leaders at service companies take new thinking and new ideas seriously. They take client projects and client service seriously. They take selling deals that are in their pipelines seriously. Note to leaders: If you want the rest of your firm to take marketing seriously, you need to as well. Marketing and lead generation are often the redheaded stepchildren, pining for, but not getting, the attention they need.

Back in the day, police in Great Britain didn't carry guns. Robin Williams once asked what they yell when they're chasing a suspect. "Stop . . . or I'll say 'stop' again!" (We're sure the suspects shook in their boots.) If you want people to follow plans and hit goals, put some teeth in the consequences for *not* delivering. When it comes time to tell people which way the bus is going, let them know that either they're on the bus or they're not. If they're not, there will be consequences. When team members don't deliver on their part of a client project assignment, they get unpleasant visits from management pretty quickly. Can you say the same when it comes to following through on your marketing commitments?

Incentives are important as consequences. Simple as it might sound, you have to reward people who implement well. You'll find treatise after treatise on how to reward successful and productive staff members. Find them. Read them. Reward loudly. If you do, the rewards for your business will be energy, passion, and growth. If not, well, there's always next year.

What happens without the right consequences and incentives? Status quo.

- No incentive compensation: "Why should I sell? I need to bill anyway."
- No consequences for not selling: "Well, I guess I'll try, but what's the worst that will happen if I don't succeed? They are not going to do anything about it."
- No consequences for not increasing leads: "Well, I work in marketing, but I guess I'll just wait to be told to do something—or work on something that doesn't produce results."
- No consequences for not delivering on any goal: "We're supposed to create thought leadership, but the subject matter expert isn't responding to me, so I guess that's off my plate for now."

Skills and knowledge

Have you ever been at a business development meeting with a newbie running the show while you sit back and enjoy the ride? How does the newbie seem? Confident in her abilities? Comfortable that she'll win the new client?

And how does she fare running that first meeting? Does she talk the right amount? Ask the right questions? Follow the well-worn protocols of first-time business discussions? How's her body language . . . confident and relaxed?

Rainmakers need skills and knowledge in order to find and win clients. With the right skills, they can walk the client through the new business development process with savvy, ease, and confidence. With the right knowledge, they can ask the right questions and craft the right solution set for the client.

Marketing skill is no different. Without the ability to implement specific tasks with alacrity and a keen eye, you'll not only get anxiety, you'll also get everything that comes with it: poor quality, poor decisions, inaction, and slow progress.

The tools of marketing are a finite list. Just because you know what those tools are doesn't mean you can do anything with them. Think about how a great heart surgeon becomes great: preparation in college, four years of medical school, years of internships and residency, rotations through many programs and different surgical areas, specialization in heart surgery and years of study under more experienced surgeons, and very high-stakes successes and failures. Then you're ready to let that surgeon work on your heart. Many don't make it that far.

Marketing and rainmaking might have their own nuances and time frames, but the parallel works.

What happens without skills and knowledge? Anxiety.

- "Do I really have to pick up that phone and say something to someone I don't know?"
- "I'm not going in there; you can't make me go in there."
- "There's no way I know what to do or say to actually bring in a new client like you do."
- "I am not ready to run a brand study . . . implement a marketing campaign . . . coach a professional in business development . . . build a marketing plan . . . build a great presentation."

Unfortunately, many professionals won't admit any of these feelings, so they never deal with their anxieties and move their careers forward.

Selection and assignment

Have you ever seen someone fail in a marketing or business development role when almost anyone (except the hiring manager) could have predicted that this person was not the right fit for the job? There are quite a number of roles that people have to play: the technical expert, the lead generator, the closer, the client relationship manager, the marketing leader, the marketing specialist, and so on. Whatever the case, you need the right people in the right roles.

For example, you may have selected someone in your firm who is going to be a great rainmaker: ready for strong relationships, ready to bring the solid new clients into the firm. But don't assign him to the cold calling: He simply shouldn't (and often won't) succeed at it—it's not the right fit.

> "It's not just about selecting the right people, it's about making sure the team continues to be the right people over time. If you do have to counsel someone out of the firm, I have rarely dealt with that issue where the person doesn't agree that it's right for them to move on. Then I hear from them a year later that they have a great position for them and they're thrilled."
>
> —Mike Sheehan, CEO, Hill Holliday

What happens without the right selection and assignment? Chronic underachievement.

- "Twenty years in the business and *now* they expect me to run my own campaigns . . . develop PowerPoint slides . . . attend networking events . . . make cold calls? I don't think so."
- "How do they expect me to sell to engineers? I'm not an engineer."
- "All ready for my first day in business development! What do you mean my territory is Aroostook County, Maine?"
- "Glad to be here as the new managing partner. What's up first? Building our marketing?!? You've got to be kidding me. How am I supposed to run that?"

Motives and preferences (attitude)
Let's say you take care of the other five influences noted in this chapter: Expectations clear. Resources available. Compensation set. Skills in place. Right people—right jobs. All of this is great, and necessary, but you still need a team with the fire in the belly. You need people with focus and drive to be successful in business development. If they're not motivated to build a practice, there's little a firm can do to light the fire of focus and drive.

What happens without motivation and preferences? Mediocrity.

- "Nine A.M. already . . . time to start working. Five P.M. finally . . . time to go home!"
- "Look at all the money I can make! Too bad I don't care about money."

- "They've trained me . . . they're paying me . . . they told me what to do. Unfortunately, I just don't want to. It's not for me."

If you're looking to build a culture of business development, make sure you attend to all of the factors that affect human performance. Miss one of these factors for any reason—inattention, lack of time, unwillingness to invest, political difficulties—and you'll severely limit your success.

Fortunately for you, it's the rare services firm that *does* focus on all six factors. If yours is the one that goes the extra mile—and plugs all the holes that would eventually have sunk the boat—better get ready to hire more billable professionals. The tide's going to come in, you'll be shipshape, and you'll need more people to get all the new client work done.

Challenge 2: Disconnect with Reality

The second factor leading to lack of marketing and business development performance is a disconnect with reality. In most service businesses, leaders are in touch with the daily realities of their client projects and their internal staffing. They're often out of touch with (1) how the landscape of their own industries has changed, (2) how the buying cycle at client businesses has changed, and (3) how their own marketing and lead generation activities need to change if they want to grow and stay competitive.

A lot of service business leaders feel pressure—from their competitors, from their shrinking revenue and margins, from internal staff, from increasing commoditization in their industry—to do more marketing and lead generation. Unfortunately, they too often take the easy ways out:

- Throwing money at advertising and graphic design.
- Redoing their web sites just for the sake of changing the look.
- Delegating billable staff who are currently not so billable to become marketers or rainmakers to 'get some new business!'
- Pushing their services rather than truly understanding why clients buy from them.

- Trying tactic after tactic without a clear idea of how the tactic connects to prospects or to real results.

Firms also often need a reality check for how much they can actually get done. One of the reasons many marketing and lead generation plans are not implemented is that they have too many priorities. When plans have too many priorities, they have no priorities.

GETTING IN TOUCH WITH REALITY

Guard 1: What?! A swallow, carryin' a coconut?!
Arthur: It could grip it by the husk!
Guard 1: It's not a question of where he grips it; it's a simple question of weight ratios! A five-ounce bird could not carry a one-pound coconut!

As this scene from *Monty Python and the Holy Grail* continues, the guard proceeds to tell Arthur that to maintain airspeed velocity, a swallow has to beat its wings 43 times per second.

Arthur's response: "I'm not interested."

Service business leaders who are interested in realistic marketing and lead generation activities, budgets, and implementation plans get them done. When we work with clients to help them build their plans, we're often presented with the plan from the last year . . . and the year before . . . and the year before that. The company leaders describe them as "aggressive" when, in reality, they're castles in the air: Insufficient budget. Ill-conceived staffing. Unrealistic time frames. No internal experience or skills to complete the work. And no commitment from the firm as a whole to make sure everyone understands expectations and consequences.

In terms of goal setting, one company might plan to spend $350,000 to "get our name out there" in advertising (a weak goal with little ROI). Another might say, "We'll hire a big-gun business developer; and after they ramp up for a quarter, they'll sell $2 million in new business" (which sounds great, but is not likely to happen—just a castle in the air). These strategies are based on gut feelings and desires for simple fixes, and supported by spurious, or spuriously applied, research and data.

Those service business leaders that get in touch with what they need to do for lead generation (and, thankfully, there seem to be more and more of them) are making serious headway. Still, there are too many service firms that aren't executing, because they're out of touch with the reality of what they need to do for lead generation and why they need to do it. Thus the lukewarm efforts at executing their own plans.

Challenge 3: Lack of Will

The third, and perhaps the most debilitating, factor leading to lack of marketing and business development performance is that the organization lacks the will to get it done. This becomes less about marketing implementation and more about the seriousness of the whole company—from the leadership through the first-year associates—about growing the firm, being the best they can be, and competing at the highest levels.

"We in the marketing department work with the 'coalition of the willing' among the lawyers in the firm. It's really a fundamental principle in our department. Lawyers who are serious about working with a purpose—rather than simply 'doing marketing'—tend to work well with us. When we receive requests for random brochures or broad market research, we look first for a clear purpose. Lawyers either lose interest or become part of the coalition," says Kevin McMurdo, Chief Marketing Officer at Perkins Coie.

How do you know if your firm lacks the will to do what it needs to do to grow? Look around for these telltale signs:

- Regardless of the planning process, people (even the leaders and planners themselves) doubt that anything is going to get done.
- There's a cynical mood at the company with a silent (and sometimes not so silent) majority who believe the company is not serious about improvement and progress.
- Energetic and focused people bent on top performance and success are hired, become frustrated, and then leave the firm.
- There's a history of flavor-of-the-month management initiatives that never seem to go anywhere.
- People put in enough hours to get by, but not enough to break new ground or achieve peak performance.
- Regardless of how many hours people work, there is an overall lack of passion, energy, enthusiasm, and hustle.

If, indeed, your marketing or business development implementation challenge is based on an organizational lack of will—the company is just not serious about growth—you've got bigger problems than you can solve through marketing planning. Challenges 1 (performance environment) and 2 (connection to reality) are things you can realistically do something about, especially if challenge 3 (lack of will) is not an issue.

That's not to say that challenge 3 isn't something you can't tackle, but it's a big mountain and it's less about marketing and more about change management.

8 | Brand—What It Is; Why Bother

"I don't know who you are.

I don't know your company.

I don't know your company's product.

I don't know what your company stands for.

I don't know your company's customers.

I don't know your company's record.

I don't know your company's reputation.

Now, what was it you wanted to sell me?"

—Famous McGraw-Hill advertisement

The concept of brand is a touchy one for most professional services firms. Unless you have millions to spend on taglines and image, spending strictly to increase your brand awareness creates hot discussion around the marketing committee or executive meeting conference tables. The debate usually goes something like this:

Brand advocate: We know our services are as good as or better than any of the other firms out there, but we keep getting beaten by well-known firms with more aggressive marketing. Just last week we came in second fiddle to one of the big-name firms. And we all know we were perfect for this deal!

I even heard last week that Acme Industrials just signed up with one of our competitors to a six-figure contract. We've been trying to meet Acme's CFO, Katherine Janeway, for a year and a half; but someone else got the call. Perhaps CFO Janeway checked out our web site after one of the calls. If she did, I don't blame her for not calling us back. The other firms are blowing us away comparatively.

We need to make sure our name is out there more, that we get known, and that we present ourselves much better than we are doing now, or we'll never grow this place like we should. We need more brand!

Brand skeptic: That brand stuff is hogwash. People buy from us because of relationships, our people, and what we have done and can do, not because of our logo, our tagline, and our web site. I can't think of any better way to waste time and money than to spend it on this marketing stuff. Repeat business, referrals, and a team networking hard in the field to make contacts—we need more energy and effort in these simple, tried-and-true areas. This brand stuff is soft.

So who's right? Mike May, former Global Managing Partner for Strategy at Accenture, puts it like this:

"The only problem with the second argument is that it assumes that the people-working-hard model is scalable in terms of getting you known. It's not. In other words, they're saying they have 'all the reach we need with personal energy. People will know us by our people,' and so on. That assumes that the people get an opportunity, are sent out for the opportunity, win the job, and get known. Brand's established and enhanced. The problem with that approach is that it's diffuse and not scalable.

"What a brand does for you is it draws clients to you. It gives you more of those opportunities. It starts to bring it all together for you in the market. So, I think the issue between the two is a matter of scale. . . . The brand basically pulls everything together for you in a very cohesive package. You know that the best client in the world can remember only a few sound bites at any one time; 150 consultants in the field, or 150,000, will never establish the reach and consistency you need.

"Thus, with the brand you have leverage and consistency."

Disagreements like the one illustrated in our brand advocate/skeptic scenario question the energy and effort that should be put into brand at a professional services firm. The disagreements often stem from a lack of understanding of what a brand can do for a firm's ability to gain new clients and grow. This is because it's difficult to make a direct and tangible return on investment (ROI) calculation based on brand and marketing. As a result, marketing in many firms still suffers from the image of marketing as soft, immeasurable, and consisting mainly of brochures and marketing fluff.

This is sometimes marketing's own brand. In one *Dilbert* coming strip, Dilbert is sent from his normal assignment in engineering to work a stint in marketing. When he arrives, he finds the marketing department to be surrounded by Greek columns with marketers floating in the clouds like angels. Above the entrance to the department hangs a sign: "Welcome to Marketing. Two-drink minimum."

What kinds of hard-nosed managing partners and CEOs are going to listen to the fuzzy, design-sensitive, "Let's make an emotional connection" marketing crowd? The smart ones will, if they know what's good for them. Both for company leaders and for marketers (who need to make a better case for marketing's effectiveness and necessity), the question comes down to this:

"What can a brand actually do for a professional services firm?" In other words, "Why bother?"

Both for marketers defending their reason for being and for the hard-nosed managing partners, here are the answers:

Brands increase sales effectiveness. If a potential buyer says, "I know your company—you have a reputation for providing great value and treating clients exceptionally well," you'll be in much better shape than if they recite for you, word for word, the McGraw-Hill advertisement highlighted at the beginning of this chapter and in Figure 8.1.

Figure 8.1　Brands Increase Sales Effectiveness

© The McGraw-Hill Companies, Inc. Reproduced with permission of
The McGraw-Hill Companies, Inc.

In addition, we all know that large buying decisions have multiple
people influencing the purchase from the buyer side. When your prospect
asks around and hears, "Yes, I've been following their research for years.
They're a leader in the space," or "I've worked with them before—they're as
solid as they come," it'll be much better for you than if they hear a chorus of
"Nope—never heard of them," or worse.

Brands help generate leads. If prospects know and respect your
company and reputation, they'll be more likely to accept an invitation to an
event, an offer to download a new white paper, or a random telephone call
inviting them to have lunch and discuss business. If they've never heard of

you, the messages can often go unnoticed and untouched (until the messages build up enough over time and they've seen these messages for a while, but then you're starting to establish—dare we say—a brand).

In the Wellesley Hills Group and RainToday.com research study *What's Working in Lead Generation*,[1] we asked 731 leaders in professional services businesses about their lead generation practices. In this study we found that the well-known respondent companies were significantly more likely than their "hidden gem" and "best-kept secret" counterparts to say they were "good" or "excellent" at generating leads for their services. (See Figure 8.2.)

In total, the 30 percent of companies that considered themselves "very well-known" in their target market benefited from the impact of reputation reach, while the 70 percent of companies that thought of themselves as "not very well-known" didn't.

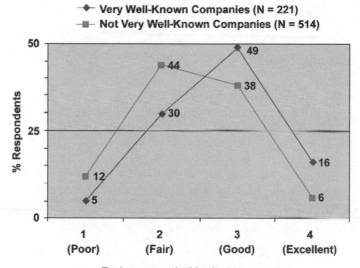

Each measure in this chart represents a
significant difference, at a 95% confidence level.

Figure 8.2   Companies' Overall Ability to Generate Leads, by Reputation Reach in Target Market

---

[1] *What's Working in Lead Generation* (RainToday.com, 2007), www.raintoday.com/leadgenreport.cfm

Lest anyone tell you differently, brand recognition and reputation help when it comes to lead generation. Fully 65 percent of well-known companies report being "good" or "excellent" at lead generation, whereas only 44 percent of the not well-known companies report being "good" or "excellent" at generating leads. If you are well-known, whatever lead generation tactics you employ are likely to work better, and the brand itself can make the phone ring.

The impact of brand on lead generation is driven home to us every day in our work for clients. One of our primary services at Wellesley Hills Group is to bring about new opportunities for clients through integrated marketing efforts, including cold calling. Our business developers love to work with clients whose names are known in the target industry. They get fewer rude responses, more people willing to transfer the call, and at least the chance to engage the prospect long enough to elicit interest. And they love to work with clients that have engaged us with robust marketing tactics *besides* cold calling. There's often a huge difference in results after only six months of integrated marketing efforts because the brand becomes familiar to the target market. (See Figure 8.1.)

Now, should you think brand is available only to the Accentures, McKinseys, and KPMGs of the world, we have clients consisting of 30, 15, and (as you read earlier) 2 professionals who have established brand in their target markets with their target buyers through their speaking, writing, content-rich web sites, direct mail, e-mail, and other marketing outreach. Each new client we work with reinforces this truth: Brand is a lead generation multiplier.

Brands generate premium fees. It may seem basic, but buyers are looking for services firms to do what they say they're going to do. If your brand and reputation (1) create a promise for what the buyer can expect from you, (2) support the belief that you deliver on your promises, (3) deliver a promise that has value to the market, and (4) position you as distinct from other offerings in the marketplace, you'll garner higher fees.

Take a look at the "Median Hourly Billing Rates" table from Wellesley Hills Group and RainToday.com's series of Fee and Pricing Benchmark Reports. It's clear the firms that are well-known in their target markets receive higher fees than firms that are not as well-known in their target markets. This applies not only to earning higher fees, but also to getting more new client opportunities. Again from our fee and pricing studies, well-known firms reported realizing higher fees per hour than those that were not brand leaders—in fact, sometimes as much as 50 percent higher.

MEDIAN HOURLY BILLING RATES REALIZED FOR THE HIGHEST-LEVEL PROFESSIONALS

Industry	Non-Brand Leaders	Brand Leaders	Percent Difference
Consulting	$250	$300	20%
Marketing, Advertising, and Public Relations	$150	$200	33%
Architecture, Engineering, and Construction	$160	$172	8%
Accounting and Financial Services	$200	$298	49%
Law Firms and Legal Services	$300	$450	50%

Brands help you beat competition. If a buyer feels confident she's going to get top quality, high output, reduced risk, the best thinkers, or whatever your brand signifies, then she is almost always certain to value that over the lowest price. Without distinct criteria for buyers to evaluate what you will do versus someone else, or a referral, or past experience, or some other previous indicator that what you say is, indeed, what they'll experience from you, price often becomes a central factor.

Brands facilitate repeat business. When buyers know what to expect from interactions with you, that you keep your promises and that you deliver at (and above) their expectations, they're less likely to switch or stop buying from you. Part of brand is the degree to which buyers prefer to purchase from you versus other options available to them.

Brands keep you competitive for top talent. In good economies and bad, services firms need to hire the best people they can possibly find. Brands are often a force in attracting the best job candidates and getting them to accept positions at your company versus the others.

Brands increase the value of a company. As discussed throughout this book, brands help create premium fees, new business leads, strong sales, and quality staff hiring. These are long-term financial advantages that translate into higher market value and company valuation, especially because of how long it takes to establish a brand from scratch. This point may interest only the owners of a business; but then again, the owners often hold the purse strings and the keys to success for brand and marketing initiatives.

How to Think about Service Brands

At the beginning of this chapter we played a scenario about an internal debate in professional services firms about brand. We have seen or heard countless others. Ask 10 people in a professional services firm to define brand, and you're likely to get 10 different answers. Common language inside a firm about brand is elusive. Let's first, then, define and describe the important concepts.

A brand is the collection of perceptions about your firm.

Among the many ways one could define brand, we like this one for a number of reasons.

First, by not defining brand as solely something in the minds of stakeholders in the market (e.g., decision makers, influencers, and referrals sources), this definition leaves room for the importance of the perception in the minds of your staff. In branding a product, the marketer worries about the packaging, taglines, and slogans that become the brand. A can of soda does not vary much from can to can. The soda can does not doubt its ability to deliver on its brand promise. In service firms, your brand is tested and delivered every day by each member of the firm. If there are doubts and confusion around what you stand for, it will come through clearly in every interaction and weaken the impact of your brand. It is crucial that you promote your brand internally as well as externally.

Second, this definition focuses on client and market perceptions about you. Earlier we stated that brands facilitate repeat business. I can imagine someone thinking, "My logo and how my web site looks will not factor one iota into repeat business." If you were thinking that, you're largely right. However, the *perceptions about you in the minds of your buyers*, which can be based on many factors, are exactly why they'd choose you to work with again versus someone else, versus doing the work internally, or versus doing nothing at all.

Third, you can look at perceptions in the minds of staff, buyers, influencers, referral sources, and the market at large from a number of important business perspectives. Influencers may recommend you or your firm; and the market at large may be important to you for investor confidence, ability to attract talent, and other factors. As long as you know what's important for your firm, the definition is easy to unpack.

"I think that many professional service firms, including law firms, too often think of brand as visual and verbal one-way communication. To me, brand is primarily behavioral. The visual reinforces the position of the firm as a player in a particular market, and that is a good thing. Some firms, however, spend more time and energy on the visual and less on the behavioral. They focus more on giving out information about firm capabilities and expertise rather than on listening to their clients and prospects and responding to what they hear.

"Firms should be less concerned with broad name recognition and more concerned about communicating with core clients and targets. Their messages should say: 'This is what it's like to work with us.' The firm then is able to concentrate on reinforcing and rewarding lawyer and staff behaviors that align with the messages."

—Kevin McMurdo, Chief Marketing Officer, Perkins Coie

For example, is there a perception *at all* about you in the market? You might have a great logo and color scheme, but like a tree falling in the forest, if no one sees your logo, do you really have a brand? According to our definition, no: You'd don't have brand recognition or awareness. (What you have is a corporate identity platform.)

Some of the other perspectives that can form the collection of perspectives that a client might have about a firm include recognition, articulation of capabilities, top-of-mind awareness, preference, and viewpoint.

CLIENT PERSPECTIVES ABOUT FIRMS

Brand Perspective	Description
Recognition (or Awareness)	Does the market know that my company exists? *Unaided Awareness:* If someone were to ask a buyer in your market, "What firms or service providers come to mind when it comes to X services?" and your name is included in the buyer's list, you have unaided awareness. *Aided Awareness (or Recognition):* If someone were to ask a buyer in your market, "Have you heard of Acme Consulting?" or "Do you know of this consultant or book?" and the buyer answers, "Yes, I recognize them and know who they are," you have aided awareness in these areas.
Articulation of Capabilities	If a buyer can say, "I know how they help companies like me solve problems like mine with X set of services, approaches, and so on," you have articulation of capabilities.
Memorization (or Top-of-Mind Awareness)	If buyers think of you or your firm at the elusive time of need, and/or they have the ongoing desire to use you and your services, they have memorized your brand and you have top-of-mind awareness.

Preference   If buyers prefer to use you when they have a need over other available options, you have achieved brand preference in their minds.

Why a buyer prefers to use you or your services can be further broken down into a number of other areas:

Performance Resonance: They really need what you do, and/or what you do for them makes a difference in their success.

Emotional Resonance: They have an affinity for working with you or your firm personally from a feeling versus a rational perspective. This is often where brand identity and graphic design have an influence. (Are they high-end? Are they edgy? Are they professional? Are they modern? Are they in my league as a peer? Are they thought leaders?)

Differentiation: They believe you are distinct from other companies or offerings.

Substantiation: They believe that you can do what you say you are going to do. In other words, they have faith in you and trust you.

Viewpoint   A buyer's perception of your firm may include thoughts on:

- Your organization as a whole.
- A service line, geographical focus, or industry expertise.
- An individual or set of individuals at your firm.

A brand can have a significant impact on your ability to grow the firm, and a brand itself is simply the collection of perceptions in the minds of buyers and influencers. That still leaves a number of questions unanswered, such as:

- How do I figure out what my brand strategy should be?
- What do I really need to know about differentiation?

- Where and when do graphic design, logos, taglines, and key messages fit in the brand equation?
- How do I go from *crafting* my brand identity and key messages to *actually getting known* in my target markets? If I have limited budget and resources, how do I do it in a way that gets me the most bang for my buck?
- What are the truths about brand that fit for my professional service business?

We'll answer these questions in the following chapters.

9 | Three Elements of Well-Crafted Brand Messaging

My aim is to put down on paper what I see and what I feel in the best and simplest way.

—Ernest Hemingway

We are a unique, dynamic, flexible firm that efficiently and effectively meets your needs. We have helped many Fortune 500 and emerging companies in your industry to increase their revenue, employee satisfaction, cost structure, cash flow, profitability, and, most important, shareholder value.

Work with us, and you'll be amazed at our intense client service levels and unyielding dedication to client satisfaction. Indeed, we don't just offer services; we offer solutions, real solutions, becoming a trusted advisor to our clients, helping them make the most difficult and important business decisions.

We've all read descriptions like this, or something close to it, describing professional services firms of all types. While the firms that offer these services may indeed be fabulous, and these messages may actually be true, marketing copy like this comes across at best as cliché.

Exaggeration, you say? A quick Google search yielded the following web site copy about a professional services firm:

> From small business to large corporations [company name] has the people, tools, and experience to meet your organization's needs.
>
> Since 1998 [company name] has provided [service type] for business. By forming long-term relationships with our clients, we provide them with time-efficient, cost-effective solutions that provide results. [Company name] has now expanded, with a wide range of services meeting today's business needs.

While this copy is all too common and most unfortunate, we understand its origins. It is the result of decades of being steered away from selling service features and being steered toward selling benefits and (dare we say) solutions. It's also an offshoot of client and market research gone awry.

Just as a brand is the collection of *perceptions*, this kind of marketing copy comes from a collection of *misconceptions* of what you're supposed to do to articulate a services brand's strength.

Firms can do a much better job to communicate value and resonate with buyers, differentiate their firms, and build marketplace credibility by understanding what drives buyers' decision making about choosing and working with a professional services firm.

What Buyers Want to Know

While no two buyers are exactly alike, and every buying situation has its own dynamics, buyers of professional services are typically asking the same questions and weighing the same factors every time they search for and engage outside help. The core buyer questions are:

- What service providers do I know of that can solve this problem (or help me achieve this goal)?
- Do I have any predisposition to buy from one company/provider over another?

- What is the business impact of solving this problem?
- What is the risk of failing to solve this problem?
- How difficult is it to find providers who purport to solve my particular problem?
- How difficult is it to find providers who can solve this problem *well*?
- What are the different options I have for solving this problem?
- What are the differences among the various options I have for solving this problem?
- How deeply do I believe (or how skeptical am I) that the service providers who *say* they can solve this problem can actually solve it?
- Do I believe any of the possible providers will be a better fit for my organization?
- What resources will my firm and I need to commit—in time, energy, and money—to solve this problem?
- How comfortable am I, personally and professionally, with the delivery teams of the possible providers?

The questions boil down to: "How comfortable am I with your expertise, your interpersonal skills, and your dedication to my success; and do I believe that you can actually do the work well?" The answers a buyer comes up with for these questions are in large part the result of substantial interaction between you and a prospective client, and less the result of marketing.

Your brand, however, can have a substantial impact in five areas:

1. Whether you get into the discussion at all when a buyer has a need.
2. A buyer's predisposition to want to buy from you as opposed to using other options to solve the problem.
3. A buyer's desire to solve the problems that you can help the buyer solve.
4. The ease of your winning the business during your business development process.
5. Expectations of the behaviors of your team in the business development process.

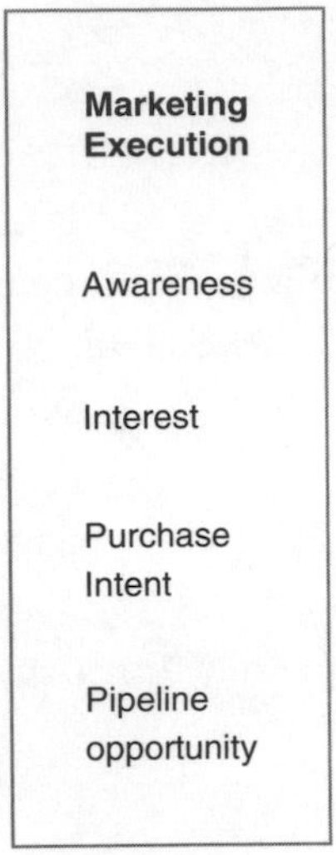

Marketing Execution
Awareness
Interest
Purchase Intent
Pipeline opportunity

Figure 9.1 Marketing Execution

The first task, then, is building the foundation upon which you can establish the strongest brand possible for you and your firm.

All buyers must go through similar stages before they become your client (Figure 9.1 and below.).

- **Stage 1.** Awareness
- **Stage 2.** Interest
- **Stage 3.** Purchase Intent
- **Stage 4.** Pipeline Opportunity

Awareness can manifest itself in a number of ways, and it's more than just "getting your name out there," as many people like to say. You need the market to know that you exist as well as that a particular service or solution exists. As Johnny Carson was wont to say, "I didn't know you could *do that!*" If buyers don't know they can solve a particular problem or don't know they can solve it in a new or novel way, you won't get any chances to sell anything.

Perhaps your service is not a new concept to the market, but it is new service for you. If people don't know you solve a particular problem, they won't come to you when the problem arises. Obviously, people who don't know that something exists (a company or something inside that company) won't even have the chance to be buyers. Awareness is a precondition for purchase.

While a buyer might be *aware* that you exist, and, as we stated, awareness is a precondition for purchase, they may have no *interest* in what you do or interest in solving any of the problems you solve. First, they might not even know what you do; thus, of course, they're not interested in buying anything from you yet. They're probably not curious about your company and probably not curious about your services and definitely not curious about the results you've gotten for others.

Assume now you've got them paying attention—*awareness AND interest*. A buyer might say, "Interesting enough. I'll check them out. Okay, now that I know that Acme Consulting exists, I see they do this kind of service for these kinds of companies in this situation. But unfortunately for them, I don't want or need to solve this problem or get help in this area right now."

This buyer has awareness and interest, but no purchase intent. The question then becomes, "Why don't you want or need what I do?" Perhaps the buyer is satisfied with his current provider. Maybe you solve a particular problem, and the buyer does not perceive that problem to be an issue for him. If it is an issue on the buyer's radar screen, it might not be important enough to solve. Maybe the buyer has a problem and understands that you *say* you solve it, but he doesn't really believe you. The reasons go on, the point being that buyers are not going to buy something unless they put it on their to-do list to take action.

Let's now assume that the buyer intends to solve a particular problem and knows you exist and that you communicate that you solve that particular problem. Next you need to *convert the buyer into your pipeline*, or, as we say in the marketing business, generate the buyer as a lead.

Unlike products or simple transactional services, buyers don't usually walk into a retail store and go from purchase intent to purchase without some kind of substantial interaction with you. It's your marketing and business development outreach in conjunction with your brand that go to work for you in translating a buyer's purchase intent into a genuine pipeline opportunity.

To create awareness, interest, purchase intent, and pipeline opportunity, you need two major components of your brand in place:

Positioning. With corporate identity, there is power in a name, a logo, and a symbol. Your brand identity serves as the

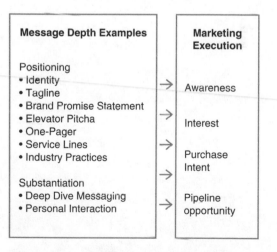

Figure 9.2   Value Proposition Delivery

foundation of the rest of the messaging and positioning with which you communicate to the market and as a launch point for delivering key messages. With positioning messages, you communicate such things as who you serve (industries, geographic areas, functional areas, levels in the organization); the problems you solve; the methods you use to solve those problems; and what it's like to work with you as a firm. Positioning serves as well in a comparative role: setting forth who you are and what you do against other options available to the market to solve similar problems. Taglines, brand promise statements, one-page descriptions, and your home page on your web site are all examples of what you can use to deliver your positioning to the market.

Substantiation. Through substantiation, you take who you are and what you say that you do (positioning) and give the market the sense that what you're saying is genuine and defensible. Substantiation can be delivered in one of two ways: deep dive messaging and personal interaction.

Seminars, speeches, webinars, teleseminars, podcasts, on-demand Internet presentations, white papers, books, articles, research reports, and case studies are all examples of deep dive messaging. With deep dive messaging, you give clients and prospects the ability to dive deeply into who you are *without you personally interacting with them*. These approaches allow them to draw conclusions on whether you seem to be a good fit for their needs.

"A message to firms of every size: Every one of your prospects and recruits looks at your web site. Guaranteed. If they're serious about hiring or joining you, they'll *really* look at your web site. We designed our current web site as a repository of detailed, specific information so that people could find the information most valuable to their particular search. Now, it needs to be more interactive and supportive of targeted communications with new, more narrow markets."

—Kevin McMurdo, Chief Marketing Officer, Perkins Coie

Personal interactions such as face-to-face discussions (sales conversations), telephone discussions, two-way e-mail exchanges, and, of course, the actual delivery of services are the most powerful way to relay to the market that you can, and do, live up to the promises you make in your brand messaging.

Taken all together, think of your positioning and substantiation as the vehicles through which you deliver your *value proposition* to the market. Assume, if you will, that prospects read and see every piece of positioning and substantiation marketing material and intellectual capital you offer. And, of course, they see it all packaged consistently with your brand identity (logos, colors, etc.). They can now answer the question, "Given the collection of my deep perceptions of this company, how much do I want or need what they do, and how strong are my preferences for engaging them in discussions to help me compared to other options?" In other words, in total, buyers now have the foundation to evaluate the extent of your likely value to them.

VALUE PROPOSITION DEFINED

A *value proposition* is the collection of reasons why a company or individual will benefit from working with a firm. Value propositions can be delivered through a number of marketing vehicles, from company names and taglines to brand promise statements and corporate overviews to deep and detailed interaction with your intellectual capital and people.

When it comes to positioning and substantiation, you should also note:

As you move down the list of ways value propositions are delivered, the delivery vehicles increase substantially in breadth and depth. Your logo, name, and color palette will begin to communicate your overall value proposition; but they often do so subtly, perhaps only implying and reflecting key messages that support how people benefit from working with you. Core attributes of your company may be embedded in your logo, but they may not be readily apparent to the viewer. What is important is that they are imbued with meaning from which you can hang the rest of your value proposition messaging. Your one-pager or corporate overview will list what you do and for whom, as well as the outcomes you can achieve; but it does not give much context as to *how* you get it done, how it has worked in the past, and how buyers can evaluate if it is right for them. Your white papers, case studies, research, and speeches will provide the deeper meaning and context. But from positioning to deep dive messaging, the messages must cascade consistently.

While they are not mutually exclusive, positioning and substantiation messages lend themselves to different outcomes. Your name and logo can be used to generate awareness. Indeed, awareness marketing without a name and logo would be useless (with a few historical exceptions). However much they are necessary for *awareness*, names and logos aren't typically very powerful in generating *interest* for your services.

Messages geared toward positioning your services serve as a foundation for generating interest in your services. Yet, by themselves, they're not the most effective for generating actual pipeline opportunities.

Let's say 1,000 people at an industry conference attended by decision makers in your industry receive your one-pager in their kit of conference materials. After reading it they say, "Good to know. If I need this kind of help, I have someone I can call." In terms of pipeline opportunities, even though you have 1,000 one-pagers in the kit of conference materials, you might get zero inquiries. However, give a speech to the same audience and follow up afterward to see if people want to discuss the topic more deeply, and you can have dozens of new business opportunities in your pipeline.

Foundation of Developing Your Value Proposition Messaging

Now that you understand the ways to deliver value proposition messages to your desired market, you will need to build the right subset of messages to communicate it. Before you can build your value proposition messaging, you need to answer this question:

What knowledge do we need in order to build the strongest value proposition messaging we can build?

The strength of your value proposition is a three-legged stool, the legs being resonance, differentiation, and ability to substantiate. (See Figure 9.3.)

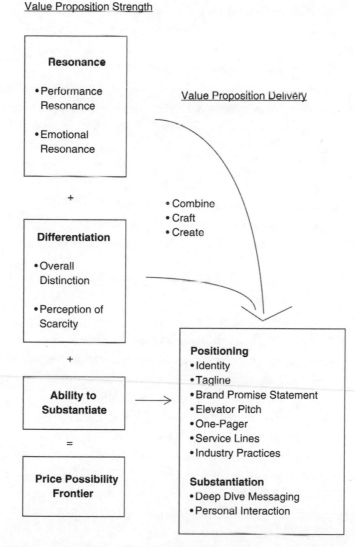

Figure 9.3   Value Proposition Strength and Delivery

Resonance

Earlier in this chapter, we posed a number of questions that buyers ask themselves. Two of those questions were, "What is the business impact of solving this problem?" and "What is the risk of failing to solve this problem?" One could argue that these two questions form the essence of the buying decision. As complex as many consultants and practitioners try to make these concepts, this is one of those very rare cases where it is actually possible to boil everything down to a one-syllable word: *need*.

A powerful but simple concept, need itself can further be broken down into two major components: performance resonance and emotional resonance.

Performance resonance

Performance resonance is a buyer's perception of the need to solve a particular problem or to engage a particular solution because of the impact that solving the problem will have on the business. For example, a decision maker might say, "Last year, 100 employees whom we didn't want to leave left our hospital, costing us $100,000 in replacement expense and lost productivity per person. In other words, $10 million walked out the door last year." If that decision maker comes across a message from a firm that says, "We have helped our clients in health care institutions reduce unwanted turnover by an average of 20 percent within one year, and we can do it for you," she could see that for her that would equal a drop in unwanted turnover by 20 people, saving the company $2 million.

While they're closely related, don't confuse performance resonance with return on investment (ROI). As you can imagine, the message of lowering turnover by 20 percent and saving $2 million will likely resonate with our buyer as something to investigate. Whether she'll get a return on investment depends on what she'll have to spend in time, energy, and money to achieve the desired results. If the engagement will cost $200,000, the ROI will seem pretty good. If it will cost $1.5 million, not so much.

While $2 million in savings would seem large by many business-people's standards, that's not always the case. One decision maker, when presented with a way to save $10 million by one of our clients, said, "I see that you can save me the $10 million, but right now I'm solving $50 million problems." What resonates with one buyer won't necessarily resonate with another.

Emotional resonance

Emotional resonance is a buyer's collection of feelings toward a particular problem, a particular solution, or a particular company.

Mike Schultz: More years ago than I prefer to count, I was working at a company that had recently made the decision to go public. Curious young manager that I was, I asked the CFO of the company why he chose a particular big-five firm (at the time there were five) to handle the preparations for our public offering.

He said to me, "Come down to my office and I'll show you." When we got there, he walked me through a decision grid he had created for the president and board of directors. After he was done, he said, "Clearly, this firm was the most qualified, best firm for us to take us public." After hearing his argument, I couldn't agree with him more. This firm was head and shoulders better for us. Then he said, "Close the door." (I did.) "Do you want to know the real reason I picked them?"

"It wasn't what you showed me?" I asked.

"Nope. I picked them because . . . I liked them better." He went on, "Three of the five had the experience, the people, and the resources to do a great job taking us public. But I'm the one who will have to work with these people for 18 hours a day for a year straight, and I simply had the best connection with the folks at the firm I chose."

It's been said that buyers buy with their hearts (emotion) and justify it with their heads (performance). This kind of statement is often associated with consumer buying, not business buying. While the contexts might be different, it's just as true with business buyers that emotions and feelings influence their decision making and budget allocations.

Differentiation

Few topics in services marketing are more misunderstood than differentiation. With differentiation, as with many topics treated in this book, the simple explanation is the best. *Differentiation* is the combination of the overall existence of (or lack of) distinguishing characteristics of one thing when compared to another thing and the perception of the availability of substitutes. That's it.

As we discuss in Chapter 13, much of the literature available about differentiation misleads marketers of professional services, suggesting that they need to tout a message of being unique, that they should position themselves as opposite as possible to the other options available in the market.

One ill-conceived school of thought goes as far as suggesting that firms approach differentiation not from the perspective of positioning but of *oppositioning*, a term they coined to connote that firms should position their messages as radically different from the other available options. (For more on how to think about differentiation for your firm, see Chapter 13, "On Being Unique and Other Bad Marketing Advice.")

Ability to Substantiate

You can deliver messages to the market about the impact and the difference you can make for clients (resonance) and your differentiation. But you won't get very far if the buyer doesn't believe you. One of the reasons those in marketing often take flak from business leaders is because, in many cases, marketing messages are just puffery. You need the market to believe what you say. In another word: trust.

You do that through substantiation.

Buyers will ask, when they read your claims of the value you can deliver (resonance) and your differentiation, "Are they *credible*?"

Do you claim:

- Your work is research based? If so, where's the research and how well is it done?

- To have delivered millions of dollars in recovered costs from insurance companies for manufacturing companies, costs that your clients didn't know they were entitled to? If so, where are the case studies and testimonials?
- To be the world's leading experts on consumer product innovation? If so, where are your articles and books? When are your industry conference keynote speeches?
- To be a unique firm—a firm like no other that exists? If so, how good is your reasoning for that?

Let's assume you claim to be the world's leading expert on consumer product innovation. You have a rich library of primary research you've conducted and case studies you've written. You have a history of publishing excellent articles in top publications on the subject, and your book on innovation is in its third edition. You run an active innovation research center. Credibility rating: very good.

On the flip side, anything that will cause anyone—be they clients, prospects, partners, or potential employees—to question the credibility of what you say puts you at a disadvantage.

> "The real-world story is you've got to get the organization to understand that there is a difference between just asserting something and real research."
>
> —Mike May, Professor at Babson College, former Co-Vice Chair of KPMG, and former Global Managing Partner of the strategy business for Accenture

Buyers will ask, "Are they *reliable*?" Buyers want reliable service providers. In your marketing and business development processes, you can do a lot to influence a buyer's perception of your reliability. And how do people judge reliability? They do so largely based on your history of making and then keeping your promises. For example, in the Wellesley Hills Group and RainToday.com's *How Clients Buy* study, we asked buyers to reflect back on the past few times they purchased professional services. Some 18 percent of buyers reported service providers being late to meetings, and 30 percent reported that the provider did not respond to their requests in a manner that they deemed to be timely.

You might ask yourself, what exactly is "timely"? For all intents and purposes, it doesn't matter. The buyer's perception of you, should you not respond to requests in what is deemed to be a timely manner by them, will likely be one of not being particularly reliable. If that's the buyer's perception of you, then it's a part of your brand.

The more someone feels they are in good hands with you, the more clout (substantiation) any claims you make will have with them. For example, in one case, someone knows you have published well-regarded research, books, and articles on the subject but hasn't read them; you may have credibility in general but no deep connection or emotional resonance (necessary to build trust) yet.

In a second case, someone has read your well-regarded articles, books, case studies, and research and is thoroughly familiar with your models and methods. Thus begins the foundation for stronger connection, emotional resonance, and trust (and, assuming your intellectual capital is good, your credibility improves as well).

In a third case, you've never worked with a buyer as a client, but you've spent a year working with the company as a prospect in your long business development cycle, talking people through important issues, providing counsel, and helping them move their agendas forward. Even before they begin to work with you, their level of security to entrust you with something important has begun to bloom.

In a last case, you've worked with someone for years intimately as a client, though thick and thin and several touch-and-go situations. You've come through for someone repeatedly in good and difficult times. This client always believes that you have his firm's best interest at heart, and you've demonstrated this to be the case numerous times in difficult situations.

Now your connection and level of trust is very deep. Your value proposition strength is based on three legs of a stool: resonance, differentiation, and

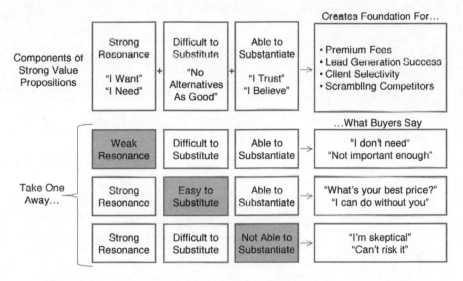

Figure 9.4   Components of Value Proposition Strength

substantiation. Figure 9.4 shows what happens when one of those legs gets taken away.

In Chapter 10 we examine how you can uncover the essence of your brand attributes that will contribute to developing your value proposition messaging.

10

Uncovering Your Key Brand Attributes

To do a common thing uncommonly well brings success.

—H. J. Heinz, printed on the back of a ketchup bottle

When it comes to marketing and branding, one very simple question seems to trip up firm after firm. That question is:

What should we say about ourselves?

We know from the previous chapter that we can deliver messages of our value to the market and clients in a number of different ways. We also know that to build the strongest possible messages, we must combine resonance, differentiation, and substantiation. With or without this knowledge, firms struggle to figure out what the core components of their messaging should be.

The diagram in Figure 10.1 offers you a review of where we have been to this point. In Chapter 14 we'll address how to approach combining, crafting, and creating your messages from a core set of building blocks. In this chapter, you'll learn how to discover what those building blocks are for you and how to categorize them. And, when you are finished, you will see how to figure out what to say about yourself.

121

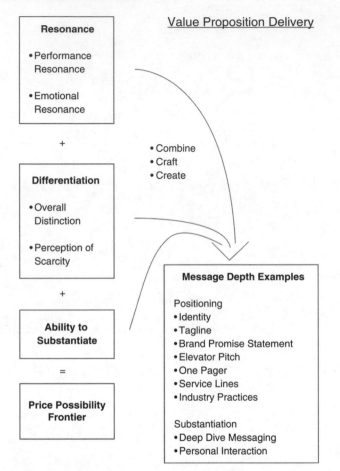

Figure 10.1   Value Proposition Strength and Delivery

Nine Questions: Finding the Strength of Your Value Proposition

In order to articulate the messages about your firm that will contribute to your growth by connecting with the market and helping you sell, you first need to answer nine questions dealing with two topics: value and differentiation.

You need to know your clients' and your markets' perception of *value* regarding:[1]

1. Your general category of firms and services.
2. Your firm.
3. The specific services you offer.
4. Solving particular problems that clients currently have.
5. Solving certain problems clients can anticipate having in the future but do not perceive as priorities.

You need to know your clients' and your markets' perception of your *overall distinction* in the market and their perception of how difficult it would be to get services similar to yours or to solve the problems you solve in other ways. Thus, you need to find out what *different options* clients and decision makers in the market perceive they have regarding:

6. Different categories of companies that can help to solve problems (or achieve goals).
7. Specific companies that can help solve problems.
8. Specific services available to help solve problems.
9. Other options available to help to solve problems, such as internal staff.

Let's look at each of the nine questions in turn in the context of different examples and see how the answers will affect your messages to the market.

Question #1: What *value* do clients and decision makers perceive about our general category of company and services?

It's no secret that the pharmaceutical industry is a large purchaser of management consulting. But the question is: *What do specific buyers in the industry value about management consulting?* Do they value functional expertise,

---

[1] Of course, you also need to know your own people's perception of your value. In the next chapter, we look at how to look at your own firm.

such as marketing or industry experience, in the pharmaceutical industry? Are they likely to buy services from small firms or large? Does it matter? Do they perceive that 6 times out of 10 they do not get the value they wanted out of consulting? When they got good value the 4 out of 10 times, what did that look like? Would they likely spend more on prestigious thought leaders, or will experiences of the team win out?

The dynamics of your firm, your industry, and your target markets will drive the specific questions you need to ask about the category of your firm. What you discover will inform the general positioning and messaging for your firm.

Question #2: What is the *value* clients and decision makers in our target market perceive about us as a firm?

If there is a fundamental question to which every service firm should know the answer, this is it.

You should know what your *clients* think of your company. The answers can, among other things, drive opportunities for service improvement, uncover opportunities for cross-selling, and shape messages of value you can bring to the market. In almost all cases when you speak with clients, you'll learn perceptions about your firm's personality and what it's like to work with your team. You'll learn how they perceive the value they receive from working with your firm. You'll learn how they think you're distinct.

It is important to stress that what *you think* you know about how clients perceive your value and how *they truly perceive* the value you offer are often worlds apart. In our work with professional services firms, we often interview our clients' clients. One of our clients, a midsize certified public accountant (CPA) firm, wanted to grow faster than just through referrals. The firm had always offered great service and believed its value was comparable to or better than what other like firms offered. In speaking to the firm's clients, we heard comments much like the following, from the president of a client firm:

> "The CPA I had 10 years ago was nothing more than a tax planner. He provided me no advice at all, not managing the business or ebb and flow of cash flow in manufacturing, no balance sheet projections, no

strategy . . . nothing. It is important for a small business to understand its risk profile and balance sheet. My comptroller and I devised a formula with our current CPA firm [our client] to be debt free. This allowed us to make some very good growth decisions, not knee-jerk. We weren't laden with debt and didn't have to chase cash flow. They were very progressive. They do think outside the box. They are very creative in the way they assist in capital planning, handle all facets of the business, and are very familiar with the finance side of manufacturing."

This is great stuff to hear from a client, but the CPA firm had no idea how strongly its value as a partner and advisor came through. Talk to clients (or have someone do it for you) to make sure you know how valuable you are.

Along with clients, you should know what the buyers and influencers across your *markets* think of your company.

- Perhaps they don't know about your company at all. While it's not impossible to reap the benefits of marketing and be successful at business development if you are not well-known among the buyers and influencers in your market, you'll always be at a disadvantage as long as you hang on to your "hidden gem" or "best-kept secret" status.[2]
- Perhaps the marketplace's perception is that you are a specialist in a particular industry or service area: "Oh, they're great at technology consulting, but they don't have a strategy capability." This is the challenge Mike May at Accenture (Andersen Consulting at the time) faced in 1993. "Think back to 1993. Andersen Consulting, with little strategy capability, was very good at and known for technology, process, change management, and systems integration. The then chairman/CEO of Andersen Consulting said, 'The new game is called "business integration." We're going to have four competencies: strategy, change management, technology, and process. Our value proposition to clients is we're going to bring those together seamlessly

---

[2]See Chapter 9 on what brand can do for you.

around client problems. But guess what? We don't have the strategy thing we need to build on.'"

Many firms are known for one thing, or known for different things by different buyer sets, and see the opportunity to grow in a number of areas. Before you answer the question of how to influence the thinking of the market, you first need to know: What do they think?

Question #3: What *value* do clients and decision makers in the market perceive about the specific services we offer?

This question gets less attention than it should (or no attention) in many service firm research initiatives.

Assume you're an accounting firm with a specialty in bank auditing. When you ask clients about the value of the banking audit service, you may find that your audits consistently find ways to save them tens of thousands of dollars in hidden areas as you help them to create efficiencies and tighten up processes. You may find that they value your auditors' commitment to their success, evidenced by the auditors' consistent extra effort and willingness to talk them through issues that help them think strategically about their business.

> "Marketing communication strategies in the legal industry are often disconnected from what the lawyers really need. We have produced our share of brochures, carefully written with, by, and about our attorneys. Our clients didn't really care about them. Firms that first take the time to understand their clients and markets (and compare them to the firm's strengths) will be better able to develop strategies that will make a real difference in the firm's ability to grow."
>
> —Kevin McMurdo, Chief Marketing Officer, Perkins Coie

For a manufacturing company, your firm's operations consulting process helped increase supply chain efficiency by 25 percent. This is a very tangible value of that service, indeed, that you can build upon in your marketing.

In another scenario, let's say your firm has five distinct service areas. You may ask clients to give you their thoughts on each service. They may know of two services, and not know of three. That may signal the opportunity (or need) for marketing the other services.[3]

Question #4: What *value* do clients and decision makers in the market perceive about solving the particular problems that they currently have?

This question uncovers the value of solving explicit needs, needs that clients already know they have. Assume you're a human resources consulting firm. If you were to say to your clients or buyers in the market, "Tell me about your priorities as they relate to people practices for the next year," you might hear that they need to:

- Decrease unwanted turnover by 20 percent.
- Increase the skill and performance of people, particularly the sales force, since the industry has been changing so much.
- Increase the effectiveness of leaders, including intense focus on developing high-potential leaders.
- Contain benefits costs, as they're rising out of control.
- Support, promote, and manage an increasingly global and dispersed workforce.

Your objective is to explore each area for specific details, learn what success looks like in each area, and discover which areas are perceived as most important to solve and why.

Question #5: What *value* do clients and decision makers in the market perceive they might get if they could solve certain problems, or get certain things done, that they aren't focusing on right now or might not perceive as priorities?

---

[3] More often than not, when we ask this question on behalf of our clients, we uncover actual needs for other services. Needs discovery is a common and welcome side effect of this kind of research.

Professors Ian MacMillan and Larry Selden argue in their *Harvard Business Review* article "The Incumbent's Advantage,"[4] "Market-leading companies get attacked when they focus on products and geographic locations rather than on what competitors and disruptors actually target—unmet customer needs."

Consider the case of Everon Technology Services. For years, small business technology industry veteran Michael Cooch saw deep frustration at small businesses that complained of:

- Difficulty managing technology problems and issues internally at businesses too small to hire a dedicated technology support team.
- Inability to get in touch with their "man in a van" technology provider when they needed to, and inconsistent levels of service quality with said man.

Mike also confirmed with business leaders that they were not reaping the benefits that technology could provide them in their small businesses because they lacked knowledge of what was possible and lacked knowledge of technology successes at other small businesses.

In 2003 Mike founded Everon Technology Services to offer the market solutions to these problems and frustrations.

SOLUTIONS TO BUSINESS NEEDS OFFERED BY EVERON

Need	Everon Solution
Business too small to have dedicated technology person.	Pricing based on number of computer desktops so companies of all sizes spend appropriate and reasonable amount.
Inability to anticipate and control costs.	Monthly cost set regardless of service usage in any given month.

---

[4] Ian MacMillan and Larry Selden, "The Incumbent's Advantage," *Harvard Business Review*, October 1, 2008.

Inability to get immediate service from hourly providers for technology emergencies and timely support for nonemergencies.	Immediate availability of technical support representatives over the telephone with the ability to access computers and servers remotely to solve most problems. Availability of technical consultants to react immediately to crises in person (if necessary) at the company's site.
Inconsistencies in service levels and quality.	Formal standards for technical service, client service, and client satisfaction to set clear expectations for clients of service levels. Surveys immediately after service as well as once per month to uncover any service inconsistencies.
Small companies not reaping the strategic benefits of technology.	"Chief technology officer" services available to companies to provide benefits such as technology assessments, business objectives meetings, annual plans, and technology project management.

Did it work? The firm was founded in 2003. In 2008 Everon was named to *Inc.* magazine's list of the fastest-growing companies in the United States.

Not all unmet need is hiding in a new or novel business model. Perhaps, for example, it's simply the case that larger accounting firms have raised the bar on their client revenue level targets. They might say to themselves, "Only clients generating over $150,000 in annual revenue for us and targets that could generate the same are our priority. We will continue to service our smaller clients, but not with the focus and energy that we serve our larger clients." What happens when firms start focusing their energy on one client base versus another? Satisfaction drops across the stepchild client base.

If you find this trend and if your accounting firm targets clients in the $50,000 to $150,000 fee range, you could tailor your messaging to capture business with firms whose needs are no longer being served as well as they could be.

Question #6: What *different options* do clients and decision makers in the market perceive they have regarding different categories of companies that can help to solve problems or achieve goals?

Let's assume you are a graphic design firm and you help clients build and implement web sites and other Internet marketing strategies. When it comes to web sites and Internet marketing, what types of companies do decision makers turn to? Would they look to a creative design firm or a Web development company? Do they think of Internet marketing primarily as graphic design, as the ability to get found on Google, as e-mail marketing, or as online public relations (PR)?

Many a branding guru has said something to the effect that if you can create a new market category and if you can be perceived as the first player in that market, you can dominate the market as its leader. As we mentioned earlier, this is generally not particularly sound advice for most service firms and serves only to muddle service firm marketing strategy process with unnecessary complexity. It is, however, quite useful to know what buyers perceive as the different categories of firms from which they can get different services.

Question #7: What *different options* do clients and decision makers in the market perceive they have regarding specific companies that can help them solve problems?

It's a fundamental question, and it has a fundamental effect on your ability to compete for business. First, do clients and the market perceive *your firm* as a company that can help them solve particular problems? Second, whether they consider you an option or not, what other firms do clients and the market perceive are available to solve particular problems?

Most buyers don't have long lists of companies in their files or in their minds for each need they might have. Even if buyers can remember names of many different firms in different categories, they typically have a handful or fewer with which they associate the ability to solve particular problems.

For example, ask us to list a number of management consulting firms, and we can start rattling off names: McKinsey, Bain, Boston Consulting Group (BCG), PRTM, Accenture, BearingPoint, Monitor Group, and the list goes on. Ask us if any of them can solve a *particular problem for us*, and the answer is: We don't think so. If we were at a billion-dollar corporation, all of these firms could probably do something for us, though we couldn't tell you right away what specifically that would be. (In their defense, these firms aren't trying to market to our firm, anyway.)

We perceive our firm, probably rightly, as too small to engage the services of any of these management consulting firms and get value from them. The list of consulting firms that might be able to help us looks much different, and it's very small.

Question #8: What *different options* do clients and decision makers in the market perceive they have regarding specific services available to help them solve problems?

A CEO may say to himself, "I believe there are hidden sources of profit here at my company, but I haven't figured out yet how to find or tackle them. I know that any number of the major consulting firms would say that they could analyze my company and find the profit. But the only company that I know that has a *specific service* dedicated to finding profit is Bain & Company through its Profit Hunt service."

Bain describes a profit hunt in its marketing materials as follows:

A profit hunt is a 6- to 12-month initiative focused on identifying and understanding a company's key drivers of profitability and then design-ing and achieving quick-hit profit improvements. Typically, more than half the profit uplift comes from revenue increases. The remainder comes from reducing both internal costs and supplier costs.

A buyer might then think, "I know that not only can Bain help me find sources of profit, but the results are quick hit (I need fast returns!), and they're revenue focused as well as cost focused (I need to drive the top line!), and they're not just going to give me a report and walk away (I need help implementing!). I know who Bain is (who doesn't?), and I read right here on the Bain web site a client success story where they back up their claims (gives me reason to believe them)."

If buyers of Bain services know about Profit Hunt, Bain has a leg up. Let's say the buyer is interested in improving his profit and knows of Bain and Profit Hunt. He expresses his interest in Profit Hunt to Bain by filling out a contact form on Bain's web site. He also contacts two other major consulting firms and expresses his need. If the other firms don't have named, well-packaged, well-described, well-supported services in the area, even if they've "done it a million times," they're at a disadvantage. If the other firms prepare a custom proposal to deliver consulting services aimed at the problems the CEO faces, they may get in the game and they may even win.

But Bain has the advantage.

Additionally, inside the Profit Hunt example, we find all the elements of a strong value proposition. And this is just what we can see on the web site.

BAIN'S ADVANTAGE

Component	Examples of How Bain Uses It Well
Resonance	
Performance Resonance	More profit.
	Higher revenue.
	Quick-hit and long-term improvement.
Emotional Resonance	Bain is a top-tier firm.
	Profit Hunt feels like it was written for me.
	On the front of the site it says that Bain's clients "outperform the market (S&P 500) by a factor of 4 to 1." I want to be a Bain client.
Differentiation	
Overall Distinction	The naming and packaging of Profit Hunt.
	The client base Bain has worked with for Profit Hunt and other services.
Perception of Scarcity	What is a buyer going to do, call another firm and say, "Show me your Profit Hunt"?
	Bain people are top-notch.

Ability to Substantiate	Mini case study on Profit Hunt web page. Other case studies on Bain web site, as well as a wealth of other thought leadership pieces.

Remember, all of the questions outlined in this chapter are meant to help you define the key elements of your value proposition and deliver that value proposition to the market in the most effective ways.

Companies often confuse the concept of value proposition with their firm's elevator pitch, a brand promise statement, or some other short sentence that describes the essence of the firm. These statements are helpful, but would an elevator pitch describing Bain include Profit Hunt? Probably not—it would be too granular. However, is Profit Hunt a part of Bain's value to the market? Of course. You just don't deliver the message or its value through an elevator pitch about Bain in general.

Question #9: What *different options* do clients and decision makers in the market perceive they have regarding other options available to help them solve problems, such as internal staff?

Quick, who is your competition for your services? Did you think of other firms? It's a natural instinct to do so. Yet the competition a professional service business faces is not always other firms.

A core service of the Wellesley Hills Group is Services in Demand[SM], our service package (à la Profit Hunt) focused on lead generation and business development. While we sometimes run into other service providers during our business development process, more often than not we're faced with two other competitors:

1. Internal staff
2. Client doing nothing

If internal staff is a major competitor, the strength of your value proposition depends not on how well you position your services against the other firms, but on how well you position the services vis-à-vis the company building the capabilities in-house with its own staff. For your particular service, perhaps:

- It's important to have a team working on something, versus only one person.
- The client needs to be able to calibrate the level of service up and down depending on business conditions.
- The client would need to build a technology and management infrastructure in-house that you already have in place.

Your team has already proven its success; whereas, if the client hired internally, it would need several years to discover whether team members will actually succeed (assuming they stay long enough to even have the chance).

Comparison is part and parcel of the concept of differentiation. Many firms sell only against other firms. For example, Sarbanes-Oxley compliance work must be delivered by an independent third party. Accounting firms that deliver services here must, by their nature, compete against each other. If, as it is in many cases, your competition is internal staff, then you need to be able to position your value against that option.

You can do this only if you understand the nature of the other option.

Consider also that your competition is often the choice of your client or prospect to "do nothing at this time" or "postpone until the third quarter." Services firm leaders in this position express to us, "Well, our clients either pick us or do nothing." In these situations, there is no other service provider under consideration. When your competition is the decision maker's indifference or lack of urgency in moving forward, your challenge is less in the area of differentiation and more in the area of resonance or substantiation. If they don't see the value (resonance), they won't take the plunge. Perhaps they see the value in your message but don't believe that you can deliver it or get it to work for them (substantiation). They perceive the risk to be too great and don't take the plunge.

Brand Attributes: The Building Blocks of Brand Messaging

The answers to the nine questions will yield a veritable cornucopia of data points about you from your market and clients. These data points are the planks you can use to build your brand message platform. It's in this area, however, that many marketers (and marketing consultants) make colossal errors. They find an abundance of great information about their firms, their competition, their services, and their value to the market, and then they jumble it up in the messages.

To translate the data you've collected into useful marketing ammunition, you need to understand how to categorize the data and then apply the data the right way.

Essentially, the data breaks down into three major areas: (1) attributes of similarity, (2) distinction, and (3) experience. (See Figure 10.2.)

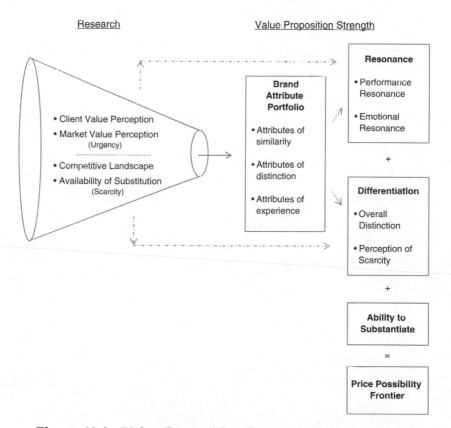

Figure 10.2   Value Proposition Research and Strength

Brand research yields a portfolio of attributes that you can sort into two buckets: things that make you valuable and things that make you distinct from other available options.

Attributes of Similarity

Attributes of similarity are things about your firm or services that are similar to other offerings or options in the market.

A quick study of the "about us" pages on the web sites of the big-four accounting firms reveals a number of emphasized key messages that are largely the same across all four firms.

ATTRIBUTES OF SIMILARITY SHARED BY BIG-FOUR ACCOUNTING FIRMS

Attribute	Ernst & Young	KPMG	PWC	Deloitte
Audit	X	X	X	X
Tax	X	X	X	X
Advisory/ Consulting	X	X	X	X
Diversity of services	X	X	X	X
Diversity of industries served	X	X	X	X
Size in people	135,000	123,000	146,000	165,000
Size in offices	X	X	X	X
Global	X	X	X	X
Great place to work	X	X	X	X
Socially responsible	X	X	X	X
Ethics/values	X	X	X	X

Depending on your type of firm, target market, and service set, certain key messages are necessary components to play the game. At the very least they are common and universally important concepts (e.g., client focus and client service, commitment to results, "people are our most important asset," etc.) that are often used as key messaging attributes but are rarely fundamentally different from the messaging of other firms.[5]

As H. J. Heinz said, "To do a common thing uncommonly well brings success." It's often your attributes of similarity, not those of distinction, that if done well, form the foundation of the strength of your firm.

Attributes of Distinction

Attributes of distinction are things about your firm that can communicate a meaningful difference when compared to others.

One of our least favorite questions that buyers ask is: "How are you different?" If we're asked this question, we'll typically respond, "Different from whom?" Are they asking how we're different from every other firm that offers services in our space? A particular category of firm? A particular firm?

As we noted earlier, difference implies comparison. Without comparison, the answer tends to be either why you're good (we win cases, our people are the smartest, we solve problems, we're big and we have global reach and assets to bring to bear for you, we're small and will treat you like gold, our foundations are rooted in our research, etc.) or something more granular that you bring to the table (we're the only firm with deep research on doing business with the financial community of Dubai, we have three former congressmen at our law firm, Dr. Emmett Brown is the world's leading expert on flux capacitor design innovation, etc.).

---

[5] Note that while the *messages* may be fundamentally similar across many firms, the *truth* may not be. You may actually be more client focused than most firms in your industry or have the best track record of results. While your reality may be distinct from other folks' realities, the messages are not.

Attributes of Experience

Attributes of experience are things about your firm that affect the perception of clients and the market regarding what it's like to work with your firm.

Is your firm buttoned-up or casual? No-nonsense or touchy-feely? Vanilla or quirky? Is your downtown office worthy of *Architectural Digest* in elegance and sophistication, or is your suburban office Spartan and work-manlike? Do you wine and dine your clients or meet up for a dog and a beer at the football game?

The one place where every service firm can, indeed, be its own special snowflake is in the experience of what it's like to work with you.

* * *

Taken together, all of your attributes—everything the market and clients say about you and everything you know about yourself—form the foundation of strength of your value proposition.

It all comes back to the question we suggest as the second most important one for you to answer as you begin marketing your practice, your firm, or yourself: "What do we say about ourselves?" (Note that the first most important question is covered in Chapter 20 on targets—"Who should we be marketing to?") By answering each of the nine questions, you will be finding relevant answers to help you articulate the value you provide to the marketplace.

11 | Your Firm, Your Brand

Look well into thyself; there is a source of strength which will always spring up if thou wilt always look there.

—Marcus Aurelius

The "visible" half of execution—the marketing professionals—can only perform as well as the "invisible" operations area allows it to. Moreover, the quality of operations can also determine an institution's ability to innovate.

—Amar Bhide, *"Hustle as Strategy"*[1]

"Who am I? Why am I here?"

—Admiral James Stockdale

In the previous chapter we looked closely at the questions you need to answer to unlock your key brand attributes. We noted that you need to find these answers from your market and your clients (assuming you are not a start-up). Before you venture beyond the firm's walls in your quest for knowledge, you must first ask the same questions of . . . yourself.

---

[1] Amar Bhide, "Hustle as Strategy," *Harvard Business Review*, September 1, 1986.

Much has been written about what makes great firms with solid financial results great in the eyes of their clients. Firms that deliver the highest level of client satisfaction enjoy the highest level of client loyalty and are most likely to get new business referred to them from their client base.[2] Being the best firm you can be is (rightly) the subject of much attention, as the better you are at doing what you do, the more likely you'll be to succeed.

Let's assume most of us believe we can always get better at what we do and deliver stronger value to the market and our clients. For the purposes of this book, regardless of universal agreement that we can get better at what we deliver in the future, we need knowledge about ourselves regarding what we can deliver *right now* and how good we are *right now* so we can build marketing messages that will support revenue generation.

Who Are We? What Do We Deliver?

Your *capabilities* are what you can deliver to clients. This may sound like it's a given, but the first thing you need to do if you want to establish a strong brand is get a grip on your capability set.

Companies often view capabilities as a list of services, but they're more than that. View your capabilities through two lenses: (1) what you do and (2) the outcomes you produce. A consulting firm might, for example, have a service that analyzes large firms' spending in corporate overhead and then implements changes to the overhead structure based on this analysis. That's the "what you do" part.

On average, this service produces 5 percent reductions in overhead spend. At a billion-dollar corporation, overhead spend might be 10 percent of revenue, or $100 million. A 5 percent reduction in spend equates then to $5 million in savings. The same capability viewed through the lens of the outcome is: "We help large corporations create lasting reductions in overhead at an average of 5 percent without changing the quality of what the company gets from its overhead investments."

---

[2]James L. Heskett et al., "Putting the Service-Profit Chain to Work," *Harvard Business Review,* March 1994.

To recap:

- *What we do:* Analyze corporate overhead and implement new strategies.
- *Outcome:* Reduce corporate overhead spend on average by 5 percent.

The distinction is important because it affects how you ask questions about yourself when conducting brand research. Firms often ask about the value of their services in the light of what they do and don't dig deeply enough around the outcomes those services produce. Ask 100 chief financial officers if they value "overhead analysis and new overhead strategy implementation," and you might get answers like this: "Overhead is necessary and we keep tabs on it closely; but we focus on building new plants, product development, and mergers and acquisitions (M&A). Analysis on administration and overhead is not an area I'm going to dedicate a space for in my brain. So, no, I don't think I'd find it valuable."

Ask about the value of reducing overhead spend by 5 percent, and you might get a different answer. "A 5 percent reduction in overhead spend at my company would mean annual savings of about $15 million. Over five years that would be $75 million. It's something I'd pay attention to, for sure."

It's all a question of how you look at what it is you are capable of delivering.

Competencies and Assets: The Building Blocks of Capabilities

Capabilities are made up of two major components: (1) *competencies* and (2) *assets*. (See Figure 11.1.)

Competencies—*What Your People Can Deliver*

Professional services firms are made up of people who do things. (Shocking, we know.) Those things are made up of the collective competence of the

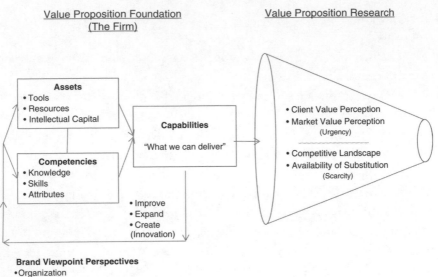

Figure 11.1   Value Proposition Foundation (The Firm) and Value Proposition Research

people in the organization. Competence itself is made up of knowledge, skills, and attributes.

How might all three of these come into play? Consider the case of the law firm with a specialty in helping clients pursue and close overseas acquisitions.

The top attorneys at the firm may have 20 or more years of experience each helping manufacturing companies acquire other companies overseas. Not only do they have the *knowledge* of the process and legal technicalities of a successful overseas acquisition, but they also have the knowledge of hundreds of deals, including what went right and how to avoid the common snake pits into which firms pursuing acquisitions can fall.

At this firm, the attorneys have personal *skills* in negotiation and meeting facilitation, technical skills so they can navigate the complex legalities of overseas acquisitions, and fluency in over 12 different languages.

The firm also has the *attributes* of extreme client focus, likable attorney personalities, and a culture of teamwork.

Together, this mix of knowledge, skills, and attributes creates the firm's overall competence in helping companies identify and complete overseas acquisitions.

Sounds like a great firm, right? If you needed to buy a $100 million manufacturing company in Europe, it might be a great fit, perhaps the best fit, for what you need.

For this firm, there is one problem—another firm has similar knowledge, skills, and attributes. From the perspective of the *competencies* of the organizations, the two look fairly much the same.

Assets—What Your Firm Has That Helps Your People Deliver to Clients

Unfortunately for our example law firm, the similar competitor also has several *assets* to support the knowledge, skills, and attributes that help it increase its overall ability to deliver to clients.

One *resource* the competitor has is an actively maintained database of 22,000 possible acquisition targets across industries, sectors, and countries that can, within hours, narrow down acquisition targets to the top 20 most likely matches given your industries and geographies of focus.

One *tool* the firm has is its proprietary 12-step methodology for acquiring overseas firms. Before the firm had this methodology in place, it created excellent client results; but those results took six months longer per deal to realize. With the methodology, results come much faster.

One component of the firms' *intellectual capital* is the annual benchmark study of overseas M&A activity. While part of the research is available to the general public, the details and certain key components of the research are available only to clients of the firm.

In this case, the competitor firm's assets clearly contribute to its ability to deliver. It's not difficult to see how.

"When acquiring firms, I've always been very reluctant to pay for any sort of future revenue or earnings stream. I've always bought them because of their assets. They have a piece of intellectual capital, a model, or a tool that if we were to develop it ourselves it would have cost us a certain amount of money to develop."

—Mike May, Professor at Babson College, former Co-Vice Chair of KPMG, and former Global Managing Partner of the strategy business for Accenture

Which firm would you want to be? Now that we've completed our short treatise on the definition of components of company capabilities, let's look at how it all applies to building a brand.

Informs client and market research. People too often view marketing as overhyped puffery that gets people to buy things. Seth Godin didn't help the image by writing books like *All Marketers Are Liars* (Penguin, 2005). No one wants to be fooled or emotionally enticed to buy something they don't want, don't need, or that isn't right for them. Like it or not, there's no question that it happens, perhaps often in consumer marketing.

Not only does this kind of disingenuous smoke-and-mirrors marketing not work well for marketing and selling professional services; but if you're the seller, you don't want it to work. Let's say a consumer sees a great car ad and buys an old hot rod on a whim. Once he buys it, as long as it's not a lemon, the person who sold him the car is done with him. If the car's in great shape, purrs like a kitten, and is just like new, then great! If it turns out the buyer needs parts, service, upgrades, and the like, he goes to a garage, not back to the seller. (Even at most car dealerships, the buyer gets shuffled off to the service department. The sales rep has moved on.) If you don't like the car or you decide you don't want it anymore, you can resell it.

Let's say you sell a consulting engagement. Who shows up at the kickoff meeting to get everything rolling? Typically, you! During your business development process, you set a number of expectations: about what is going to happen, how long it is likely to take, what the process will be like, and what will happen when you complete the engagement. If what you promised would happen doesn't match what actually does happen, your client won't be happy. Unlike a car, if the client doesn't like the consulting engagement, he can't sell it to someone else on eBay. You just have to face the music.

What firms should do with branding and marketing is similar to what they should do when selling. Marketing works best when it sets expectations that the firm meets. Before you start your market and client research processes, you must do so in the context of the realities of your firm. Too often service firms engage research to find out what messages will resonate with the market for their type of firm, find out what those message are, and adopt them without enough attention regarding how well those messages match up with the realities of the firm itself.

By engaging research couched in the reality of your firm, you will find the intersection of what the market wants and the reality of what you deliver.

Marketing amplification effect. Assume you work at a business law firm, Jones Jones and Jones. While you have a broad set of capabilities and can service many different types and sizes of client organizations, you are relatively unknown in the market.

One day you're at a yard sale, and you buy an old bottle. You give it a few rubs and out comes the genie, who promptly tells you about your three wishes. Since you've been dying to expand your marketing and your brand, you wish for $100 million that you can use for marketing outreach. (If you do, you really need to work on your wish list. But back to our example.)

Bam! Your messages are everywhere. You're now reaching every decision maker, influencer, and referral source that could be important to you; and you've achieved top-of-mind awareness. You get inquiries directly, but somewhere along the line almost all buyers start checking you out by asking around. It goes something like this:

Scenario 1: Steve is the CEO of a midsize technology manufacturer. He meets Angela, another CEO buddy of his, for golf on Saturday. He asks her, "Have you ever heard of Jones Jones and Jones?" Angela says, "I have. They're terrible. Horrible. Run for your life. They were my law firm four years ago; and not only did they mess up everything, they were miserable people to work with."

Scenario 2: Same setup. Same question. Angela responds, "I have. They're amazing. Fabulous. I have heard all the promises that professional services firms make about smarter people, extra service, fair treatment, and value added. Rarely have I gotten said benefits, but Jones Jones and Jones is the poster child amazing firm. I trust them completely. They always get it right."

Somewhere in the middle (you probably think closer to scenario 2) is the truth about your firm. By creating conversations in the market among the various stakeholder groups, your marketing outreach amplifies whatever people actually think about your firm. (See Figure 11.2.)

Before you start communicating your value proposition to the market— a value proposition you want to resonate with buyers, differentiate your firm, and substantiate your claims—you want to make sure it's true. You can only

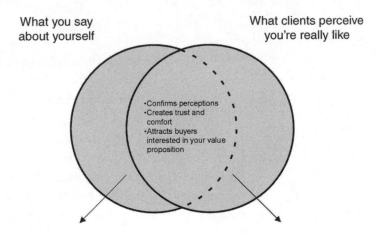

Figure 11.2 Intersecting Circles

do that if you base your messages on a solid foundation of what your firm is all about.

> "Someone from another organization once told me about their marketing message: 'Oh, the marketing team came up with this great thing and plastered it all over the wall. Too bad it was a meaningless slogan.' I'll never forget that as long as I live, and I told myself, 'I'm never stepping in that trap.' Make sure anything that becomes a core component of your brand messaging reflects what the internal organization believes they deliver. Do that, and it's going to resonate all the way through the firm."
>
> —Paul Dunay, Global Director of Integrated Marketing, BearingPoint

Uncovers opportunities for innovation. At almost all firms there's an ongoing discussion about what the firm needs to be doing that it's currently not doing. Even without research to indicate changing needs or client dissatisfaction, firm leaders often see areas where the firm can improve current services, expand the scope of services, or create new services and capabilities.

Ultimately it's up to firm leadership to create an environment where innovation and improvement can actually take hold. And not every improvement or new service idea is the right one to implement. If you ask your staff about where the opportunities lie, you may find the next big thing, and a number of the next small things, that will make your company more competitive.

Uncovers barriers to brand strength and revenue growth. We once worked with a human resources consulting firm whose stated value proposition didn't match up with its actual value proposition because of an internal disconnect. The value proposition suggested that no matter what the human resources issue might be, this company could solve it. If they needed exposure to new thinking and vendors, they could go to company-produced conferences. If they needed learning, they could work with this firm's executive education division. If they needed consulting, they could work with the firm's consulting arm. And so on.

> "Professionals go along with creative and messaging processes and nitpick, but they don't really focus where they need to: asking themselves, 'Is this really us?' Then they see an advertisement in print and they don't feel right. Have the discipline and honesty—the kind of intellectual and emotional honesty you need—to say up front who you are and who you want to be, and then be consistent about it. If it's not reflective of who you are, it will be rejected."
>
> —Mike Sheehan, CEO, Hill Holliday

The firm had a centralized business development function that maintained relationships with buyers. This group was charged with uncovering client need and crafting solutions to meet that need, given all the firm's capabilities.

One manager at the firm noticed a major variation in how often certain business development executives guided their clients toward executive education. When he looked into it, he found that about half of the business development team had been burned when their clients reported poor experiences with executive education: "I've sent clients to our executive education programs, and then I had to recover them as clients because they were quite dissatisfied and upset."

Regardless of the reasons behind the underlying problem, the lack of trust from one department to another inside this company (1) made it unlikely this firm could deliver on its brand promise of solving human resources problems through multiple service areas and (2) hindered revenue flow to the firm by probably several million dollars a year.

As you look seriously at the truth of your service (and don't lie to yourself), you can uncover the barriers to building your brand, such as:

- Quality issues that create internal lack of trust and inability to deliver on company brand strategy (see preceding example).

- Lack of internal knowledge of company strengths.
- Lack of interest in the rest of the company. ("Why should I care about the other practices and capabilities? I have numbers to hit.")
- Morale issues that can dampen or undermine the strength of any real brand effort.
- Need for assets to help the firm deliver better to clients.
- Underutilized assets that will contribute more to client delivery and marketplace differentiation.
- Misalignment between what the firm currently says about itself and the truth about what the company is like and what it delivers.

Builds an army of brand advocates. Including your team in brand research can uncover lack of knowledge, lack of interest, and other challenges, as noted earlier. Couple staff inclusion in research with internal marketing programs, and you'll also build knowledge, guide staff behavior, and connect staff to the firm's brand messages.

At most (not some, not quite a few, but most) firms, there's a gross deficit of staff knowledge of a firm's overall capabilities and value proposition.

> "There are really three levels of brand. The 'big B' brand is the corporate brand, which tends to be identity, tagline, letterhead, web site, overall standards, and the like. The 'little b' brand is the specific industry focus, channel, or specialty. And the third level is faces of the brand . . . the people who are walking into client sites every day. The trick is getting them all to work together."
>
> —Paul Dunay, Global Director of Integrated Marketing, BearingPoint

Don't believe us? Take everyone at your company right now—no preparation, no warning—and ask them to list every capability the firm has, who the firm serves with that capability, where the firm serves people with that capability, and the major outcomes of that capability. We provide a chart format for you to record everyone's answers. Perhaps everyone will do amazingly well. (But that's rarely our experience.)

FIRM CAPABILITY CHART

Capability   **Industry**   **Geography**   **Outcomes**

Recently we delivered a cross-selling training session to 40 or so senior staff at a superregional accounting and consulting firm. The essence of cross-selling is discovering need over and above the need you're currently addressing and then creating solutions using the firm's overall service set to solve the additional need.

The first thing people have to know, then, is what the firm can do. We asked them to list on sticky notes the services of the firm and the industries the firm focused on. We also requested that they work alone—no peeking at their teammates' lists—and that they put only one industry and one service per sticky note.

The company listed 64 major services on its web site and 33 specialty industries. All in, the folks listed about 50 services and 20 industries. Not bad—except that that wasn't the average; that was the aggregate of what all 40 people could come up with! The most any individual person could list was 20 services and 15 industries.

The original purpose of the training session was to give people the *skills* to ask questions to uncover need, but what they needed first was the *knowledge* of what they could actually do for clients. It's not much use to uncover need and then not know if the firm can even help.

From the perspective of brand, you have an opportunity to leverage your team every day to communicate what you can do for clients and what you can help them achieve. If they don't know what that is, or have inconsistent knowledge, you miss that opportunity anew each morning. (See Figure 11.3.)

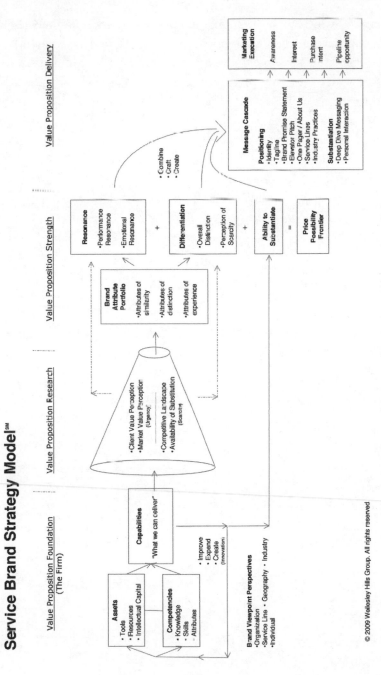

Service Brand Strategy Model℠

Value Proposition Foundation (The Firm) — **Value Proposition Research** — **Value Proposition Strength** — **Value Proposition Delivery**

Assets
• Tools
• Resources
• Intellectual Capital

Competencies
• Knowledge
• Skills
• Attributes

Capabilities
"What we can deliver"

• Improve
• Expand
• Create
(Innovation)

Brand Viewpoint Perspectives
• Organization • Service Line • Geography • Industry
• Individual

• Client Value Perception
• Market Value Perception (Urgency)
• Competitive Landscape
• Availability of Substitution (Scarcity)

Brand Attribute Portfolio
• Attributes of similarity
• Attributes of distinction
• Attributes of experience

Resonance
• Performance Resonance
• Emotional Resonance

+

Differentiation
• Overall Distinction
• Perception of Scarcity

+

Ability to Substantiate

=

Price Possibility Frontier

• Combine
• Craft
• Create

Message Cascade

Positioning
• Identify
• Tagline
• Brand Promise Statement
• Elevator Pitch
• One Pager / About Us
• Service Lines
• Industry Practices

Substantiation
• Deep Dive Messaging
• Personal Interaction

Marketing Execution
Awareness
Interest
Purchase Intent
Pipeline opportunity

Figure 11.3 Service Firm Brand Strategy Model

By now, if you have been asking and answering the questions about brand as we have suggested, you should have a good understanding of:

- What your clients and prospects value.
- Who you are as a firm.

The next step is to put this knowledge together to form the messages for your marketing efforts and for strengthening your brand.

12 | RAMP Up Your Brand

The man who whispers down a well
About the goods he has to sell
Will not make as many dollars
As the man who climbs the tree and hollers.

—Lord Leverhulme

As we have discussed, brand perception has a tremendous impact on a buyer's attitude toward a company and disposition toward purchasing goods and services. In addition, we have shown how to craft the right messages based on your markets' needs and perceptions of value and your reality as a firm. In this chapter, we provide a way to think about your brand goals as you lay out your marketing plans.

In the Cahners Advertising Research Report, *How Important Is the Reputation of a Brand Name?*[1] 79 percent of buyers agreed that a company's brand reputation is as important as the actual specifics of what is being purchased.

Specifically, among the buyers:

- 85 percent agreed that familiar brands provide good postsale service.
- 82 percent agreed that buying an unfamiliar brand is often risky.

---

[1] Cahners Advertising Research Report (CARR) 120.13

- 81 percent agreed that a familiar brand usually guarantees selection agreement among internal stakeholders.
- 53 percent agreed that a familiar brand usually ensures good value for the money.
- 44 percent agreed that unfamiliar brands often indicate unreliable companies.
- 34 percent agreed that unfamiliar brands are of lower quality.

In our own research we found that 73 percent of buyers of professional services stated they are likely to consider engaging service providers of whom they already have "personal recognition or awareness." Among the top 20 ways buyers searched for providers, "previous awareness of the provider" was one of the most commonly cited, second only to referrals.

Brand works. But, as we have stressed, mistaking "getting your name out there" by engaging advertising and brand outreach like business-to-consumer marketing is an expensive mistake that too many professional services firms make. The reason behind the mistake is a misconception about how to approach becoming well-known in your target markets.

If business-to-consumer advertising campaigns and business-to-business product marketing tactics mislead the professional services firm marketer because the thinking is fundamentally flawed, how then should a service firm think about brand building?

Imagine you are playing the strongman game at the carnival. You lift the sledgehammer over your head and swing it down onto the platform. When it strikes the target, a metal cylinder rises up and up—20 feet up the pole until it rings the bell. On its way down the pole, the cylinder passes the same words it passed on the way up: strongman, tough guy, athlete, junior, and weakling.

In a way, establishing a services brand follows a similar process. You swing the hammer (your marketing tactics, the marketing mix you employ, and the quality of your company's services), and the strength of your efforts determines whether your brand moves up the pole and makes it to the top to ring the bell.

The question is: What stages must your brand pass through in order to ring the bell?

Strip away the apparent complexity around what building a service brand is all about, and you find that the stages you have to reach with your own strongman efforts are quite straightforward:

- *Recognize:* Your target clients must recognize you.
- *Articulate:* They need to be able to articulate what you do.
- *Memorize:* When they need your service, your company should be the first option they think of.
- *Prefer:* Your target clients should prefer to use your service versus all other options available to them.

While there are several interim stages in the services branding process through which you must travel, the desired end result—the golden goose

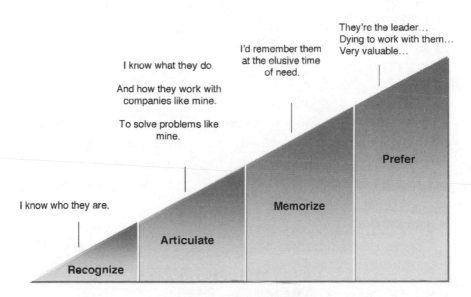

Brand RAMP^{SM}

Figure 12.1 Wellesley Hills Group Brand RAMP^{SM}

of branding—is to establish strong preference for your brand over your competitors. (Can you hear the bell ringing?)

To help you visualize your steps to a stronger brand, follow the Brand RAMP. Within the RAMP framework and methodology (recognize, articulate, memorize, prefer), branding becomes approachable as a process and, at the same time, focused on a worthwhile business outcome.

Let's take a brief look at each stage of the Brand RAMP and see how it leads to establishing a powerful services brand.

Recognize

Question: What's the purpose of this marketing campaign?
Answer: Well, we really need to get our name out there. You know, establish our identity.

We are about as impressed with this answer as we are with the salesperson who has a meeting with a prospective client and says the purpose "is to have a get-to-know-you meeting." The purpose of a sales meeting is to find sales opportunities and to advance a sale. Getting to know the client is part of what is done in that process. It's not a goal in and of itself.

In services branding, getting your name out there and establishing an identity is something that you do in the process of branding; it is not the goal. For most firms, focusing on stand-alone brand recognition leads to inefficient use of money, time, and effort in the marketing process. You work hard to get your name out there, but you do not generate actual business development activity.

WHO WAS THE AD WIZARD?

John Wanamaker famously said, "I know half the money I spend on advertising is wasted, but I can never find out which half."

We've found both halves. They're in the *Boston Business Journal* (or any similar newspaper in cities throughout the United States).

Nothing against the *BBJ*—all it does is accept the ads that professional services firms send in. The problem is with the firms themselves; they craft such weak ads.

From just the perspective of the offers the companies make, these ads need some serious work. A quick review of 25 or so ads in a recent *BBJ* from accounting firms, law firms, management consulting firms, commercial real estate, investment banking, technology services, and other like firms revealed the following offers:

- Free cost-saving analysis . . .
- Call me if you have a project . . .
- To schedule a meeting, call . . .
- To take advantage of our expertise, call . . .
- For more information on our services, call . . . (Offered three times.)
- Visit us at our web site . . . (Offered one time with a main home page URL and one time with a landing page URL.)

No offer made occurred 16 times.
What does this tell us?

1. A whopping 16 times, there was no offer at all! We can hear Adam Sandler now: "Who was the ad wizard who came up with that one?" Of course, companies have to make good offers for the ad to have any chance at being effective; but without any offer at all, these ads aren't doing much.
2. The "call for more information," "visit our web site," and "schedule a meeting" offers aren't much better than no offer. One might as well just say, "But enough about me . . . let's talk about me!" or "I couldn't think of anything to offer that you might find worthwhile, but if you want to buy something, I'm around."
3. In the "enough about me . . . let's talk about me" vein, many of the offers had announcements. Some popular ones were

"we've merged," "we just hired some staff," and "we did some work that we're proud of." Me, me, me . . .

4. The "cost-saving analysis"—the only offer that even remotely hinted of potential value for the respondent—didn't have any detail about the analysis itself. This could easily have been taken care of by providing a landing page on the company's web site about the offer itself and a Web form where the visitor could sign up for the analysis. Plus, by providing a landing page and response form, the company could have analyzed the effectiveness of the ad (is it worth the money?) by tracking landing page visits and acceptances of the offer.

5. If we were to ask the people who came up with the strategies to place these ads to explain to us what they were doing and to defend their budgets, they'd probably give us the "brand building" argument. Not only could the ads be much better, but if we were most of these services firms, we probably wouldn't spend our money on ads in business journals. For most of these firms, there are better ways to generate recognition for their services.

Companies without enough outbound activity leave their business fortunes to serendipity. Worse, they never know where the next lead will come from or how to plan for growth.

You need your prospective clients to recognize you. Without recognition you are at the whim of your referral base. As you start to generate recognition proactively, though, you need to do it in a way that serves other, higher return goals (namely the rest of the RAMP process).

Articulate

Let's assume you make it past the recognition phase of the Brand RAMP. At this point, you want to avoid the following:

Question from your firm: So you've heard of us. Do you know what we do?

Answer from prospect: Yes, I've heard of you. What you do . . . I'm not sure.

A core goal of brand messaging is getting your prospective clients to be able to state, in clear terms, what you deliver. This serves multiple ends:

- By knowing what you do, they will know how, where, and when to apply your services.
- They will now be able to refer you to others who can use your services.
- They are able to explain your services internally so they can create a coalition (if it's necessary) to purchase your services.

It's so important, yet so many services firms struggle with how to articulate what they do. Regardless of your situation, whether your firm is large or small, singularly focused or with a range of complex services, you need to get the message across.

The litmus test of whether it is getting across is asking a prospect, "Do you know what we do?" and hearing the answer you want to hear.

Memorize

At some point we've all had the following thought: "This is a sticky problem. . . . Oh, I remember there's a firm out there that focuses 100 percent on fixing this problem, and I've heard they're great. What was its name again? It slipped my mind. Oh, well. On to other things."

The type of brand messaging you employ and how often you employ it will affect how well people remember you at the time of need. If they know who you are and they know what you do, but your marketing mix and your communications plan drop the ball in terms of creating a lasting impression, your business development efforts will never perform to their fullest potential.

It's common sense that if buyers can't remember you when they have a need, they can't buy anything. Even if you have had aggressive marketing in the past, if you discontinue aggressive outreach or take a break if the economy or your business goes through a rough patch, you will lose much of the business impact of your historical outreach.

Research from well-respected consumer brand marketing company Millward Brown bears this out:

> The longer-term effect [of discontinuing aggressive marketing outreach] can be far more damaging. A good example comes from the U.K. insurance market. A regular and reasonably heavy advertiser, this insurance company came off air, with only one subsequent burst two years later. Consideration levels plummeted over the next few years.[2]

HOW MANY IMPRESSIONS DOES IT TAKE?

How many marketing touches does it take to affect buying preferences and to increase your brand preference? In going through some old files, we ran across an all-time favorite piece of advice. It goes like this:

> The first time people look at any given ad, they don't even see it.
> The second time, they don't notice it.
> The third time, they are aware that it is there.
> The fourth time, they have a fleeting sense that they've seen it somewhere before.
> The fifth time, they actually read the ad.
> The sixth time, they thumb their nose at it.
> The seventh time, they start to get a little irritated with it.
> The eighth time, they start to think, "Here's that confounded ad again."

---

[2] "What Happens When Brands Go Dark?" Millward Brown, 2007.

The ninth time, they start to wonder that they may be missing out on something.

The tenth time, they ask their friends and neighbors if they've tried it.

The eleventh time, they wonder how this company is paying for all those ads.

The twelfth time, they start to think that it must be a good product.

The thirteenth time, they start to feel the product has value.

The fourteenth time, they start to remember wanting a product exactly like this for a long time.

The fifteenth time, they start to yearn for it because they can't afford to buy it.

The sixteenth time, they accept the fact that they will buy it sometime in the future.

The seventeenth time, they make a note to buy the product.

The eighteenth time, they curse their poverty for not allowing them to buy this terrific product.

The nineteenth time, they count their money very carefully.

The twentieth time prospects see the ad, they buy what it is offering.

—Thomas Smith (published in 1885)

As much as things change over the course of a century, many things stay the same as well.

Prefer

Prospective clients recognize you, can articulate what you do, and remember you at the elusive time of need. Still, all of this may be for naught if they do not have a compelling reason to want to work with you and your firm.

Brand preference is created in many ways. Your marketing activities and actual service experiences with your company are the two most common paths to building brand preference. Thus you should engage branding and marketing activities with the idea of creating preference for your services with your prospective and current clients.

Developing a brand identity without the RAMP methodology firmly embedded in the beginning of the process often leads to graphic design and marketing campaigns in a vacuum. You don't want logos, web sites, brochures, presentations, and marketing tactics developed without the end goal in mind: creating a client's preference for your firm.

Back to the strongman game at the carnival . . .

The carnival is your market.

The sledgehammer is your brand implementation program.

The words on the pole are (from bottom to top):

- Recognize
- Articulate
- Memorize
- Prefer

If you swing the hammer with the right force and hit the right spot, the prizes you win are more new clients and increased brand loyalty. And, unlike at the carnival, these prizes can be worth a great deal more than the cost of playing the game.

> "There's a buying cycle. Before anyone is likely to buy, they've got to know who you are. The more aware they are of your name, the more that awareness breeds familiarity. Familiarity builds trust. Trust generates brand preference."
>
> —Ed Russ, Chief Marketing, Grant Thornton

13 | On Being Unique and Other Bad Marketing Advice

The problem with the marketing concept is a persistent tendency toward rigidity. It gets dogmatized, interpreted into constantly narrower and inflexible prescriptions. . . . There is not, and cannot be, any rigid and lasting interpretation of what the marketing concept means in the specific ways a company should operate at any given time.

—Theodore Leavitt

I got a bad grade on my final paper in entrepreneurship class in graduate school. The professor said, "The business you're proposing to launch . . . it's not different. Other people do it. While the plan seems well thought out and well researched, due to the simple truth that this business has been largely done before and there doesn't seem to be anything truly unique about it, I wouldn't advise launching the business." (So long, stellar GPA.)

Being different and unique seems to be highly regarded by those who think about, write about, and teach business. Professors Terrell and Middlebrooks of the Northwestern University's Kellogg School of Management and the University of Chicago Graduate School of Business, respectively, say it well:

> Service companies need to dare to be different. To find a leadership position in the market . . . and then to lead. The key strategy is to be different from competitors. . . . They break free from "be better," internally oriented initiatives to "be different," externally oriented strategies. Being different is grounded in providing customers with unique value that they cannot get from any other competitor.[1]

They then cite McKinsey as their first example of a "different" business.

The need for being different is so well accepted, it's considered simplistic to even make the case for it. Why make a case for something everyone already knows? Many conversations on being different thus center more on *how* to be different and *how radically* to be different. (Terrell and Middlebrooks go as far as to say you should position yourself so far opposite competitors that they coin the nifty term *oppositioning* to describe it.)

That we need to be different at all . . . is accepted without further thought.

Well, put some further thought in it. The pursuit of being unique and different has done disservice to many a service firm.

On Unique Selling Propositions

Among the favorite platitudes of marketing moguls is that every business—nay, every person—must have a unique selling proposition (USP). Having a USP can be defined as doing or saying something about yourself or company that is unlike what anyone else does or offers. In other words, unique . . . one of a kind.

Between us, we deliver over 50 speeches per year. During speeches, we frequently ask the members of the audience to take a few minutes to deliver

---

[1] Craig Terrell and Arthur Middlebrooks, *Market Leadership Strategies for Service Companies.* (NTC Business Books, Chicago: 2000), p. 31.

their elevator pitches: They use a minute or so to describe themselves to the CEO of the company they would like to win as a client.

When they're done, we ask people to raise their hands if their partner delivered a fabulous elevator pitch. Many hands go up. When we ask what was so great about them, we typically hear things like: They were clear about what they do, exactly how they bring value to their clients, and which industries they serve. Often we hear of stories told that truly bring their companies to life.

We then ask who has heard of the concept of a USP and who has been told at least once in their business lives that they need to have one. Almost all hands go up. We then ask whose elevator pitch partner said something unique. At first no hands go up, but then here and there a bold person jumps into the fray. In the end, as the brave volunteer tries to describe the uniqueness of the accountant or lawyer or consultant, they end up backing off their stance that their partner was unique—good elevator presentation, compelling value, but rarely unique.

The "Unique and Different" Label

Too often in elevator pitches, and in marketing messages in general, professional services firms ill advisedly label themselves as unique and different. A quick Google search for "unique consulting firm" (with the quotes, so it would get results that only had these words in a sequence) yields close to 4,000 sites—think about that—4,000 unique consulting firms.

The copy is generally terrible. Tempted as we are to reproduce some of it here, we decided against it. Suffice it to say that a lot of firms describe themselves as unique and different, but support those claims more with expressions of value than of difference. Call yourself unique and fail to support the claim, and you lose credibility. Firms that label themselves "unique" don't usually come across as unique. It just seems as if someone read in some marketing or sales textbook that they have to have a unique selling proposition. Voilà . . . there it is!

> "There aren't a lot of silver bullets out there, but if you can find some that highlight at least some crack of differentiation, you should shine the spotlight there."
>
> —Paul Dunay, Global Director of Integrated Marketing, BearingPoint

Many admit later how amateurish their USPs sound and sometimes acknowledge that they thought their USP sounded amateurish before they launched their unique-speak publicly. Firm leaders tend to have good common sense radar but check common sense at the door when it comes to self-designated uniqueness.

WHAT CLIENTS REALLY WANT

Much as they might hear otherwise, being different isn't much of a factor in winning or keeping clients. Often, the "we're different" message affects them negatively. Consider the following scenario: Your tooth hurts and your dentist is out of town. You need an oral surgeon and you need one fast; so you ask two trusted close friends, Trip and Beverly, if they know anyone.

REFERRAL #1: CLOSE FRIEND TRIP SUGGESTS DR. PHLOX

Trip says that his Aunt Deanna needed oral surgery and went to Dr. Phlox, who has been in the town next door for 20 years and has a very busy oral surgery practice. Word on the street is that he's pretty solid. When Trip's Aunt Deanna went in, the doctor took the time to explain the surgery and what was going to happen and answered all the questions she had.

The surgery went fine (as far as they know), and Deanna hasn't had any problems since. Dr. Phlox is a little more expensive than average; but Deanna says he's very booked up and established, so it's understandable.

REFERRAL #2: CLOSE FRIEND BEVERLY SUGGESTS DR. McCOY

Supposedly Dr. McCoy is well-known throughout the nation as a cutting-edge oral surgeon, often going where no other oral surgeon has gone before. He has a unique blend of people at his office, and a process for oral surgery and tooth technology that he has pioneered. His results, according to his brochure and web site, are 22 percent better than all other oral surgeons, which is how he justifies his very high prices.

Beverly's Uncle Pavel went to Dr. McCoy, and all went well with the surgery (as far as they know), though Uncle Pavel met Dr. McCoy for only about 30 seconds, as he was so busy.

At a gut level, even with Uncle Pavel's satisfaction, few people would choose referral #2. And many of the dynamics of how clients buy business-to-business professional services are similar to how people choose dentists:

- Should failure happen, the consequences are painful.
- You don't need the world's greatest outcome. You just need a very good outcome.
- Since you can't sample a service like you might sample a piece of gum, you have to rely on reputation, experience, and expertise as proxies for expected results.
- Price is a factor, but you'd rather not skimp when the outcome is important. (Side note: If I had said that Dr. McCoy's innovations enable him to charge less than half of what other oral surgeons charge, would you have been more interested in buying his services or less interested?)

Innovation in the sense that the doctor does something *different* than others, or is somehow unique, by and large won't tip the scales of purchase preference in the favor of the innovator.

So what is it that clients are, indeed, looking for? In our experience and research, such as Wellesley Hills Group and RainToday.com's benchmark report, *How Clients Buy*, most buyers want to tell service providers the following:

- **Reliability.** Do what you say you are going to do, and be on time about it. (This is first because it's so important. "If only the service providers I've worked with in my life were better at keeping their commitments . . . ")
- **Accessibility.** Be there when I need you.
- **Impact.** Help me buy the most helpful and impactful services from you, and help me translate your services into success for my business and my industry.
- **Fit.** Be a good fit for the specific needs that I have. If you're not the best fit, help me find a provider that is. Don't shoehorn your service into something that, in the end, won't meet my needs as well as something else.
- **Importance.** Make me feel like I am, as a client, important to you and your team.
- **Service.** Deliver great service as well as great services.
- **Prudence.** Be careful and do your homework before you suggest a course of action for me.
- **Research.** Stay on top of the developments and trends in your industry and in mine.
- **Listening.** Understand my business, my team, and my clients or customers so you can come up with ideas relevant to me.
- **Teaching.** Help me understand what you're doing. I might not be an expert in your area, but I'm pretty bright and I make the decisions here. Help me understand what's new in your area of expertise so I can apply that knowledge in my business.
- **Business management.** Run an efficient operation and constantly improve so I don't pay for your inefficiency.
- **Relationship management.** Be pleasant and fair, and work with me through communication or other breakdowns on your end or mine. In essence, treat me like a person.

Different situations warrant different mixes and degrees of these client wants. For example, with many necessary services like Sarbanes-Oxley compliance, efficiency is important as well as expertise. In contrast, buyers looking to hire product innovation consultants are likely to be less concerned about efficiency, and more concerned about the impact from the creativity and innovative thinking of your team.

One last question—how often do you think a buyers says, "I need to hire some unique, different than every other provider out there." In our experience, it's rare.

Some firms take the quest for being different literally, creating spates of "we're different" messages. Consider a top law firm with the following message: "At [*firm name*], we practice law differently. While our attorneys agree that results drive our business, building relationships with our clients and providing value-added service are the keys to our success."

This firm might be amazingly good; and from what I know of its reputation, it is. However, results driving business, building relationships, and providing value are pretty much par for the course from both firm goals and marketing copy standpoints.

Regardless of the mix of attributes that are most important to your buyers, you probably won't see many of them inserting this into the list of client wants: *Unique. Be one of a kind, offering something that no one else in the market offers.*

So be different: Stop listening to the continuous pleas from consultants, marketers, and textbooks to be unique . . . one of a kind . . . a shining beacon of newness in a sea of same old, same old.

Focus instead on actually delivering the value to the market that you say you deliver (which, in and of itself, can be uncommon, if not unique), and find ways to create a conversation with buyers around that message. Not only is it better marketing, it's less lonely than being unique.

Five More Branding Laws That Need Breaking

"If [a law] is of such a nature that it requires you to be the agent of injustice to another, then I say, break the law."

—Henry David Thoreau

Along with being unique, there are quite a number of branding maxims tossed about in the marketing world. These maxims, accepted as unquestionable gospel and law, simply are not valid for almost all professional services. At least they are not valid for everyone and every business.

When we read any piece of business advice that confidently declares, "Always do this," or "This is true 100 percent of the time," or even "You should . . . ," the warning lights flash. The high priests of branding and marketing are particularly prone to heading down this all-or-nothing path. So, we thought we would throw in our two cents' worth and add to the list of branding absolutes:

- Always seek to understand the underlying dynamics of your own industry and company before making decisions on how to brand your business.
- Never forget that, in the right situations, laws are meant for breaking.

Consider the following commonly held branding beliefs that may be meant for breaking for those of us in the world of professional services.

Maxim 1: Law of the Opposite

"The Law of the Opposite: If you're shooting for second place, your strategy is determined by the leader."

—Al Ries and Jack Trout[2]

---

[2] Al Ries and Jack Trout, *The 22 Immutable Laws of Marketing* (New York: HarperBusiness, 1994).

The overall argument is that if you are not number one in your market and you want to hold the number two spot or below, analyze the company that holds the number-one spot, look for holes in its strategy, and position yourself as very different from it. The Law of the Opposite is a good example of what Terrell and Middlebrooks, whom we discussed earlier in the chapter, would call "oppositioning."

Think about the positioning of the following types of companies that you know about:

- CPA firms
- Law firms
- Financial advisory firms
- IT consultants
- Strategy consultants

Of the companies in these fields, what are their positioning strategies? Are they directly opposite each other? Do you really even care?

Here in Boston there are quite a large number of CPA firms. Sure, some are known to have a bit of a stiff personality, while others are somewhat more casual. Some are known to have strong practices in certain industries like education, nonprofits, and biotechnology. I would hardly call having a personality or competent industry presence a "hard-hitting positioning strategy that differs significantly from a competitor's." Looking around at their web sites, no one is shooting for opposite.

As seemingly similar as many firms in actuality are (though we are sure some of them would argue otherwise), many of them are also quite successful.

Don't get us wrong. It's important to have a strong value proposition that resonates, conveys distinction, and is defensible (see Chapter 9). But the concepts of being different for difference's sake and unique selling propositions are just not helpful.

Maxim 2: Law of the Category

"The most effective, most productive, most useful aspect of branding is creating a new category. In other words, narrowing the focus to nothing and starting something totally new. That's the way to become the first brand in a new category and ultimately the leading brand in a rapidly growing new segment of the market."

—Al Ries and Laura Ries[3]

Imagine this conversation:

IRS: Ms. Jones, this is the IRS calling. I have a question about the tax return you filed.

Ms. Jones: Yes?

IRS: Well, we don't understand the return. The forms you sent in are unfamiliar to us. We also do not understand your calculations.

Ms. Jones: Oh, I'm not surprised. You see, I used a new category of CPA firm this year.

Do you really want a new category of:

- CPA to do your business taxes?
- Lawyer when you need to win a case?
- IT consultant when your server is down?
- Plumber when all you want is a promptly returned phone call (as the water rises in your sink)?

Or do you just want a reliable, consistent, high-quality job done by trustworthy people who treat you well?

Maxim 3: First Mover Advantage

"There's one critical thing to know about position: Whoever grabs a position first pretty much owns it forever. Position is in the minds of the collective market. Reality hardly counts."

—T. Scott Gross[4]

---

[3] Al Reis and Laura Reis, "Law of the Category," *The 22 Immutable Laws of Branding* (New York: HarperCollins, 1998).

[4] T. Scott Gross, *Microbranding* (Dulles, VA: Leading Authorities Press, 2002).

Branding guru after branding guru echoes this "first mover advantage" maxim.

We ask you, who grabbed the position first and now owns high-quality investment advice in Boston?

John Hancock • Citigroup • Brown Brothers Harriman • Fidelity Investments • Charles Schwab • TD Waterhouse • TD Banknorth • Citizens Bank • RBC Dain Rauscher • Wainwright Bank • Eastern Bank • Sovereign Bank • Prudential Financial • Legg Mason • Merrill Lynch • Morgan Stanley • PaineWebber • Bank of America • Boston Private • Fiduciary Trust International • Edward Jones • A.G. Edwards • Goldman Sachs • Bank of New York Mellon • USAA • JPMorgan • Dozens of smaller banks • Hundreds of CFPs, CPAs, and insurance firms • Hundreds of others

(Once again, we show our New England roots.)

Does it matter who was there first?

Maxim 4: Word Ownership

"If you want to build a brand, you must focus your branding efforts on owning a word in the prospect's mind. A word that nobody else owns."

—Al Ries and Laura Ries[5]

In industries where there is a limited number of players because of the nature of the industry (e.g., there are only so many car manufacturers), it is possible to own a word. Who owns safety? Volvo, of course.

In service industries it's different. There is typically an overabundance of providers of all sizes, and there are few generic words one can own:

Achievement • Advice • Balance • Confidence • Control • Creativity • Execution • Fame • Independence • Influence • Integrity • Loyalty • Peace

---

[5] Al Reis and Laura Reis, "Law of the Word," *The 22 Immutable Laws of Branding* (New York: HarperCollins, 1998).

- Performance • Pleasure • Power • Prestige • Recognition • Respect • Safety • Service • Smartness • Solution • Tradition • Trust • Wealth • Wisdom[6]

Sometimes service firms use specific words that focus on need areas or hot buttons. Among CPA firms these words might be:

Advisor • Assurance • Audit • Cash management • Compliance • Estate planning • Family business • Forensic accounting • Internal controls • International • Sarbanes-Oxley • Small business • Transition • Valuation

In your area, who owns any of these terms so much that other firms can't also associate with them? Can't think of any firms? Or maybe you just think of a number of CPA firms that play in these fields. Even if you could own a word in a service industry, we suggest that it should be a side benefit of winning and satisfying clients, not a goal in and of itself.

Maxim 5: Being Number One in Revenue or Market Share

"Your company doesn't belong in any market where it cannot be the best."

—Philip Kotler[7]

"Be number 1 or 2 in your business or get out."

—Jack Welch[8]

What CEO heads into his board meeting and says, "Next year our big, hairy, audacious goal is to become number 16 in our market!" You simply wouldn't hear it. Being number one is a natural strategic target to set, and it certainly sounds good. However, in service businesses, being number one is

---

[6] See page 181 in Chapter 14 for an expanded list.

[7] Philip Kotler, *Marketing Management*, 11th ed. (Upper Saddle River, NJ: Prentice Hall, 2002).

[8] Robert Slater, *Jack Welsh on Leadership* (New York: McGraw-Hill, 2004) pp. 31–32.

usually neither a feasible nor a desirable goal to set. Revenue and market share are not necessarily the answer to greater success and higher profits.

Service firms should focus on client loyalty and reputation if they want greater revenue and profit growth. Publication after publication (however, not branding publications!) by well-respected authors and academics, such as James Heskett et al. in "Putting the Service-Profit Chain to Work" (*Harvard Business Review*) and Fred Reicheld in books like *Loyalty Rules!*[9] echo this mantra. For some reason the messages of these publications are not making enough of an impact on the hearts and minds of the advertising and marketing community.

The idea here is not to make the argument for client and employee loyalty. We merely want to point out that not everyone agrees with the "being number one" law—one of the most taken-for-granted laws of branding that business people blindly follow.

Be unique . . . be opposite . . . own a word . . . be number one . . . be first . . . create a category . . . the list goes on. These guiding principles are easy to remember (good job in branding, branding gurus) and easy to latch onto.

Take care, however, that you act only on the guiding principles that will do the most justice to your business and the people that comprise it. In the end, it is up to you to know which laws apply to you and which laws are meant for breaking. Of course, as much as it pains us to say it, even the laws we espouse should be evaluated based on the particular circumstances of your own firm.

---

[9] Fred Reicheld, *Loyalty Rules!* (Boston: Harvard Business School Press, 2001).

14 | Building Brand and Marketing Messages

The poet is the sayer, the namer, and represents beauty.

—Ralph Waldo Emerson

Once you have a sense of the value you want to convey, you begin the task of announcing who you are to the market in a manner that is compelling, distinct, and to the point. Unfortunately, too often, the following is the result:

> If you're looking for a different kind of accounting firm, look no further than Smith and Jones. With our focus on specific client industries, our energetic and hardworking professionals, and our deep financial experience, we help our clients achieve what they truly need: results. While results are the goal, it's our commitment to building relationships and delivering value-added service that helps our clients succeed and sleep better at night. At Smith and Jones, your success is our number-one priority. When it comes to your unique accounting needs, we have you covered.

You might be thinking as you read this value proposition:

The book's authors visited my web site and used our marketing copy for inspiration! Those sneaky little devils. In truth, we did and we didn't. Over and above visiting service firm web sites every day for this book's research, we visited over a thousand web sites across professional services fields, including law, accounting, consulting, architecture and engineering, technology services, and others. For the most part (but not always . . . read on), firms sound relatively the same from a brand promise perspective.

So should you hang it up and not bother? Hardly. You should spend serious time and energy figuring out exactly what you want to say. A core brand promise statement is essential as an umbrella for the rest of your marketplace messaging.

Firms often develop messages that they believe are unique and potent because they worked so hard to get there. But they engage marketing message development exercises without understanding the special dynamics of messaging for professional services. What do they end up with? A "different kind of [*insert service type*] firm" that suggests their focus on relationships, results, and trust—a firm you can depend on for your mission-critical needs—and a message that sounds like so many others.

We understand how firm leaders and marketers come up with this kind of wording. Ask 20 clients and hear the same comment about your firm as to what buyers find "different" and "valuable" about you, and—tah-dah!—insert into your messaging.

Whereas the concepts you include in your message might be what your research shows to be *true* about your firm, they're not always as *helpful* from a marketing perspective as people think they will be. For example, 20 out of 20 clients might say that your attorneys, accountants, consultants, and the like are "different from other firms they've worked with because of the level of service . . . quality of people . . . delivery of results . . . on-time delivery." (True. You heard it.) The problem is 10 other firms in your space asked the same thing, and that's what their clients said as well. Once 10 competitors in the space decide to hang their hats on "different because of the level of service" or "different because of results" or "different because of our people," the message of difference loses its potency. (Not helpful.)

What's a firm to do, then?

How to Think about Brand Messaging

We assume you have an understanding of your attributes of similarity, attributes of distinction, and attributes of experience. (If you don't, you're not ready to start crafting brand messages yet.) You know what it is about those attributes that resonate with buyers and are different from the other available options in the market, and how you can substantiate anything you claim to be true.[1] (See Figure 14.1.)

Now you have to take these concepts you know about your firm and combine them in the right mixes to create an overall messaging strategy and craft various marketing messages.

The first concept most firms need to grasp is how marketing messages cascade from most basic to most detailed and what's appropriate to have in each message type.

First, you have positioning messaging. This type of messaging should largely be used to establish initial fit and connection with buyers. For most firms, it can be used to set the stage for differentiation but, by itself, doesn't deliver diffentiation.

With your identity—logo, firm name, and your corporate look and feel on web sites and in brochures—you can establish (or fail to establish) an initial connection. Buyers (and influencers, referral sources, and potential employees) make quick decisions as to whether you are in their league. People can often tell from looking at you whether you are small-time, big-time, or somewhere in between. They typically know which they need. If you are in their league, but you don't *look like* you're in their league, you've got a large hurdle to jump.

Buyers also can tell the difference between a quality look and feel and a cheap or home-done look and feel. You can think of look and feel quality as shining your shoes and wearing a nice suit. Show up to a client's office with old scuffed shoes and a wrinkled suit that doesn't quite fit, and you have an initial-impression hurdle to jump.

Why jump these hurdles if you don't have to?

---

[1] See Chapter 9.

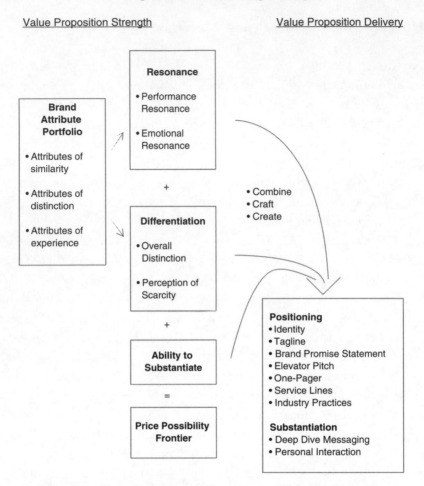

Figure 14.1   Value Proposition Strength and Delivery

At the same time, don't assign more weight to corporate identity than is warranted. Assume you show up to a client meeting with shined shoes and a nice suit. You still haven't gotten anything done for the client yet. Corporate identity is similar. It's simply something that you need to do in order to put yourself in the right league and thus establish initial fit.

Corporate identities often include taglines: brief phrases or slogans that serve to set a premise for a brand. Taglines are typically given too much weight in a professional service firm's identity development process.

Can a tagline convey a key piece of performance resonance? Yes.

- Timex takes a licking and keeps on ticking.—Timex
- When it absolutely, positively has to be there overnight.—FedEx
- Engineered like no other car in the world.—Mercedes-Benz

Emotional resonance? Yes.

- You are now free to move about the country.—Southwest Airlines
- L'Eggo my Eggo.—Kellogg's Eggo waffles
- Just do it!—Nike

Can a tagline make much of a dent in either performance or emotional resonance for a service firm? Not usually. Unless you have a very large advertising spend, it's just not worth the effort (and the effort that can be excruciatingly painful) for a service firm to go through a long and involved process to develop a tagline.

> "I firmly believe that unless you're spending over $100 million a year in media, you don't need a tagline."
>
> —Mike Sheehan, CEO, Hill Holliday

This is not to say we're anti-tagline. Do we think Ernst & Young will be negatively affected by its "Quality in Everything We Do" tagline? No. But we hope the firm didn't spend too much on coming up with that one. Do we think KPMG is negatively affected by its "Audit ▪ Tax ▪ Advisory" tagline? No. It helps to establish initial fit—an umbrella under which the company can describe the rest of its services.

Even with smaller firms, taglines can often serve to help establish initial fit.

- Circadian Technologies: 24/7 Workforce Solutions ("We work around the clock at my nuclear power plant. I'm guess Circadian might be a good fit.")

- Everon Technologies: Your Virtual IT Department ("I need IT help. I'm in the right place.")
- Holland and Hart: The Law Out West ("I live out west. I need a law firm for my business.")

Taglines that focus on emotional or performance resonance don't necessarily do firms a disservice, either. But they often fall flat because the concepts behind them are so common (see the "Common Themes for Taglines" list).

A brand promise statement is a concise declaration that an organization, service line, or person uses to convey the essence of the value it delivers to clients. Companies often use this as the foundation statement about the firm. It's usually a paragraph or two, but it can also be a short series of concepts, bullets, or sentences that describe the firm. Brand promise statements are often accompanied by other "about us" – type blurbs with headings like "what we believe," "our mission," and "our values." They're also accompanied by overall firm descriptions, often referred to as one-pagers, and descriptions of service lines and industry specialties.

You can use any and all of these marketing-type statements to describe the essence of your firm.

Overall, these high-level, not in-depth communications serve more to position and describe your firm than anything else.

With these types of messages you establish your overall fit. Especially as you get to the elevator pitches and one-pager types of descriptions, firms typically address five W's and one H:

- What you do.
- Whom you work with.
- Where you operate.
- When it's the right time to work with you.
- How you go about things.
- Why clients should care.

COMMON THEMES FOR TAGLINES

Menu of common performance and emotional resonance words and themes used by service firm taglines and brand promise statements.

Achievement	Focus	Prestige
Advancement	Future	Recognition
Advantage	Global	Reliability
Balance	Health	Respect
Care	Ideas	Results
Change	Independence	Sense
Clarity	Influence	Service
Client	Innovation	Solution
Commitment	Insight	Specialist
Comprehensive	Integrated	Strategic
Connection	Integrity	Strength
Control	Knowledge	Success
Creativity	Leader	Teamwork
Dedication	Leverage	Thinking
Drive	Local	Total
Empowerment	Loyalty	Tradition
Exceed	Partner	Trust
Excellence	Passion	Unique
Expectations	Performance	Value
Experience	Personal	Vision
Expertise	Pleasure	Wealth
Extraordinary	Power	Wisdom
Fame	Practical	

Review the marketing messages of almost any firm, and it's fairly easy to take their core messages and put them into these buckets. Regarding message construction, there is no rote formula or specific path you should take. If you can be clear and have a solid architecture to deliver this messaging, you're in great shape. Eloquence is even better, but clarity and intelligent message construction go a long way.

A few examples of the key components of positioning messaging for different types of firms are shown in the table. As you look at them, don't take them to be examples of excellence or examples of mistakes to avoid. Think of it like this: How do you get across at a high level your five Ws and one H so you can establish an initial fit with buyers?

Accenture is an example of how this all works together. The firm does a fabulous job of cascading its marketing messaging from positioning messaging through substantiation messaging.

The name Accenture is derived from two words, *accent* and *future*. A team member at Accenture came up with the name as part of an internal contest to help the firm rename itself. Thus the name is based in the realities of the perception that at least one internal staffer had about the firm—a good start, for sure.

MARKETING MESSAGES CASCADE

Positioning Messaging	Substantiation Messaging
Establishes initial fit and connection.	Strengthens resonance, establishes differentiation, and substantiates messages.
Where you establish fit, with whom, what, where, when, why, and how.	Where you establish and deepen the senses that:
	"We fit"—Continues positioning.
Should focus on attributes of similarity	"We fix"—Performance resonance.
Should focus on attributes of experience.	"We get it"—Performance and emotional resonance.
May or may not focus on attributes of distinction.	"We get you"—Emotional resonance.
Few key points of performance resonance.	"We can do it"—Substantiation.
Few key points of emotional resonance.	Sum of numerous messages and interactions establishes differentiation.
	Deep and sustained engagement strengthens resonance, differentiation, and substantiation.

KEY COMPONENTS OF POSITIONING MESSAGING

What	Who	Where	When	How	Why
Audit/Tax/Assurance	Public companies across industries	Global—156 offices in 37 countries	All the time—different for each of our 42 service lines	Deep industry experience Deep technical experience Teamwork	Results Decision making support Insight Commitment to quality and service
Innovation Consulting	Consumer products and medical device companies	Serving North America from Atlanta headquarters	When you need fresh ideas and new thinking When competitors are cleaning your clock	Proprietary database on scientific innovations across industries	Results Outside thinking breaks logjams Creative genius
Technology Consulting	With companies that have an installed base of IBM servers	14 cities across the U.S., most heavily in the Southeast	Major implementations Break/fix Application upgrades and integrations with other technologies	Acme Innovation Framework Intense engagements Deep technical expertise Experienced technicians Server analysis and improvement tools and technologies	Service excellence Listening On-time commitment No long-term contracts Our eight core values

(Continued)

185

(CONTINUED)

What	Who	Where	When	How	Why
Law	Midsize to large organizations, typically with more than 200 people 16 industries of focus	Chicago, Houston, New York, Miami, and Charlotte	Whenever your organization has legal needs	Deep industry experience Deep technical experience Global connections	Satisfaction Trust Results Thinking Collaborative firm with a personality Commitment to community
Telecom Specialty Consulting	Companies with over $250k in telecommunications spend per year	Serving U.S. from Cincinnati headquarters	When you want to streamline your telecommunications spend	Analyze your spend Renegotiate your contracts Take percent of savings as our fee	Results No risk Trustworthy, honest team It's never top of mind, but might as well save the money
Marketing	Technology firms of all sizes	Serving U.S. from Atlanta, Seattle, and Boston offices	Ongoing for marketing communications Product launches Lead generation campaigns	Experienced team Proprietary methodologies for marketing strategy and product launches Media and analyst relationships in place	Results Creative genius Make you the leader Ideas for the future Commitment to client success

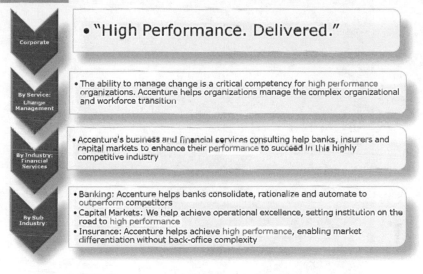

Figure 14.2 Accenture One-Pager

As Figure 14.2 shows, the Accenture logo is simple, and the tagline "High Performance. Delivered." has two key concepts. The first, performance, is obviously an umbrella for topics that focus on performance resonance. The second, delivered, seems to make a statement about a core value (we get things done) as well as emotional resonance. A buyer might say, "I've hired so many firms that don't do what they say they're going to do. They don't deliver the results they say they will deliver. If Accenture can, I'll be so much happier." And, of course, if you deliver, there are obvious implications for performance resonance.

If, indeed, the buyer has had experiences with other firms that don't deliver, don't perform, and don't help the buyer perform, then the tagline sets the stage for differentiation as well.

But it doesn't actually differentiate because it's very easy for another firm to say the same thing. And it doesn't make the case that Accenture can actually deliver performance. It just sets a stage to do that later.

Continue in the overall positioning and stage setting, as the messages get deeper and more detailed, the same umbrella structure works.

Figure 14.3   Accenture Advertisement with Tiger Woods

Consider an advertisement of Accenture's—also an example of positioning messaging. (See Figure 14.3.)

Tiger Woods is a perfect choice, as he epitomizes high performance and winning. He's also the right celebrity to make an emotional connection with buyers. "He's the best. I want to associate with the best. I want my company to perform in my industry like Tiger does in golf." From a graphical perspective, the advertisement is designed with simple but impeccable copywriting and art direction.

Figure 14.4   Accenture Ad Copy

You think we are impressed with the Accenture example so far? What we really like is shown in Figure 14.4.

The copy has an offer! The offer is an asset that substantiates a research-based, analytical approach! Other firms may have research, but they don't have *this* research, so it's distinct! Deep dive messaging connected to positioning messaging! In the research, Accenture then has the ability to connect deeply with buyers and to demonstrate its insight and ability to deliver high performance.

What happens with many firms that are willing to spend good money and effort to get in this marketing excellence league, even those that have done the right brand research to come up with the right messages?

- They spend amazingly disproportionately on graphic design and copy-writing versus outreach. Firms spend a year coming up with messages and designs, then buy brochures that sit in boxes, build web sites that make no effort to generate visits, and do little sustained outreach to the market.
- They skip the deep dive messaging (no white papers, no events, no research) and lose the ability to make a connection other than a glance at a logo.
- If they do create interactions with their firms through various marketing offers available to them, follow-up is anemic or nonexistent.

Through substantiation messaging, the key to establishing overall distinction in the minds of buyers, you have the opportunity to communicate and substantiate the key messages you need buyers to understand:

- "We fit"—Through our overall positioning and messaging you understand that we're the right firm for you. You start to connect with us and want to engage us.
- "We fix"—Here are the problems we can solve and the future we can help create for you. We fix these problems.
- "We get it"—We really stand out to you because we get it, and other people and firms don't. And we get you, and other people and firms don't.
- "We can do it"—Through our research, case studies, references, books, client list, speeches, and personal interactions with you, you not only get the sense that we *say* what we can get done and what it will be like to work with us, but you *believe* it to be true.

Messages and Graphic Designs

Now, here is some advice about developing messages and the graphic designs that support them.

> Dither (n): A state of indecisive agitation: *Company management was in a dither about the new round of graphic designs, marketing copy, and corporate messaging. Everybody had strong opinions on what they liked and didn't like.*
>
> Dilatory (adj): Tending to postpone or delay: *The graphic design and messaging process had a dilatory effect on our ability to do anything in marketing besides work on designs. Could this drag out any longer?*
>
> Delusion (n): Psychiatry. A false belief strongly held in spite of invalidating evidence, especially as a symptom of mental illness: *The team seemed under the delusion that choosing between possible brochure trim colors of papaywhip, peachpuff, or peru would[2] make any difference in marketing results.*

When firms build new web sites, brochures, and logos for their organizations, they scrutinize them with fanatical zeal. "Everyone is going

---

[2]Three actual colors. Who knew?

to see them and form an opinion about us based on them. They must be . . . they will be . . . perfect!" (Even if the process of doing so kills us.)

This intense graphic design and messaging scrutiny is especially true in service organizations. Why?

- Aggressive, proactive marketing is just catching on with some service industries.
- Besides answering the phone, service firms have always put great stock in very nice brochures. Thus, much of the marketing attention was focused on them.
- Service businesses are run by experts in their field. Thoughtful and experienced as they are, they haven't spent years in the marketing department at a major corporation; and they aren't schooled, and often aren't interested, in graphic design excellence.
- The people who deliver the services tend to associate themselves personally with any ad or graphic design that depicts their service. Thus, they identify the quality of the marketing piece as a reflection of the quality of their own work.
- Service firms are filled with smart people. They all have opinions and, indeed, would consider it a failing if they didn't add intelligent, constructive criticism to everything. Graphic design and messaging are simply easy targets.

As a result, when a service business decides it's going to "really do some marketing," everyone gets overly caught up in the graphic design and development process.

The same pathology happens over and over. It goes something like this:

- Marketing initiative is kicked off with vigor and enthusiasm.
- New design of something—branding, brochures, or web site— becomes a central component of the marketing effort.
- A large group of stakeholders becomes part of the design review team.
- The process takes forever.
- People lose energy as the process drags on.

- Nobody focuses on the "let's get new clients" part of marketing with the same vigor they do when choosing web site trim colors and deciding whether they're more results oriented, performance oriented, or return-on-investment (ROI) oriented.

The purpose of marketing—the end prize—should never be anything but the following: Attract and retain profitable clients. All too often we see companies getting so caught up in the visible and sexy part of the marketing process (design, copy) that they forget about the important-but-mundane part (lead and revenue generation).

Here are five pieces of advice that could save your marketing initiatives from the graphic design and corporate messaging pit of despair.

1. Keep Your Eyes on the Prize

Is it possible that you should disregard this chapter and pore over your designs and copy for months, all the way down to the last comma, pixel, and Pantone color? Sure—if you're about to spend tens of millions of dollars on an advertising campaign that will create hundreds of millions of impressions.

You can be sure that companies executing campaigns this large are also doing the following: extensive market research, testing each ad for customer response, researching each market, and many other steps before the launch. And they're prepared to turn on a dime if they find a new creative approach that will work better to help them win the prize: attracting and retaining profitable customers.

2. Collaborate with Care

Most design processes have too many people involved. In the name of collaboration, companies make the design process muddled and painful. Balance the benefits of collaboration with the knowledge that too many cooks make for bad soup.

3. Apply Ockham's Razor

Fourteenth-century philosopher William of Ockham is famous for a statement known as Ockham's razor: Plurality should not be posited without necessity. In other words, unless proven otherwise, less is more. Apply this to your creative process by asking yourself questions like:

- Do we need eight people here when, in the end, the design will be just as good (if not better) with three people involved; and we will get finished two months earlier?
- Do we need another round of design edits in order to help us attract and retain profitable customers, or can we stop now and move on?
- Do we need more design features such as Flash introductions on our web sites and a six-color process for our brochures when they won't make a difference to our clients?

Applying Ockham's razor to the design process will help you save time and money and will prevent a good deal of heartache.

4. Don't Rewire the Network Yourself

Let's say you are a CEO at a leadership consulting firm and your company is replanning its technology infrastructure. Would you tell the technologists where to put the wires? Whether to use fiber optics or something else? Whether version 6.3 of one software package is more robust than version 3.2 of another? You'd be laughed out of the room. If the technologists don't do a good job of listening to your business needs and implementing technology that will help serve those needs, get new technology people. Don't try to fix it yourself.

If you are not a designer, ask questions like "We're going to use this at a trade show. Will this help us attract attention and generate leads? How so?" and "How does this design compare to designs of companies you feel are best in breed?" instead of questions like "Don't you think a hunter green would be better?" In the end, if you don't think your designers are doing a good job, get new designers. Don't try to be one of them. As Emerson said, "The poet is the sayer, the namer, and represents beauty." If you're the client, hire the poet and help direct the poetry. Pick up a pen yourself, though, and it's rare you'll do anything but muddy the composition.

Many people may have the following titles: attorney, consultant, and doctor. If you need to win a major case in court, or if you need to figure out whether you want to spin off a $500,000 subsidiary in Central America, or if you need a liver transplant, you need credentials, experience, and talent. There's simply no substitute for the same when it comes to graphic design and marketing messaging.

5. Stop the Insanity

If you find yourself spiraling into design, messaging, and copywriting process despair, it's time to stop the insanity. If the current discussion is either overkill or distracting you from that goal, put an end to it. Do what you must to save yourself and your company from wasting time and energy on discussions that won't make a difference in results.

Dither (n): A state of indecisive agitation: *We don't dither about design, messaging, and copywriting. We run the process well, have the right people and skill sets on the team, and make decisions that help leverage graphic design to grow our revenue.*

Dilatory (adj): Tending to postpone or delay: *Others tried to slow us down by distracting us from our marketing goals and focusing too much on superfluous discussions. Their dilatory tactics won't work on us!*

Delusion (n): Psychiatry. A false belief strongly held in spite of invalidating evidence, especially as a symptom of mental illness: *I drank the punch and no longer operate under the delusion that marketing equals graphic design. Marketing equals growing our revenue. Graphic design is a great tool in the process, but not the process itself.*

The definitions are the same, but you have the power to change how you use them in a sentence.

15 | On Becoming a Thought Leader

Thinking is easy, acting is difficult, and to put one's thoughts into action is the most difficult thing in the world.

—Johann Wolfgang von Goethe

Jim, a CPA, wanted to grow his business and create new clients. Years ago, partly by accident, he discovered that there was a whole little world—condominium associations—in which he could become a thought leader. He already had a few condo association clients, and realized:

- They had special tax, financial, operational, and management needs from an accounting and business perspective.
- Condo associations made similar mistakes that, if avoided, could save them a lot of money and heartache.
- Well-managed condo associations had a lot in common from a management and financial perspective.

He started speaking and writing about the nuances of condo association accounting, management, and reporting.

Soon he became known as "The Condo King." As his royal reputation grew, condo associations all over the region would call him, because anything written on the topic had his name associated with it. After some time, he could barely keep up with the speaking engagement requests and new business opportunities. It became a very nice, successful practice for him.

His Highness the Condo King shared his story with us. "People call me all the time now; but when I started out, I did not think I would corner the condo association market. I did recognize the niche where I could make a difference, and I found it interesting. Plus, I was willing to put in the time and effort to do a good job speaking and writing. The rest just followed."

There are thought leaders of all kinds in the business world. Some are the "big T" Thought Leaders, the names many recognize: Tom Peters, Seth Godin, Peter Drucker, Michael Porter, Bill Gates. Others are "little t" thought leaders, who reach their defined niche market and do it well (His Highness, King of Condos).

Regardless of their ultimate reach, thought leaders share their ideas with their target markets. They are writing books, delivering seminars, and leading panels in industry organizations. They are writing columns in journals read by the people in their field. By speaking, writing, and teaching, they inspire and influence people and create new business opportunities for themselves and their firms.

Thought leadership itself is not a new topic in professional services, but it's becoming much more prevalent. The emergence of thought leadership as a mainstream marketing topic creates both a challenge and an opportunity for would-be thought leaders.

The challenge: Articles, white papers, webinars, teleseminars, seminars, podcasts, and books are everywhere on almost every business topic.

The opportunity: Much of what purports to be thought leadership is not very good; it is "sound and fury, signifying nothing." Lightweights are everywhere with weak writing, retread ideas, lack of rigor, poor presentations, specious arguments, and flimsy research.

Ten years ago fewer people were publishing and speaking, and fewer firms had thought leadership on the priority list as an explicit marketing strategy. Succeeding with thought leadership was a bit easier, as the decision was more binary than anything: speak and write, or don't speak and write. Professionals who journeyed down the path of speaking and writing, assuming a modicum of competence, were apt to succeed.

"I think that marketing, at a minimum, should help lawyers become thought leaders in clearly defined markets, particularly those markets tightly aligned with a firm's experience, expertise, capabilities, and growth goals."

—Kevin McMurdo, Chief Marketing Officer, Perkins Coie

Not so anymore. As Fiona Czerniawska wrote in an article on RainToday. com, "If you look at the web sites of the world's top 40 consulting firms (in terms of revenue), there are almost 3,500 articles and reports positioned as thought leadership—and that's leaving out the tens of thousands of case studies and descriptions of services that don't justify the label."

She goes on to say, "Around one-third of the bona fide material addresses strategy-related issues—studies of new or emerging markets, planning tools, and so on. Another third focuses on more operational topics, such as business process efficiency, technology, procurement, and outsourcing. The remaining third is made up from a whole host of topics, from leadership to cost control."

With fewer and fewer people in the don't-speak-and-write category, turning the switch from "off" to "on" is now just the price of entry. Once you're in, it's a dogfight to get traction. For those who succeed, thought leadership as much as ever can be one of the greatest competitive marketing advantages to your firm.

Two Keys and Eight Pillars of Thought Leadership

Thought leadership is one of those topics that engenders never-ending "what you need to do" lists. At the 50,000-foot level, thought leadership works when your ideas resonate with decision makers and influencers. Doing that requires only two key things:

1. Quality of intellectual capital.
2. Exposure of intellectual capital to the market.

One without the other doesn't work very well.

THOUGHT LEADERSHIP KEYS

Key Combinations	What Happens
Exposure *minus* Quality	You want to be known in your market, and you have fabulous market exposure and reach . . . but something's missing, and your audience knows it. Most empty speeches, empty books, and empty suits get judged correctly and set aside.
Quality *minus* Exposure	If a great white paper falls in the woods and nobody is there to hear it, does it make a sound?
	You may be the real deal when it comes to your quality ideas and relevance to your market. But if you're known by no one, you'll influence no one. The "leadership" part of thought leadership implies that there are people who follow you to action. Without the followers, you're out of luck.
Quality *plus* Exposure	Your ideas are relevant and helpful. When people engage your "real deal" thinking, it makes a positive difference in their businesses.
	You've connected with the market, broadened your sphere of recognition and reputation, and marketed your packaged ideas in a way that allows your ideas and contributions to disperse among the people in your market. You win.

Some of the current and aspiring thought leaders we interviewed expressed distaste for setting an explicit goal of establishing a personal brand and maximizing market exposure.

Let's assume you come to the table with the passion for your field and the guts to make an impact with your thinking. If that's true, why shouldn't you plan explicitly to use all the marketing, public relations (PR), and branding tools that you can to maximize your reach? If you want to change hearts and minds and show the world a better way, you need the spotlight. If you have good-quality intellectual capital to share, there's no room for sheepishness and mixed feelings about standing out.

An *asset* is an item of economic value owned by an individual or corporation, especially something that could be converted to cash. Thought leadership is an asset[1] for you and your firm. You have to capitalize on your asset, or you're not getting the type of return you can.

> "What I've done over the years is I've made a huge investment in long-term success. All those articles I've written that you've read, I didn't get paid to write those articles. Many of the conferences and speeches I've given, I've done for free. All the boards I've been on, I don't get paid. Like the Drucker Foundation—I don't get paid for that.
>
> My web site: I give away all the materials, and I don't get paid for that. So I've made a huge investment. . . . Be willing to invest for the long haul. Be willing to invest when there's no short-term payoff, and be willing to make personal sacrifice for long-term positive brand enhancement. Most professionals are not willing to do that."
>
> —Dr. Marshall Goldsmith

Quality of intellectual capital is, of course, subjective. With notable exceptions, too much so-called intellectual capital doesn't deserve the label. People dive in to write articles, write a white paper, or deliver seminars because these are "good marketing things to do." Without rigorous inquiry and attention to quality, they're bad marketing things to do.

Assuming quality is your goal, you can use the following list of pillars as a litmus test. Pass each test, and you will be in good shape.

---

[1]See the Chapter 11 section "Assets—What Your Firm Has That Helps Your People Deliver to Clients."

Eight Pillars of Intellectual Capital Quality

1. Distinction

Contrary to popular thought, intellectual capital doesn't need to be new in the sense of the breakthrough new idea or the unique, totally novel concept.

In *What's the Big Idea? Creating and Capitalizing on the Best Management Thinking*, authors Tom Davenport and Larry Prusak suggest, "Almost all ideas share one or more of three business objectives: improved efficiency, greater effectiveness, and innovation in products or processes."[2] They go on to say, "In describing the role gurus play in business ideas, 'create' isn't exactly the right word. Gurus tend to assemble, package, and broadcast business ideas; they will rarely create the whole thing from scratch."[3]

Great thought leadership is, however, distinct; it can stand on its own as a worthwhile contribution. While intellectual capital may contain new models, new case studies, new stories, and new research, as Davenport and Prusak suggest, the creation can be as much assembly and packaging as it is pure originality.

2. Salience

The word *salient* can be defined as "conspicuous" or "noticeable," and that gets the idea about right, but there's another definition more apt. Something is salient when it "has a quality that thrusts itself into attention." Your thought leadership might be everything else in this list, but it won't be contagious if it's not salient.

Think of your intellectual capital as a spark waiting to start a fire. If it's not salient, it's like a spark in the middle of a damp swamp; much as you might try to keep it going, it's more likely to go out than anything else. But

---

[2] Tom Davenport and Larry Prusak, *What's the Big Idea? Creating and Capitalizing on the Best Management Thinking* (Boston: Harvard Business School Press, 2003), p. 50.
[3] Ibid., p. 71.

if it is salient, your spark is sitting on a pile of tinder. Just the slightest breeze . . .

> "Rather than push, push, push, I shifted my entire organization to enticing pull. I figure if content is king, then let it be king. Get some very interesting content that's provocative enough to pull them in."
>
> —Paul Dunay, Global Director of Integrated Marketing, BearingPoint

3. Relevance

Change management. Leadership. Supply chain. Innovation. Entrepreneurship. Activity-based costing. Coaching. These ideas are on the minds of many. And with these ideas, you can be a thought leader with a capital *T*. You can also be a niche thought leader—a leader with a "little t"—and choose ideas that are relevant to only a select few (think Condo King). If the market you target is big enough, niche thought leadership may not be a bad idea. But, like any service you may offer, there needs to be a market of worthwhile size for your ideas.

4. Consequence

Consequence works with relevance. Your ideas may have a market, but then they must pass the "so what?" test. For your thought leadership to have impact, your ideas must be worthy of people's to-do lists. If you can't answer the "so what?" question clearly, brilliant as your ideas might be, you're not going to get decision makers to pay attention.

5. Defensibility

Even the greatest business ideas have their detractors. While few business ideas will be bulletproof (as much as you might think they are), you do need to be able to defend the ideas on their merits.

People often confuse defensibility with rigor. Good intellectual capital may be rigorous in the traditional sense with impeccable research and testing, but many ideas aren't rigorous in this sense. Many of Peter Drucker's observations, while based on his experiences, aren't rigorous in the traditional sense. Dr. Spencer Johnson moved all of our cheeses and took the business world by storm with four mice named Sniff, Scurry, Hem, and Haw. Helpful? For many, yes. (Just by being helpful, it's defensible.) Salient? For sure. Rigorous? You be the judge.

6. Realism

The kiss of death for thought leadership is when people say, "That's not realistic." It's perfectly fine if some people think it's not realistic—perhaps it will take a visionary to bring your ideas to life. Your ideas do, however, need to be able to make the leap from theory to implementation.

7. Elegance

Unpack the word *elegance*, and you'll find such flavors as simplicity, effectiveness, refinement, grace, and even dignified propriety. Perhaps it's your conceptual model, perhaps it's your writing, or perhaps it's the simplicity of the ideas you advance. Wherever it is, elegance in intellectual capital is the tide that raises all boats, as elegant intellectual capital is often salient, distinct, and defensible. Elegant ideas are easy to judge relevant and consequential. Its simplicity often makes it seem more realistic. And the marketer in you will have a great time packaging it up for the world to consume.

8. Presentation

Like Supreme Court Justice Potter Stewart famously said about pornography, he might not succeed in defining it, but "I know it when I see it." While it's certainly easier to define the elements of a top-quality speech, white paper, research report, or book, most people don't pick one apart by its elements. They simply observe the presentation of your intellectual capital (in whatever form they see it) and make judgments that range from "amazing and life-changing" to "amateurish and uninteresting."

The problem with presentation is this: Not everyone knows a great speech, white paper, or book from a good, fair, or poor one. Many professionals are paranoid perfectionists and they *underestimate* their speaking and writing skills. The opposite problems all too often exist as well: either inflated views of speaking and writing quality, or simply allowing A-minus material out the door when it needs to be major league.

Thought Leader Mind-Set and Motivation

- Not everyone is suited to become a thought leader. The thought leadership marathon route is littered with people who started with the best of intentions, made it only so far, and dropped out before they finished the race. In our research and interviews with various thought leaders,[4] we found that those who make it are from diverse fields of expertise, firm types, and personalities but tend to share the following characteristics:
- They *enjoy what they do*, which gives them a deep source of energy and motivation.
- They feel *driven to teach* others what they know.
- They realize that in order to make an impact, build their reputation, and grow their business, they need to *reach out and communicate* with their market at large.
- They *take risks* with their messages. They're contrary, controversial, and edgy.
- They *balance confidence* in their skills and opinions with a genuine interest in *learning* from others (their clients, colleagues, and market).
- They are willing to *risk today's time*, giving speeches, writing articles, doing interviews, leading for industry organizations, often for little or no pay, *for tomorrow's potential benefit*: new business, public affirmation,

---

[4] "How to Become a Thought Leader," RainToday.com and Wellesley Hills Group, 2007.

high-profile invitations, and generally solid market esteem built on the reputation they've grown over the years.

- They *keep working, connecting, and communicating* long after they've achieved relative fame and success. They don't take their success for granted, and they approach their work with the realization that there is no end point to being a thought leader.

> "Most real thought leaders in my field never retire. Warren Bennis, Frances Hesselbein, Richard Beckhart, Peter Drucker—they never retired. We all retire when we die! So my first thing is, love what you do."
>
> —Dr. Marshall Goldsmith

In their actions and beliefs, each of the thought leaders we analyzed and interviewed for this research possesses a goodly subset of these characteristics.

Building your professional services business through thought leadership takes time, sustained energy, and focus. But the impact is worth it. Get it right, and you will see substantial impact on your business when you become a thought leader in your field.

What Thought Leaders Can Expect

Like an actor who puts in his time waiting for his big break, when you, after years of toil, arrive as a bona fide thought leader, here is what you can expect.

Greater Recognition, Demand, and Reach in the Market

You will notice signs that you're accomplishing greater recognition, demand, and reach outside your initial circle of business, including:

- Speaking requests.
- Meeting people who have already heard of you.

- Receiving calls from trade magazines for interviews.
- Getting article publishing requests.
- Increased service inquiries outside of your normal area of expertise.
- Generating interest from leading publications, top industry associations, and exclusive speaking venues.
- Shifting from working locally or regionally to working nationally or globally.

Writing a book (a powerful tool for an aspiring thought leader) creates significant impact, from anecdotal reach to real opportunity for your business:

- Boarding a plane and seeing your book being read by other passengers.
- Being approached by publishers to write a book, since your audience is already established.
- Improving your brand, generating more speaking engagements, more clients, more leads, higher fees, a more desirable client base, and closing more business.[5]

Easier Business Development, More Desirable Clients

Thought leaders can experience an easier business development process with potential clients, including:

- Shorter sales cycles.
- Higher-quality conversations.
- Less or no fee pushback.
- Access to higher levels within organizations.

---

[5] Schultz et al., *The Business Impact of Writing a Book: Data, Analysis, and Lessons from Professional Service Providers Who Have Done It* (Framingham, MA: RainToday.com, 2006), http://www.raintoday.com/writeabook.cfm

Appreciation Inside Your Firm

Thought leaders build credibility and esteem among colleagues. Not only are you bringing in business, but you're also creating a brand for yourself within your company, furthering the firm's success as well as your own.

HOW SPEAKING RATES WORK FOR ONE ROAD WARRIOR

Dr. Martha Rogers rates at the top end of the thought leader speaking spectrum, with roughly 60 to 70 speaking engagements per year. In the beginning, she spoke many times for free. As she became better-known and more experienced, her rates changed dramatically. She shared with us her own experience with how speaking engagements grew from a strict marketing tool to a serious revenue generator for her and her partner, Don Peppers:

> It really boils down to supply and demand. Motivational speakers make about $3,000 a day. They go all the way up to about $75,000 a day, which I think is what Tom Peters is at, and he's the best-known business name there is.
>
> We started around $3,000. I remember the first time we asked for $3,000 and I thought, "Oh, nobody's going to pay this." They did! I thought that was amazing.
>
> It didn't take long before the speakers' bureaus found us. That's what their job is, to figure out who's speaking for money. They came and said, "Are you busy?" Don and I were thinking, "Oh, my gosh, I can't believe it, yes." They said, "Well, don't you think you should be charging more to reduce the demand?" And we said, "Wow, do you think people will pay more than $3,000?" Before long, they had us up to $10,000; and before long after that, they had us up to more.

By the way, after 2001, they were very good about saying, "Okay, you've got to cut your rates now." The business has never come back after 2001 the way it was before. In fact, a lot of events now don't even pay their speakers. They actually demand that speakers pay the events.

I don't pay to speak. But sometimes, at a very, very, very favorable conference, I might go in and speak for free, which means I didn't have to pay the $30,000 other events might be charging. If it's an audience I really want to talk to and if there's a lot of really valuable publicity around it, we might negotiate a deal.

I'll tell you what. I gave a lot of free speeches those first couple of years. A lot of them. And then, the people who were in the audience call you to come speak for a different group, so it's worthwhile. You do pick and choose.

Higher Speaking Fees

While many professionals speak to build business, some speak *as* their business. When you publish a book on your topic of expertise, you're likely to receive higher-paying speaking invitations.

Less Push and More Pull

We would be remiss if we didn't say more about one of the best ways of promoting your thought leadership. In our benchmark research study *The Business Impact of Writing a Book*,[6] we surveyed close to 200 authors of business books who together had published a total of approximately 600

---

[6] *The Business Impact of Writing a Book*, (Framingham, MA: RainToday.com and Wellesley Hills Group, 2006).

books. Professional service provider authors reported the outcomes resulting from business book publishing, shown in the table.

BOOK PUBLISHING OUTCOMES

Benefit from Book Publishing	Any Influence from Publishing	Strong or Very Strong Influence from Publishing
Improve my brand	94%	85%
Generate more speaking engagements	95%	75%
Generate more clients	96%	63%
Generate more leads	94%	56%
Charge higher fees	87%	53%
Generate more desirable client base	87%	48%
Close more deals	76%	38%

RESEARCH RESULTS

Simply the act of publishing a book didn't have the impact. The books had to sell a lot of copies. Those authors who sold the most copies of their book reaped the greatest business benefits. When we reviewed the results, we were struck by the impact that selling a certain number of copies of books had on various areas of authors' practices.

Overall Effect: Authors who reported a "positive" overall effect on their practices sold a median number (at the 50th percentile) of 5,000 copies of their first book, whereas those who reported an "extremely positive" overall effect on their practices sold a median number of 10,000 copies of their first book.

Raising Fees: Authors who reported a "strong influence" on their ability to raise their fees sold a median number of 4,000 copies of their first book, whereas those who reported a "very strong influence" on their ability to raise fees sold a median number of 20,000 copies of their first book.

Generating New Clients: Authors who reported that publishing books had "some/a little/no influence" on their ability to generate new clients sold a median number of 9,000 copies of their books, whereas those who reported publishing books had a "very strong/strong influence" sold a median number of 20,000 copies of their books.

Generating Better Speaking Engagements: Authors who reported that publishing books had a "very strong influence" on their ability to generate better speaking engagements sold a median number of 25,000 books over their careers, whereas those who reported a "strong influence" sold a median number of 8,200.

It's clear that selling 4,000 to 5,000 copies of your book can bring measurable success to your practice. What we found even more impressive only emerged after analyzing all the measures of success in the study. To reach the strongest positive impact on their practices, the authors seem to need to jump two critical hurdles when it comes to the numbers of books they've sold:

> *Hurdle 1 = 10,000 Copies:* Authors who sold over 10,000 copies of their books by and large reported strong positive effects on their businesses as a result of publishing books. This group of folks seemed very pleased with the return on their investments in effort, time, and money for writing and publishing books.

> *Hurdle 2 = 20,000 Copies:* Authors who sold over 20,000 copies of their books reported phenomenally positive effects on their businesses. In most categories where we studied this data, the results achieved by authors who sold over 20,000 copies of their books were far and away stronger than results of those who sold fewer than 20,000 copies.

> If you're an aspiring author, you should note that when it comes to book publishing, the authors we studied for the report found that book publishers themselves do very little to market books. Selling books is up to the authors. Those authors who embrace marketing and do a good job at marketing reap the benefits for their practices. Those that don't, don't.

But you're not going to get your book published by a major publishing house if you don't have a marketing platform set up, anyway.

Mary Glenn, editorial director at McGraw-Hill Publishing Company, says, "Sometimes [the marketing platform] surpasses the importance of the actual topic of the book. Authors need to have a robust speaking circuit or be out there meeting the public somehow. We look for people who are go-to experts in the field."

Thus, having a marketing platform is very often a *prerequisite* for getting a publisher to even consider taking on your book. Once again, marketing is the key to success.

16 | Marketing Communications and Lead Generation Tactics

Sometimes I lie awake at night, and I ask, "Where have I gone wrong?"
Then a voice says to me, "This is going to take more than one night."

—Charles Schulz

Perhaps the easiest thing to do in professional services marketing is spend money. Whether you get any benefit from that money often depends on three factors:

1. The tactics you employ given your situation and goals.
2. How well you employ those tactics.
3. Your expectations of what you should get from employing those tactics well.

Unfortunately for most firms, they don't get the benefit they can from their marketing efforts because of avoidable missteps. We know. We've seen

211

millions of dollars swirl down the drain, gone forever, leaving marketing teams to wonder, "Where did we go wrong?"

The charts in Figure 16.1 highlight the results of our research on *What's Working in Lead Generation* concerning what tactics worked for over 700 different professional services firms. As you can see, not all tactics work for everyone; yet every tactic (even television advertising) works, but sometimes for only a select few.

The challenge of definitively sorting out which marketing tactics work from those that don't is almost impossible, because what works for one firm in one situation may be wholly inappropriate for another firm in a different situation. Though marketers often ask us for one, there is no silver bullet. The questions you need the answers to are, "What is most likely to work *here*?" and "What do I need to do to give us the best shot at success?"

This book would be very long, indeed, if we covered how all of these tactics work and how to implement them. What we have provided in this chapter is an overview of the major marketing tactics employed by professional services firms, along with guidance on when and how to employ the tactic well.

As you move along in this chapter, heed this caveat: While there is much you can learn about employing marketing tactics here and from other books, there's no substitute for experience, skill, and talent. Medical students spend years in grueling medical school before they're allowed to see a patient. Then they spend years seeing patients under the highly regulated guidance of more experienced physicians. Watch an episode of almost any TV medical drama, and you'll hear the requisite, "Oh, my! Who did the hatchet job on these sutures?" admonishment from a senior doctor directed at a resident. (See Figure 16.2.)

Marketing (and anything, really) is not dissimilar. Many a hatchet job has been done on marketing campaigns: Bad copy. Embarrassing creative work. Missing pieces. Overspending and underspending. Unrealistic expectations. Taking two weeks to do something that should take two hours. These mistakes and more are made every day in professional services firms large and small.

As you employ your marketing tactics, make sure you have the right experience and skill to help you in proportion to the importance of the task and the outcome you desire. Most parents are qualified to take splinters out

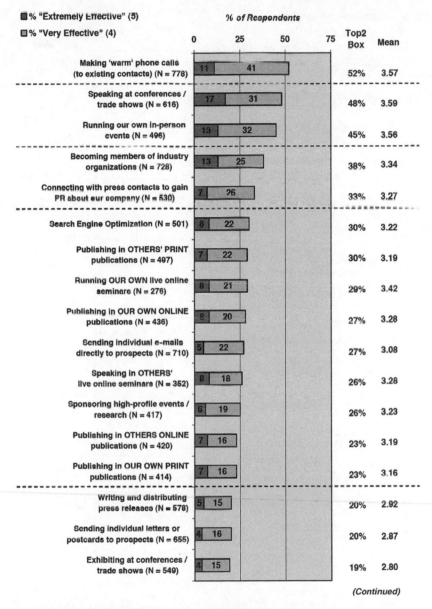

Figure 16.1 Effectivness of Lead Generation Methods Used by Particpants—by Percent Rated Extremely/Very Effective

(Continued)

	% of Respondents	Top2 Box	Mean
■ % "Extremely Effective" (5)			
□ % "Very Effective" (4)	0 25 50 75		
Publishing a company-authored or company-affiliated blog (N = 266)	9 9	18%	3.22
Running our own telephone-based events (N = 296)	6 10	16%	2.94
Search Engine advertising for our web site (N = 363)	4 12	16%	2.80
Sending professionally designed direct mail packages to prospects (N = 514)	4 12	16%	2.75
E-mailing ONLINE company newsletter(s) (N = 486)	5 11	15%	2.83
Joining online communities related to our field (N = 465)	3 12	15%	2.82
Participating regularly in blog-related online conversation (N = 333)	3 8	11%	2.73
Sending emails to prospects via a 3rd party referrer (N = 422)	3 8	11%	2.57
Making 'cold' phone calls (to new contacts) (N = 676)	1 9	10%	2.50
Mailing PRINTED company newsletter(s) (N = 428)	2 7	9%	2.50
Advertising in ad-supported web sites and online publications (N = 368)	2 5	7%	2.44
Advertising in print media (N = 503)	2 6	7%	2.37
Sending mass e-mails directly to prospects (N = 530)	2 5	7%	2.27
Advertising on the radio (N = 247)	2 5	7%	2.07
Sending mass letters or postcards to prospects (N = 560)	1 4	6%	2.23
Advertising on TV (N = 183)	1 2	3%	1.68

Figure 16.1 (*Continued*) Effectivness of Lead Generation Methods Used by Particpants—by Percent Rated Extremely/Very Effective

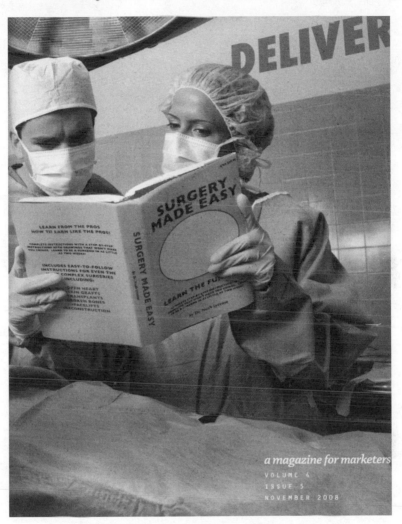

Figure 16.2 *Deliver* **Cover**

Deliver® magazine and the United States Postal Service.

of their children's fingers when they are young. When it comes time to take out wisdom teeth, much as Dad might want to do it himself, most people take their children to see the oral surgeon.

The marketing tactics that follow are broken down into several categories based on characteristics the tactics share. While you could categorize the marketing tactics in any way you like, and you could make the argument that some tactics could fit in multiple categories, we've found this typology helpful to people as they deepen their understanding of the landscape of marketing tactics.

Outbound Communications and Research Methods

Direct Mail

Communicating with your clients and prospects through snail mail[1] has been dismissed as useless by many a marketing consultant in the professional services field. Practitioners inside companies also find many reasons not to mail. They say things like, "You can't develop business through the mail." "We've tried it and it hasn't worked for us." "We're using other tactics. E-mail is cheaper, so we're shifting communications in that direction." "No one sends mail anymore."

The truth is direct mail is still an effective tactic. With mail volume for professional services and other business-to-business industries dropping, for some buyers it's even novel again.

Typically good for:

- Communicating regularly with clients and key targeted prospects for outcomes including lead generation, lead nurturing, and relationship nurturing.
- Improving all parts of Brand RAMP:

  - Mail familiarizes your audience with your company and services.
  - Clear copy and connections to deep dive offers articulate your services and value propostion to buyers.

---

[1] Before the advent of e-mail, we used to be able to call mail "mail." Now we add the "snail" in front to make sure everyone knows we're talking about physical mail and not e-mail.

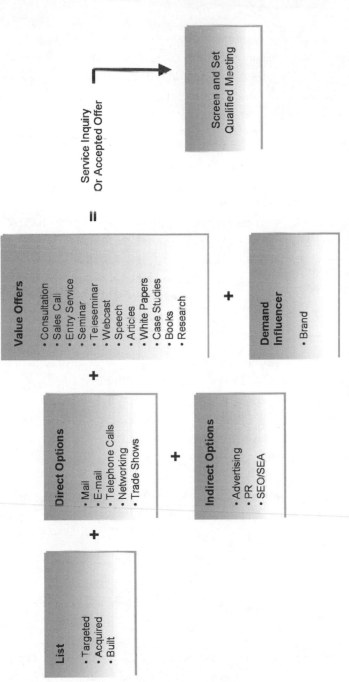

Figure 16.3   Wellesley Hills Group Summary of Marketing Tactics

217

- Regular, ongoing touches help buyers remember you at the elusive time of need (and help referral sources remember to refer you when asked for a referral).
- Messages of value and connection to value-based offers create and enhance preference for your company and services.

- Breaking through the noise; if you want direct mail to get through, you typically can make sure it does, even at the highest levels of corporate leadership.
- Getting response to value-based offers ranging from event attendance to white papers to research to one-on-one introductory meetings.
- Creating urgency by telling an ongoing story, staying top of mind, and creating deeper connection to the value of solving problems with your services.

Words of wisdom

- Establish your direct mail metrics and expectations (but be patient, as results typically build over time and multiple mailings).
- Constantly test the effectiveness of your campaigns.
- Reuse successful campaigns. Just because they're not new to you doesn't mean they won't work over and over again with clients.
- Use mail in conjunction with other tactics, such as telephone and e-mail, to increase effectiveness.
- Like advertising, think of direct mail as an ongoing communication mechanism, not an event. It's more powerful when it continues over time to the same audience.
- Direct mail is both art and science. Take care to know the science side very well (or get someone who does).

Common mistakes

- Expectations for direct mail success that are unrealistic. For example, we constantly see people mail 300 invitations hoping to get 25 people to their seminar, only to be disappointed when they get only a handful (if they are lucky). You might have read, "Average response rates for direct mail are 1 percent to 2 percent." These averages are useless. Responses can be as high as 10 percent and as low as 0.05 percent due to factors that start with the list and include offer; message and copy; package (letter, postcard, three-dimensional mailer, etc.); price of offer (if there is one); and all the rest of the direct mail success factors.

- Lists and databases that are old, small, and inaccurate. You can only be as successful as your database is clean and fresh. There is no cutting corners in this area.
- Direct mail without an offer or, even worse, offers like "buy my service" or "let us be your trusted advisor" that are often not appropriate for direct mail.
- Weak copy and creative that hurt your brand.
- Direct mail as a one-shot effort.

Telephone

It's not hard to find arguments against cold calling in professional services. We have even seen cold calling compared to ramming your head repeatedly against a wall. Srong imagery, indeed, but misplaced when it comes to cold calling.

For the most part, anti–cold calling sentiment stems from:

- Poor cold calling skills.
- Bad reputation (business-to-business telephone selling is not like the telemarketing call you might get during dinner).
- Inapprorpiate implementation.
- Personal and emotional desire of individuals not to use cold calling, especially if they must make the calls themselves.

Much like direct mail, cold calling can, and often should, be a major part of lead generation and business development. Add the right skill, strong implementation, and positive energy and desire, and cold calling can be a major factor in your firm's growth and success.

Keep in mind as well that the telephone can be used for more than cold calling. It can be used for research, warm calling, and general relationship development and maintenance. This may sound rather obvious, but people don't use the telephone to reach out to prospects or reconnect with clients often enough.

Typically good for:

- Making introductions with top prospects and referral sources.
- Developing, maintaining, nurturing relationships.
- Getting responses to specific offers.
- Generating event attendance.
- Reaching a highly targeted, well-defined audience.
- Jump-starting your pipeline.
- Selling complex, high-end services.

Words of wisdom

- Don't ask your professional staff to make the initial calls unless they have the skills and desire to do so. Not much good usually happens.
- Prepare a good reason to call from the buyer's perspective; don't just pitch services.
- Deliver value in the telephone call itself.
- Choose the right person to do the calling: right experience level, right skill, right attitude.
- Call in blocks of time; getting on a roll is important.
- Call each target, client, and referral source with the right frequency; too much and you can annoy them, not enough and you don't break through.

Common mistakes

- People who lack skill and desire make the calls and fail.
- Call reluctance creates procrastination and dulls cold calling activity.

- Robotic calling and calling from a script.
- No value for the prospect in the phone call.
- Poor target lists.
- Poor follow-up; lack of follow-up.
- Poor record keeping and database management.
- Calling with nothing else in your tool kit. Brand and integrated marketing such as thought leadership, direct mail, e-mail, strong web sites, and so on make calling much more effective.

E-Mail

Along with the telephone and direct mail, e-mail is the third major leg of the direct communications tool kit. Use of e-mail varies in frequency and level of sophistication, but it's a part of almost all professional service firms' marketing and sales strategies.

You can view e-mail in two major categories: personal and bulk. Personal e-mail involves opening your e-mail program, typing an e-mail, and sending it to a person yourself. Bulk e-mail is sending similar e-mails to many people, typically using an automated program.

That we call it bulk e-mail does not mean you should equate it with spam, and it may also be "from" you and "to" a specific person with that person's name identified in the actual e-mail. For example, your e-mail newsletter may be 100 percent opt-in, and each issue may be packed with content and value that the readership looks forward to. It may be extremely well-done bulk e-mail, but it's still bulk e-mail.

Typically good for:

- Communicating directly for lead generation, lead nurturing, and relationship development.
- Delivering value-based content such as company newsletters.
- Generating responses to offers.
- Promoting event attendance.

Words of wisdom

- Choose the right application for your situation and goals. Your e-mail strategy may include newsletters, the sending of 200 personal communications per day by your business development staff, automated e-mail seqences, targeted third-party e-mails, and much more.
- Don't spam. Follow spam laws.
- Choose the right look and feel for your e-mail that supports your brand and your objectives. Sometimes a simple, typed, text e-mail will do. Many e-mail marketing programs are the core messaging platform for the company and should fit in with your corporate identity.
- E-mail is a response generation media and is eminently trackable. Like direct mail, you should test different variables for improved reactions and responses from readers.
- E-mail as a communication type is changing more rapidly than many others. New applications and rules of the jungle for use such as automated communication sequences, tracking and testing, and e-mail deliverability issues are springing up every day. You have to stay on top of it.

Common mistakes

- Spamming. Spam at your own risk.
- Overreacting to a single negative reader reaction. Once your list gets large enough, someone is bound to forget that they signed up at one point and send you an annoyed reply. If you're operating your e-mail strategy the right way, these will be few and far between. But when they come up, don't overreact and stop your efforts completely.
- Too little attention to your list and list building. At many firms, disproportionate effort goes into the e-mail communication design and message, leaving e-mail list building and list maintenance to wither on the vine.
- E-mail communications that are too focused on the sender, and not focused enough on the reader. Make sure your e-mail communications are valuable to readers.

- E-mail communications that leave the readers saying, "What are they saying? What do they want me to do?" Be clear. Like any communication, make sure you're clear about what you're saying.
- No attention to e-mail deliverability. Spam filters catch e-mails that otherwise could get through if you take the time to make sure your e-mail content and e-mail delivery system are in keeping with the latest technologies.
- Sloppiness. Take the time to copyedit, fix broken links, and make sure you send out generally error-free e-mails.

Networking

Networking is a means to an end, not an end in itself. That end is building and sustaining relationships with people. The word *networking* may bring to mind thoughts of busy bars with rapid-fire business card exchanges, insincere glad-handing, and constant elevator pitching. This isn't what you should think about.

When we refer to effective networking, we're talking about creating authentic and honest relationships. By focusing on how we can help others to succeed and prosper, we contribute to their success, as well as our own. But first things first: We have to meet people of similar minds who will be good connections.

While networking can happen at events with explicity stated networking times, it can also happen anyplace: at conferences, charity and association board meetings, sports events, places of worship, social media, and networking web sites.

Many professionals' best leads come from referrals. The reasons are twofold:

1. People ask for referrals when they have a need.
2. When people ask for referrals, they ask a trusted source.

It's the relationships that drive the referrals. Networking is a great way to begin, develop, and nurture strong relationships.

Typically good for:

- Making initial connections.
- Generating referrals.
- Building relationships.
- Maintaining and nurturing relationships over the long term.

Words of wisdom

- Networking is about creating relationships, not gathering business cards. We said it before, but it bears repeating.
- If you get involved with a trade association, become a leader.
- People like people who are good conversationalists. Don't be too self-focused. Learn to connect with people in conversation.
- Givers gain. It's the golden rule.
- Focus on important people who are interesting to you and to whom you have something to offer.
- Learn to use the social networking on the Internet (see more on this later).

Common mistakes

- Selling as an objective. It's possible you may uncover an actual need in a first conversation with someone. More likely than not, though, you won't. But if you are constantly pitching your services or asking needs-based sales-type questions, you often turn people off who could become good connections, because they perceive you as having a heavy selling agenda.
- Viewing networking as an event versus an ongoing effort to nurture relationships. Constantly feed and nourish your network, pruning it and keeping it healthy so it doesn't wither. That doesn't mean flooding your contact's in-box or mailbox with useless information about your company or sending an article or news item just because

you find it interesting; it does, however, mean sending information that is important or relevant to your contacts and sending news items that pertain to their current issues.

- Asking without giving. Remember the golden rule of networking: givers gain.
- Attending versus working at networking events. If you're at an industry conference, work the conference. Meet people. Look for opportunities to spend more time working, not less. Often people at networking events spend too much time with people from their own companies and with colleagues from competitors. If you're not creating and enhancing relationships that are important, you're not working hard enough.
- Expecting a quid pro quo all of the time. Your goal is to meet people and make connections. Don't expect immediate gratification— getting to know people now will often benefit you later. Build your relationships before you need them.
- In conversation, don't worry too much about elevator pitches and stilted deliveries of what you do. You should know how to describe what you do in 20 seconds, two minutes, and longer; but don't go into RoboProfessional mode every time you meet someone.
- Networking with people who don't share your values or whom you do not like. As a general rule, you should like the people in your network. It will make contact easier and more beneficial.
- Confusing your network with your holiday card list. Networks are relationships built over time. Having a network is not the same as having a list of people you send holiday cards to once a year.
- Letting your network get stale. You must constantly add to your network while continuing to provide value to those who are already in it.

Social Networking

Along with face-to-face networking, social networking and social media sites like LinkedIn, Plaxo, Facebook, Spoke, Twitter, and others are fast becoming a core part of the service firm marketing and selling mix.

Typically good for:

- Reconnecting with old business and personal connections.
- Staying in touch and nurturing relationships.
- Finding immediate need. Often in sites like LinkedIn, businesspeople will post questions to their network as they look for providers, solutions to problems, and answers to questions.
- General marketing and brand communications.
- Event promotion.

Words of wisdom

- Be natural. If you're connecting with and reconnecting with people, just be yourself. Allow your personality to come through (while you also keep it professional).
- Social media is changing all the time. Keep your eyes open and your ear to the ground for new opportunities.
- Analyze social media sites for where companies of your type can find opportunities and how you can utilize the major sites to your advantage.
- Join special subnetworks based on your interest within each site.

Common mistakes

- Blatant selling.
- Overdoing it. Some folks get caught up in social networking and end up spending too much time online and not enough time on other activities.
- Not keeping up with trends.
- Not utilizing social networking at all; being the laggard.

Trade Show Marketing

Industry trade shows are often an underutilized source of lead generation and brand building potential. Like direct mail and telephone, people generally understand the concept of what a trade show is, but rarely have all the pieces in place to make the tactic work for them.

Typically good for:

- Lead generation. The first thing anyone wants to know from a trade show is, "Did you come back with any good leads?" Trade shows can, indeed, be very good for leads if you work the show right.
- Brand RAMP. Selecting the right trade shows and working them correctly can lead to advances in all areas of the Brand RAMP.
- Database building and rapid-fire connections. At many trade shows, you'll get exposure to a lot of people in a condensed period of time.
- Generating and maintaining relationships. Some shows are the must-attend shows for leaders and buyers in all types of industries. If you're at the trade shows, you can both engage and enhance relationships with these buyers.
- Competitive positioning. While it's not enough to say, "My competitors are there so I have to be there," trade shows offer the opportunity to position your firm versus the others.
- Introducing new services and entering new markets.

Words of wisdom

- What you do before and after the show makes a big difference. At many shows, you can get the list of attendees for preshow marketing activities. Many people go to a show with 1,000 attendees "hoping to meet 20 or so of the 100 bigwigs who will be there." Why not call the 100 bigwigs beforehand and set meetings with 20 of them?
- Your follow-up from the show can often mean the difference between success and failure.
- Work the trade show with the same focus and persistence you bring to everything you do.
- Aggressive and forward-thinking companies can make running trade shows a part of their strategy. But beware: Many a company has lost a

lot of money and spent a lot of time for little return because it wasn't careful.

Common mistakes

- Being there because the other guy is there; being there because you have to "do something," so you sign up to go to or exhibit at a trade show. You've got to have a strategy for each show. Don't just go.
- Not working the show. Too many people show up at a trade show and look forward to a vacation away from the office. Trade shows are for working.
- Focusing solely on trade shows to the detriment of other marketing tactics. Make sure trade shows fit in your marketing and selling mix in balance with other tactics.
- Setting unrealistic or no expectations. Shows can be good for lead generation and exposure, but you have to work to get the most out of them.
- Picking the wrong shows. Make sure your target buyers are in attendance.

Identity, Collateral, Presentations

"Sounds interesting—can you send me something?" "Will you need a projector for slides?" We all get these questions, and we all like to have good answers for them. We all like to look good as we put our first foot forward.

Brand identity and collateral material play a large part in all of our marketing and business development activities and can make a big difference in a firm's ability to get in the door and win new business.

Typically good for:

- Creating emotional connections and positive impressions on buyers.
- Competive positioning.

- Connecting with and educating clients, prospects, and internal team members.
- Brand recognition and articulation.
- Providing a backdrop for deeper interaction for your firm.

Words of wisdom

- Your corporate identity and graphic design define what league you're in. Buyers need to connect with you before they buy. Regardless of the specific messages you want to communicate, does the quality of your brand look and feel world-class or simply classy or done on the cheap?
- Calibrate the amount of collateral material with the actual needs of selling at your firm. For some firms, all they have is a business card and a web site. No other materials are necessary. For other firms, elaborate presentations and various pieces of support materials are necessary.
- Use a good graphic designer and art director, and let them do their jobs. While you will undoubtedly have suggestions, don't try to take over the design process yourself. If you don't like their work, dismiss them and get a new team. Don't try to do their jobs yourself. That doesn't usually turn out well.

Common mistakes

- Using collateral materials as crutches. Especially people who are new at business development feel the deep need to go in with a lot of high-quality materials. People usually err on the side of bringing too much when they don't need it.
- Excessive pitching. Professionals often feel the need to walk people through their materials, and then they find themselves going on for 40 minutes without stopping. This typically isn't helpful for connecting with people and developing business.
- Too much energy and focus on design and wordsmithing. Firms can spend a year of energy and debate on new logos, new web site designs,

and new materials. Then the materials are done and nobody ever thinks about them again. Collateral materials are something to get done, get done well, and get out of the way so you can focus on activities that will actually make a difference in your firm's growth.

- Overreliance in the selling process. Buyers might say to you, "Sounds interesting. Can you send me some info?" This can be serious, but it can also be a brush-off. When you send material, don't think, "Okay, they'll read it and then get back to me." Send it. Wait the appropriate amount of time, and keep on the task of building the relationship and winning business. Don't expect collateral materials to sell for you.
- Calibrating your design needs incorrectly. If you're selling to world-class firms, your materials should look the part. Perhaps a common-place logo and a trifold brochure are enough, and you don't need to spend serious budget money on design. But keep in mind, as Dad always said, "Dress for the job you want, not the one you have."
- Paying too little attention to your web site. For most firms, far and away most of the effort should be spent making their web sites as good as they possibly can be.

Advertising

Traditional advertising is typically broken down into five major areas: TV, radio, print, outdoor, and direct. Now, of course, there is also online. We cover direct marketing and online marketing in other areas. For our purposes here, the questions are: Should you advertise in traditional media? If so, what should you be aware of?

Typically good for:

- Brand recognition and articulation.
- Overall firm and company branding.
- Larger firms, or firms needing to reach a large, hard-to-pinpoint, diverse audience.

Words of wisdom

- Choosing to advertise in print, TV, radio, and so on at all is the first important step. Most firms should *not* consider advertising to be a main part of their marketing mix. Yet, when they feel the need to market the firm, this is one of the first tactics they engage. Typically that's a mistake.
- Creative is important. You'll find advertising campaigns that failed due to poor creative and advertising mechanics.
- Media choice and placement are of extreme importance. Many firms don't investigate media options with the zeal they should. They end up making poor choices in easy-to-identify publications that may not be the best for them. Choose your media wisely.
- Have an offer, and make it worthwhile. It's not enough to say, "Coke is it" or "Wendy's—It's better here." Take a cue from the Tiger Woods ads from Accenture. Each of those ads has an offer similar to, "For a deeper look at our research and experience with the world's most successful companies, including our landmark study of over 500 high performers, visit accenture.com/research."

Common mistakes

- Spending too heavily on advertising. Firm after firm spends thousands to millions on advertising for the benefit of "getting our name out there." Even the most basic marketing tactic choice analysis points to greener pastures elsewhere.
- Advertising that is focused only on brand. If you're going to advertise, you should combine brand implementation with lead generation.
- Disproportionate amounts spent on the creative and design aspects versus media and outreach.
- Weak design and advertising mechanics.
- Weak copy or copy focused on messages that are too broad (e.g., "We are a different kind of firm," "We offer solutions, not just services," or "Here are our 15 practice areas").

- Poor media choices.
- Advertising not connected to the rest of the media mix.

The list of common mistakes is long and keeps going. Few firms, even those firms that should be doing it, get advertising right.

Publicity

"I'm a thought leader," says the person from the firm. "Oh, where have you been published, and what media have picked you up?" asks the buyer. "Oh, I've been published on our web site, but I don't have any media mentions."

Publicity can play a big role in the professional service firm marketing mix, as it can lead to a veritable cornucopia of positive outcomes. Mostly because good publicity is expensive and hard to come by, the pitfalls of generating publicity can be great.

Typically good for:

- Building credibility in your target markets.
- Creating collateral for other marketing activities.
- Competitive positioning.
- Building a reputation as a thought leader.
- Generating actual leads (sometimes, but difficult to plan for).
- Driving Web traffic and overall impressions of you and your firm.

Words of wisdom

- Make sure your content and stories are of supreme interest to the media, prospects, and buyers—news has to be newsworthy. What many firms think is newsworthy the press doesn't.
- Implement each public relations (PR) tactic well. How bloggers pick up your stories is a different process from how you get a mention in

major business press. How you get a story placed in trade magazines is different from getting links to your web site.

- Implement intensely and rigorously. It takes financial and human effort over a long period to get the most out of publicity efforts.
- Keep at it over long periods of time.
- Develop relationships with the media you're targeting, or hire people who have them already.
- Use PR in the rest of your marketing. If you get a great mention or interview in the press, you can use this in your other marketing efforts for years to come.
- The stronger your brand, the more strongly your publicity efforts will work. When a Harvard Business School professor has something to say, it's much more likely to get picked up than when a professor from Jim's House of Higher Education has something to say. Brand matters in PR as well.

Common mistakes

- Expecting results quickly. It can take a long time to get a PR engine working.
- Going dark on PR efforts. If you get started and then stop, you will probably need to rebuild the foundation before the efforts will gain traction again. If you have a good press strategy in play, discontinuing it can often send you back to square one if you want to restart later on.
- Equating publicity with putting out a press release. Press releases are a tool, not an outcome. The outcome is publicity, and a press release (unless people track your firm closely already) typically does nothing, even if released on a major wire with all the bells and whistles the wire service offers.
- Expecting more leads than you get. It's quite possible that your publicity effort will yield a major flurry of leads and leads for years to come. If you get the right story in the *Wall Street Journal*, the *Harvard Business Review*, or on the *CBS Evening News*, that may happen. More often, even if you make it into a major publication in a major way, little in the

way of leads follows. Many of the "I got flooded with business after publicity" stories are business-to-consumer. While you can expect leads from publicity to happen over time, you should take leads from publicity as a bonus.

- Expecting to get into the *Harvard Business Review*, *BusinessWeek*, and the *Wall Street Journal* right out of the gate. Once again, unless you've got something really special or you're already a well-known thought leader, don't expect to get into the top publications right away. Even thought leaders with a track record have to lobby and work hard to get into the right publications with the right content.
- Focusing only on traditional media. Online publicity is up-and-coming and can yield major benefits. The right blogger mentions can get you links into your web site. The links into your site can yield conversions for your offers and higher Google weighting (meaning that someone searching for keywords that are on your site might be more likely to find yours versus some other site). Keep abreast of what's happening currently in PR before you decide on the specifics of your strategy.

Offers, Content, and Experiences

Articles

Many a professional has built a reputation and a following as a thought leader by writing and publishing articles. Articles, whether published in newsletters, the trade press, or industry web sites, are a staple of most firms' communications tactics with the market.

Typically good for:

- Presenting a point of view.
- Connecting people to your personality and thought processes.
- All components of Brand RAMP.
- Providing the base for longer intellectual capital, such as white papers and books.

- Marketing collateral.
- Generating credibility and thought leadership.
- Generating publicity.

Words of wisdom

- Come up with an idea and start writing. Many a writing strategy is thwarted when the would-be author simply doesn't sit down and start typing.
- Edit your work meticulously. Errors and ambiguity can quickly turn someone off to you and your writing.
- Be a tyrant about thought leadership quality. Your writing might be clear and straightforward; but if someone reads your writing and says, "So what?" or "That's not helpful," then your efforts are for naught. (See chapter 15, "Eight Pillars of Intellectual Capital Quality.")
- You don't have to come up with something new. Many would-be authors think, "Everything I'd like to write already has something good on the topic." Perhaps you have a good way of positioning the same topic. Perhaps folks in your industry need to hear about something widely used elsewhere but not yet in your field. Much like being a professional services provider, buyers don't need you to be totally different from what else is out there; they just need you to be helpful.
- If you're looking to publish in other people's publications, read their editorial guidelines carefully and craft articles that they'll accept. Editors are short on time. If you provide them what they need and it's good quality, they'll publish it. If they look at it and say, "This isn't bad, but it doesn't meet content guidelines 3 and 6," then they'd have to put more work into it. That might kill your insertion in their publication.
- Market your articles. Once you have something written, you can use it in direct mail, on your web site, in your collateral materials, and in your newsletter. Articles can endure, but they'll endure only if you use them.

Common mistakes

- Bad writing. Nine out of ten articles submitted to us at RainToday.com for publication by would-be authors are rejected due to subpar writing. You have to write well.[2] You might think your writing is good, but it still might not meet the standards someplace else. While sometimes you get rejected because the editor just didn't see the beauty and quality of what you wrote, more often your writing quality killed you.
- Ghostwriting that takes away your own point of view. If you have something to say, the best way to say it is to get your ideas down on paper. A good developmental editor can turn your good thoughts that have not been cleaned up yet into a good article. Unless the ghost-writer is extremely skilled, the process of "interviewing an article out of you" tends to lead down a fruitless path.
- Trying to write here and there. Like anything, the more you write, the better you'll get at it. Writing is a craft that takes time to develop. Keep at it, and you'll get better over time.
- Not leveraging what you write. Once you have the article, use it over and over. Get the most out of it. Don't let it sit around gathering dust on your web site.

White Papers

A white paper is an educational tool in the form of a persuasive essay. At its best, a white paper provides the kind of useful information about your service, thought process, or methodology that will bring you new clients.

It is best to think of a white paper as a credible source of information for your clients that will reach them before they need to make decisions. Reading a paper that contains logical arguments backed by facts fuels interest and desire.

---

[2] If you're looking to improve the quality of your writing, read William Zinsser's *On Writing Well*, 7th ed. (New York: HarperCollins, 2006).

In RainToday.com's research report, *What's Working in Lead Generation,* we surveyed 731 leaders of professional services firms. In it, we asked them, "What offers are most effective in generating new leads?" White papers were among the most effective offers, as 28 percent of respondents rated white papers as "very" or "extremely effective."

Another industry study confirmed the following information regarding how white papers get passed along:

- 69 percent of prospects who download and like your white paper PDF will actively pass it on to their colleagues.
- 36 percent of total downloads will be passed on to a direct supervisor.
- 57 percent of IT purchase decision makers said a white paper influenced at least one buying decision in a yearlong cycle.[3]

Typically good for:

White papers have the same uses as *articles,* plus:

- Lead generation in the form of an offer that people can request or download, and as an inquiry-generating tool after people read it.
- Foundation for speeches, books, and publicity.

Words of wisdom

The same advice applies as for *articles,* plus:

- Choose the right topic and title. Getting nuances right with the topic and title can mean the difference between thousands of people downloading or requesting it and virtually no interest.
- White papers are versatile marketing assets. Use your white paper for lead generation, lead nurturing, and thought leadership development.

---

[3] MarketingSherpa, "How to Invent & Promote White Papers That Fortune 500 Prospects Find Irresistible," November 11, 2004.

- Make sure your white paper gets to as many people as possible. Like advertising and graphic design, some firms spend months and years developing the asset and then get no use out of it. If you're going to write white papers, make sure you get them out to the world through your own lists, through third-party lists, though white papers syndication, through placement in other people's publications, and a whole host of other outreach methods.

Common mistakes

- Same as *articles*—poor writing, not interesting, no reach and leverage, and so on.
- Sales pitches thinly veiled as white papers. Make sure every word has value to the reader and isn't puffery for your firm. At the end of the white paper, you should let folks know what you do and how you can help, but don't mix your sales pitch inappropriately with the content of the piece.
- "That's not a white paper." While parameters of white papers do vary widely in terms of length and content, many things (like two-page marketing collateral pieces) are erroneously labeled white papers.
- Not targeting or marketing your white paper. As you seek publicity, downloads, and requests for your white paper, make sure you target well. You can spend months trying to get people to pay attention to your white paper who will simply have no interest in it.

Books

Commonly heard advice on the street: "Write a book. It'll do wonders for your practice. It's perhaps the best marketing tactic you could ever employ." Alan Weiss calls a book the gold card of lead generation.

What the advice giver often fails to mention is that the act of writing a book is an enormous investment in blood, sweat, and, all too often, tears. Writing and publishing a book is a time-intensive, laborious process that begins long before the actual writing of the book and continues through the lengthy editing, publishing, and book marketing process. Aspiring authors may have to deal with finding agents, marketers, and publishers; negotiating contracts; and, ultimately, the marketing and publicity of the book—all while keeping up with their everyday business activities. This often leaves the professional service provider wondering, "Is it worth it?"

Being in the business of figuring out "what's worth it" in marketing for professional services, we at Wellesley Hills Group and RainToday.com conducted research to find out. The result was our report, *The Business Impact of Writing a Book*. In this research we surveyed 200 professionals across industries who have themselves written a book, or books, in order to answer that all-important question: "Is the investment in blood, sweat, and tears required to write a book worth it to my practice?"

Our conclusion: a definite and resounding "yes." While the report did not evaluate the merits or quality of the books the participating authors had written, the vast majority of authors who participated in our research realized a significant positive impact on their business or practice as a result of publishing one book or multiple books.

Typically good for:

- Thought leadership and credibility.
- All components of Brand RAMP enhancement.
- Lead generation.
- Generating speeches.
- Opening doors to write for prestigious publications.
- Publicity.
- Passive revenue generation.

Words of wisdom

- Write a *good* book. This may go without saying, but many a contribution to the business bookshelf has been less than stellar.

All things being equal, a good book will sell more and reflect better on you and your practice.

- Publish with a major publisher first. There's a lot of buzz about self-publishing, but our research and experience strongly suggest that publishing with a major publisher for at least your first book has more positive impact than self-publishing.
- Sell as many books as you can. Authors who sold more than 10,000 copies of their first book had much more positive impact across their businesses than those who sold fewer copies. Authors who sold more than 20,000 copies of their first book had significantly greater impact on their businesses than those who sold between 10,000 and 20,000 copies. (See Chapter 15, "Research results," pp. 208–210.)
- Get all the leverage you can from your book: Articles placed in major publications. Speaking engagements. Marketing campaigns. Webinars. Clients. Books are platforms that you can use to buoy all of your other marketing and client relations activities.
- Expect to be the one to do a good portion of the marketing for your book. The biggest factor that publishers look for from new authors is their marketing platform. How many books will you sell yourself?

Common mistakes

- Poorly written books; sales pitch masquerading as a book.
- Thinking your good idea and good writing will get picked up by a major publisher on its merits. Publishing is a business. Typically your ability to get a book accepted by a major publisher is a reflection on your marketing and sales platform and what you'll do to sell books, not your content or skill as a writer.
- Believing your content has to be 100 percent breakthrough new. It just has to be helpful. The "what's different" request from most publishers is more for how they can position it for sale, not that they care if it's the first time anyone has written about the subject.

- Self-publishing disappointments. Sure, it seems easier to self-publish. And you can make $25 per book instead of only $1! But the folks we know, and the participants in our research, who did not have at least their first book with a major publisher did not get the sales or the ancillary benefits to nearly the same degree as folks who got a book contract with a reputable publisher.

Seminars

Seminars are one of the most powerful marketing tactics for professional services firms. You can get paid for attendance at public seminars, and your fabulous delivery and value should yield leads for both on-site seminars and consulting services. Many a firm has build up a major consulting operation on the back of its seminar engine. The challenging part is getting a paid-seminar engine up and running. Many firms have tried and failed. Regardless of *how* you get it done, *if* you can get it done, it can be a major competitive advantage.

Running paid seminars is not the only path to success. You can offer free seminars produced by your firm. You can deliver seminars for major seminar companies, as many of them subcontract delivery.

Whatever your path, keep in mind that after referrals and brand, seminars are the top method buyers are likely to use to identify potential service providers.[4]

Typically good for:

- Lead generation.
- Thought leadership.
- Brand RAMP.

---

[4] Sixty-six percent of buyers are "likely" or "very likely" to attend seminars to identify their potential services providers. [Mike Schultz and John Doerr, *How Clients Buy: 2009 Benchmark Report on Professional Services Marketing and Selling from the Client Perspective* (Framingham, MA: RainToday.com, 2009).]

- Offering that goes along with outreach (advertising, direct mail, e-mail, telephone, etc.).
- Getting paid for marketing.
- Initial service to offer to a company that can lead to additional services.

Words of wisdom

- Seminars require commitment. It's rare to find a company that can run a successful seminar just here and there.
- Be paranoid about attendance. Most firms believe they can do a good job delivering. Most firms have the cash to deliver in a decent venue. Getting decision makers to attend your seminars—that's tricky.
- Know the metrics of seminar attendance generation. It's different from almost any other type of marketing. What many books say about generating seminar attendance is misleading.
- Make the content draw irresistible.
- Include clients and other credibility enhancers like guest speakers.
- If you don't want to run your own seminars, consider delivering for other companies. It's not that easy; but if you work hard enough at it, and if a seminar company exists in your space that uses subcontract facilitators, it's worth the effort to work your way in.
- If you're planning on making money with your public seminars, that's not easy to do. You might strike gold and get margin from public seminars, but the money will come (assuming you can get the public seminars up and running) in the form of on-site seminars and consulting engagements.

Common mistakes

- Believing most of what the "run seminars and grow rich" books tell you about attendance generation. Most of them are extremely optimistic.
- Engaging in spreadsheet fantasies. Don't play the "Wow, we'll make so much money if we just get X attendees" game. Attendees are tough to

come by, and marketing and sales costs at seminar companies can run very high.

- Underestimating what it takes to generate attendance. Poor targeting, lists, and databases are usually the main culprits in low attendance. If you don't have great lists to leverage, you're at a major disadvantage.
- Getting caught up in the "it's new, it'll be huge" trap. There are thousands of leadership seminars for a reason: People buy leadership seminars. Do something totally new and you have to ask yourself, "Is there a market to support this?" Oftentimes, no.
- Not following up after the seminar. Don Schrello noted in *How to Market Training and Information*[5] (the only worthwhile book we have ever read on the subject of seminar marketing) that results from follow-up are best in the first two days after the program. Your ability to generate follow-up meetings after the seminar drops off significantly after a few days. "Let's wait a week and then call them all" is not a good idea.
- Pitching while delivering. The best selling you can do is to deliver an excellent seminar. Weaving in your capabilities and how you can help is a subtle nuance. Pitch too hard too fast, and you'll turn people off. Once you've done a great job delivering, most attendees give you license to mention what you do.

Variations on Seminars: Webinars and Teleseminars

The same uses and advice apply for webinars and teleseminars as for seminars, but the personal and emotional connection isn't as strong.

Common mistakes

- Boring, poor delivery. Delivery is different than in seminars and live speeches. You need a lot more energy to keep people's attention.

---

[5]Don Schrello, *How to Market Training and Information,* 4th ed. (Schrello Direct Marketing, 1994).

- Technology problems. There are many new technologies for running webinars and teleseminars. If you want a smooth delivery, use a major provider. You can always find great, unknown niche players, but you are taking a chance.
- Overestimating how many people will come. Not only is attendance as hard to come by online as it is for live programs, but it's also hard to get them to show up and stay once they've registered.
- Not using modern follow-up methods such as automated e-mail sequences based on attendance activity and area of interest.
- Poor slides and collateral material. Slides do become more important for webinars, and teleseminars run more smoothly and generate higher satisfaction when you provide quality material for attendees to follow along.

Public Speaking

Along with seminars, public speaking is the marketing linchpin of many a professional services provider. Buyers use speeches to identify service providers quite a bit.[6] Like seminars, with speaking you can get paid for your marketing. Build a reputation as an expert and an excellent speaker, and the fees you can garner can be significant. Nothing beats getting paid to generate leads while you touch many people and build your reputation as a thought leader.

Typically good for:

- Lead generation.
- Thought leadership.
- Brand RAMP.

---

[6]Sixty-two percent of buyers are "likely" or "very likely" to use speeches to identify their professional services providers. [Mike Schultz and John Doerr, *How Clients Buy: 2009 Benchmark Report on Professional Services Marketing and Selling from the Client Perspective* (Framingham, MA: RainToday.com, 2009).]

- Offering that goes along with outreach (advertising, direct mail, e-mail, telephone, etc.).
- Getting paid for marketing with speaker fees.
- Selling books and other products.
- Building a platform that will help you be attractive to major book publishers.
- Creating an initial service (in-house speeches) to offer to a company that leads to additional services.

Words of wisdom

- You've got to make speaking a strategy. "Let's get some speaking engagements" isn't usually enough to make the best inroads into good events.
- Finding the events and getting on event planners' radar screens is no easy task. Like any marketing and lead generation activity, the strength of your targeting and list development underpins your ability to succeed.
- It's great to generate paid speaking engagements. Many consultants suggest that you shouldn't accept speaking engagements unless you're getting paid. However, we know many a service provider that has generated millions of dollars' worth of revenue from unpaid speaking engagements. You've got to make your own decisions about your speaking strategy and what will work for you.
- If you want to generate speaking engagements, you have to build up your sparkle. Event planners want to know why, especially if you're not well-known, you will make their event that much better. Like any kind of marketing, you've got to stand out and get your message across.
- Until you're a highly sought-after speaker, getting speaking engagements takes marketing and selling. You need to develop relationships with folks at the conferences, put together good speaker and press kits (including well-done video clips of you speaking), and the like. You'll be able to get engagements at some places without these; but the better the event, the more challenging it is to jump the hurdle to get in.

Common mistakes

- Poor delivery. Everyone thinks they did a good job at their speech. That's what their friends tell them, after all. Ask people there and they'll say, "You did great." If you want to really know how well you're doing, you need to find someone who knows what top speakers do and then will evaluate you with brutal honesty against that standard.
- Poor event selection. Your audience has to be filled with buyers, influencers, and referral sources.
- Not matching your brand to your event and your speaker slot. Most top speakers will speak at schools and charities for less than their corporate fees, or even for free. That's okay. But if you're speaking at small, local events, you'll probably be viewed as small local talent. The keynote speakers at the general sessions at conferences establish stronger, longer-lasting impressions from a speech and a brand perspective than speakers not in keynote spots.
- Wanting speeches immediately, and then realizing that speakers for major events often get booked a year in advance.
- Wanting speeches, but not doing what it takes to go after them.
- Expecting speeches when you have no book, no platform, no following, and no history of speaking.

Search Engine Optimization/Search Engine Advertising

There's no question that most roads in marketing will lead clients and prospects to your web site. Search engine optimization (SEO) and search engine advertising (SEA) can be your version of a superhighway leading right to it.

Search engine optimization is the process of getting more and better visitors to your web site through the natural (unpaid) search results in search engines like Google, Yahoo!, and MSN. Getting indexed on these sites doesn't mean much unless your site shows up very high in the results for specific keywords that prospects for your services might key in to a web search. You don't have to pay to get included in the natural search results (so it's not a toll road to your web site), but it takes a lot of work to obtain a high listing for good search terms.

Search engine advertising is the process of purchasing certain keywords and keyword sequences so you can show up in the paid search results on search engines. The ability to show up only in the results of searches using specific keywords makes for highly targeted marketing for professional services firms.

While (like most tactics) they're not for every firm, SEO and SEA are gaining importance and influence in many professional services marketing mixes.

Typically good for:

- Lead generation.
- Gathering prospect contact information for further marketing.
- Brand recognition and articulation through the SEO and SEA themselves.
- Brand memorization and preference through the conversion activities on your web site.

Words of wisdom

- If you're going to engage in SEO or SEA and you don't have an in-house expert, get someone else who knows what he or she is doing to guide you. What you need to do to get results is changing all the time; and little things that you might not see can get you higher in the rankings, produce more results for your keyword spend, and save you months of time.
- While it happens here and there, don't expect people to go from Google search to client in droves. However, they will go from Google search to white paper download; and from there, you can follow up as well as engage an ongoing conversation through e-mail and other tactics to draw them into the seduction of your services. (Note: If your services are not major purchases, you may find that you *will* go from

Google search to client often because the risk of engaging you is on the low side.)

- Send people to landing pages, special pages on your web site designed to get visitors to take the action you want them to take. Send them to the front of your site, and your chances of getting them to do something diminish significantly.
- Integrate SEO and SEA with the rest of your marketing. Have white papers? Use SEO to generate downloads. Publish a major industry newsletter? Use SEO and SEA to generate subscriptions.
- Keep up with the evolutions. SEO and SEA need constant attention, as change is the order of the day.

Common mistakes

- "Let's get someone to fix the metatags on our site!" is something I still hear here and there. Metatagging was very important . . . in 1998 when AltaVista was a premier search engine. Unless you really know what you're doing or you've done your research well, what you think will get you to the top of the search engine rankings is likely to be off target.
- No conversion activities.
- Weak web site.
- Poor application. For example, if you're an accounting firm in Duluth, you don't want to purchase the term *accounting firm* or you'll overspend, getting clicks from all over the country when you can serve only a 75-mile radius around your office. *Accounting firm Duluth* might get fewer clicks, but it will work better for those that you get.
- Not giving SEO and SEA constant effort.
- Beginning to spend on SEA or hiring an SEO firm to help you and then just letting money flow out the window. You've got to evaluate whether you're gaining traction and getting what you want out of it. Don't just spend because it seems like a nifty new tactic.

17

Introduction to Lead Generation

If I can get in front of a decision maker at a company that fits my target profile, I've got a great shot at winning it as a client. If I get 10 at bats, I'll get my fair share of hits! The trouble is, it's hard to get the at bats.

— Almost any experienced professional services provider

Clients Are Waiting to Buy—It's Your Move

In our *How Clients Buy* research, we found that 52 to 72 percent of business-to-business professional services buyers are willing to switch to new service providers across professional services specialties.[1] These buyers are indifferent, at best, in their affinity to their current providers. While you may be the exception to the rule, this probably includes you. Consider the specifics of your field in Figure 17.1.

Fortunately for the weak service providers, clients typically find it a risky and painful experience to switch. They don't know if the provider down the street—or across the country—will treat and serve them better. They may

---

[1] Mike Schultz and John Doerr, *How Clients Buy: 2009 Benchmark Report on Professional Services Marketing & Selling from the Client Perspective* (Framingham: RainToday.com, 2009), Figure 3.1, 22, http://www.raintoday.com/howclientsbuy.cfm

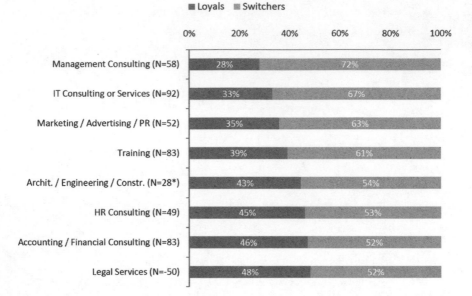

Figure 17.1   Likelihood of Buyers to Switch Providers

* N = > 30

not know who the other players in the field are. So, while buyers perceive that they're not getting everything they can from their current provider, at least with someone familiar they can predict what they will and won't get. "Perhaps that's enough," they might think. Thus most buyers don't switch.

The fact remains: Buyers are *ready* to switch. Their openness to consider switching to a new provider represents a huge opportunity for the leaders of professional services businesses. It's an opportunity for those who are willing to do what it takes to convince buyers to work with a new firm: them!

Switching, however, is only part of the story. Many buyers aren't using any services from your field of expertise at all, or they are tackling problems internally rather than seeking outside help. *You* may know the amazing positive effects, the millions of dollars you can save, the growth your services can create for the clients in your market; but those *buyers don't yet see the value* of working with a firm like yours (or, specifically, your firm). To gain them as clients, you have to help them to see that value.

The first step in converting these potential buyers into clients is to get them interested in what you have to say. In other words, first you have to *generate them as leads*.

To do so, you must:

- Identify these buyers.
- Get them to pay attention to you.
- Seduce them with your value.
- Engage them in a meaningful and valuable discussion about how you can help them.
- Nurture them to the point where they will actually engage your services.

SHORT VERSUS LONG?

By and large, our experience and research with proactively generated leads shows that:

- 25 percent are short-term leads.
- 25 percent are bad fits.
- 50 percent are long-term leads.

If you're focused only on the short-term leads, you might be missing out on three-fourths of your opportunities.

Whether through lack of resources, poor strategy, insufficient energy to implement plans, or lack of will, many professional services firms fail to make marketing and lead generation work for them. In the name of generating leads and improving brand, they spend and spend on the wrong tactics (or the right tactics implemented poorly) and get little in return. This doesn't have to be the case, if you know how to make marketing and lead generation work for professional services.

What to Expect from Lead Generation Done Well

In Chapter 1 we discussed the overall concept of what marketing can do for a firm. Let's look more specifically at what you can expect from lead generation.

CHARACTERISTICS OF A QUALIFIED LEAD

A common acronym used to describe a qualified lead is BANT: budget, authority, need, and time frame. For professional services firms, BANT works, but you also need to add *fit* to the equation.

Budget, or ability to spend: Everyone understands intrinsically what it means to sell to an existing budget, but many professional services aren't budgeted for (e.g., do you budget for getting sued and defending yourself? Do you budget in for a consultant to help you deal with a new technology that hasn't yet even come out on the market?). Regardless of whether or not there is a budget, you need to sell to a company with the ability to spend on your services.

Authority: The person (or group) you're selling to needs to be able to (1) make the decision to work with you and (2) authorize the funds to pay for you.

Need: Buyers must have a need to work with you. You may be selling to someone with a budget, or ability to spend, and with the authority to make a decision; but they won't buy anything unless they perceive a need.

Time frame: A lead is a long-term lead if there is no set time frame for working with you or if the time frame is whatever you deem to be long (e.g., greater than 30 days, greater than 90 days, greater than one year, etc.). If a lead has a set time frame to buy in the near future, it's a short-term lead.

Fit: A lead may have BANT; but if you are *not the right firm to help them*, you should say so. It's not best for them, because they'd be served better elsewhere (even if you don't know where, but you know

---

it's not you). It's not best for you because if you're not the best firm to help, it can, and often does, come back to bite you in the form of inefficiency, low margins, unsatisfied clients (and bad reputation that comes with dissatisfied clients), and bad will with your staff.

The dollars you spend on marketing can, and should, lead to strong and measurable return on investment (ROI) over a reasonable period of time. From your investments specifically in lead generation, you should get short-term leads, long-term leads, and Brand RAMP impact.

Short-Term Leads

Most services firms want short-terms leads. A professional services firm leader might put it this way: "If they have a need, the funds, decision-making authority, and a short-term buying time frame and if they are the right type of company, I can close them." Your lead generation efforts should yield these short-term leads.

But beware: Short-term leads aren't always the best leads. Often, these short-term leads are already preparing to buy services from another provider. If you call them at just the right time or if they call you with an immediate need, you may be one of the other potential providers they bring into the process. Meanwhile, they have been working with another firm (or maybe someone's brother-in-law or an internal group) for many months on what they *really* want to do.

Great professional services businesses can still win in this situation . . . sometimes. More often than not, however, the prospect says something like, "Wow, you were really good and made this a much tougher decision than we expected, but we've decided to go with another option." (The one they had in mind all along.)

With that caveat out of the way, short-term leads are still great. They can turn into strong, ongoing client relationships, especially if you set the right context for the lead from the start.

Long-Term Leads

While many firms focus exclusively on creating leads *now*, the best service firms also focus on generating and nurturing long-term leads. These long-term leads often produce the best business. Most professional services firms cannot motivate a prospect to buy their services on impulse, but they can do it over time.

Many of these service business leaders also lament the fact that they have 3-, 6-, 12-, or 24-month sales cycles. Pull back the curtain, and you see a different story. The sales cycle—once the client is a ready buyer—can be a few months or less. The long sales cycle is really the months and years that it takes for them, and for their companies, to be in the right position and time to buy.

To entice these long-term prospects (typically buyers with authority and need, but no budget or explicit time frame to buy) to *become* ready buyers, or to keep your company in consideration when the prospects become a ready buyers, is a function of sustained lead generation and lead nurturing. These functions cross the traditional line between marketing and business development (or sales). If you can work this part of the process with rigor, the long-term leads will make the biggest difference in your service firm's growth.

Brand RAMP Impact

Branding for professional services is a big trend. In pursuit of brand excellence, many service businesses waste big money on graphic design, tagline development, brochures, and awareness-based media campaigns.

Done right, lead generation can build your brand and can build it *more effectively* than most traditional branding strategies.

Keys to Professional Services Lead Generation

Follow these seven rules for professional services lead generation, and you will be well positioned to generate qualified leads, to convert those leads into new clients, and to grow revenue for your firm.

1. Plan for outcomes and ROI. (See Chapter 4.)
2. Offer value in marketing and selling that will resonate with buyers and differentiate your firm. (See Chapters 9 and 18.)
3. Create and leverage offers and experiences like thought leadership (see Chapter 15) in the form of books, white papers, seminars, speeches, and other tactics (see Chapter 16).
4. Use the right lead generation tactics for you. (See Chapter 16.)
5. Sustain lead generation and lead nurturing efforts. (See Chapter 18.)
6. Measure, test, and improve your lead generation and nurturing efforts.
7. Build brand through lead generation.

18

Value and Offers in Lead Generation

"I'm gonna make him an offer he can't refuse."

—Don Corleone

Most professional services providers seek to win clients based on delivering superior value, not on having the lowest price. (Caution: If you're the rare professional service provider who sells to win a client on lowest price, stop reading. This chapter is not for you.)

When you interact with a prospective client or send any message to a prospect, that prospective client is evaluating what it might be like to work with you and what you can do for her firm.

For this reason, you need to offer value *directly in your marketing and selling efforts themselves*. The goal is to help prospects to understand that working with you as your client is much the same as what it's like to work with you *before* they become your client—except, of course, at some point they start paying you for the privilege of your company.

A consulting firm executive once told us that he needed to get his prospects and clients to perceive that his firm was credible and distinct. A lot of professional services executives have this same thought; so they end up sending messages that say, "I'm credible and distinct," or "I'm trustworthy," or, "I'm innovative, yet solid." They think, "If this is what our clients value, we need to tell them that this is what we're like."

Sorry, saying it doesn't help much. If professional services firms want their clients and prospects to believe that they're credible and distinct, they need to *demonstrate* that they are credible and distinct. Simply stating the words "I'm credible and distinct" is not only insufficient but can even create the wrong impression. (Messaging with these self-centered messages is at the very least bad marketing and can cause buyers to ask, "If they're this bad at marketing, how good are they really at their core services?")

> "If you've got a good, well-known reputation, even if they don't know who any of your people are, they will be predisposed to say yes when someone from your firm calls and says, 'Hey, can I come out and see you and talk to you about this?'"
>
> —Ed Russ, Chief Marketing, Grant Thornton

Steps to Demonstrating Value

To demonstrate value to prospects, you must:

- **Understand your value.** As we describe in Chapters 9 and 13, your value doesn't need to be unique. But it does need to resonate with the market. For example, you don't need to be the only person to have innovative financial consulting processes. Yours just need to be worthwhile in specific situations, at the right times, to specific clients who might need them.
- **Make the value tangible.** The value a client eventually realizes from your firm's services might well be your efficient and effective solutions that helped them grow their revenue and strengthen their business. However, before they work with you, most buyers don't have an idea of what that means specifically or how it applies to them. Instead of

using vague language, communicate that your innovative approach to financial restructuring has successfully freed up over $2.2 billion that had previously been tied up in your clients' working capital due to poorly designed financial instruments.

- **Explain your process and the expected outcomes.** Potential clients want to know what you are going to do, how you are going to do it, and what outcomes they can expect. It's easier to lead the prospects down the path you want them to follow when you show them both the destination and the path.

- **Don't market the relationship.** It's tempting to offer a "trusted partner" relationship in your marketing. It's similar to dating. You want the life together; but if you go directly to "Let's get married, have eight kids, and retire to a nice condo in Boca," you're not likely to get too many takers. "Coming on like gangbusters" isn't a good a approach to building a long-term relationship (assuming that's what you're looking for . . . not everyone is.)

- **Create experiences with you.** Instead of marketing the whole relationship, start simply. At first, the experience might be that you make an offer to them to read your white paper. Perhaps you offer attendance to your seminar. Maybe you meet to discuss a particular business topic of interest to them.

In the research report *Evaluating the Cost of Sales Calls in Business-to-Business Markets*,[1] over 90 percent of buyers stated they wanted sellers to be more of a resource to them. Sellers that demonstrated they understood their prospects' businesses, need, and pressures were 69 percent more likely to come away with the sale versus those who did not. However, only 39 percent of buyers said that the people marketing and selling to them actually understood their needs and weren't just trying to sell, sell, sell. Professional services providers fall into this trap as often as any other sales people do.

---

[1] Cahners Research, *Evaluating the Cost of Sales Calls in Business-to-Business Markets*, 2001 (23,341 businesses surveyed).

> ## A PREVIEW FOR THE PROSPECT
>
> The marketing and sales process is a preview for prospects of what it's actually like to work with you. If you want to be seen as a valuable provider, offer value directly in your lead generation and sales efforts.

In the Wellesley Hills Group and RainToday.com research report *How Clients Buy*,[2] 80 percent of buyers reported that professional services providers made critical mistakes when selling to them. Some of the top errors the professional services firms made were "not listening," "not understanding the client's business," and "not understanding the client's needs."

It's no secret that repeat clients are the best clients and referral sources. They already know the value they get from working with you. They know that you are trustworthy and will do what you say. Because of this, the risk of buying from you is much lower than bringing in a new provider. To generate new clients, you need to help them see you in a similarly trusting light. Your task is to be as valuable, as reliable and as energetic when communicating with them *before* you win them as clients as you are *after*.

Engaging any new professional service company is a leap of faith. Clients are never certain what they will actually get—whether the service provider is reputable and reliable and whether the process will work in their culture. Your prospects consider all of these questions before they buy from you.

Marketing and Selling the Invisible

Services are intangible by nature. You can't see, touch, smell, or taste them before you buy them. This intangibility often makes services difficult to depict in clear and meaningful ways. Many companies' inability to depict their

---

[2] Mike Schultz and John Doerr, *How Clients Buy: 2009 Benchmark Report on Professional Services Marketing and Selling from the Client Perspective* (Framingham, MA: RainToday. com, 2009).

services tangibly leads to conditions such as difficulty picturing processes and outcomes, difficulty conceptualizing leads, uncertainty about risks, and so on.

RESULTS OF INTANGIBILITY OF SERVICES

Condition	Description
Difficult to conceptualize	Clients and prospects have difficulty picturing, in their mind's eye, service processes and outcomes.
Difficult to evaluate	The difficulty in conceptualizing leads to difficulty in evaluating the service. They don't know what they'll get, the value it might offer, or when it will be successful.
Uncertainty and perceived risk	Without a clear evaluation framework, the clients' level of uncertainty and perceived risk rises. Added uncertainty and risk is anathema to selling services, especially in new client generation, where you have yet to establish sufficient trust.
Difficult to promote the offering	Difficulty conceptualizing also leads to difficulty in creating focused marketing communications (from the firm's perspective) and difficulty selling the services internally to colleagues (from the client's perspective).

How do you make the intangible tangible? Take a cue from your local ice cream shop: Let your clients and prospects have a taste. Professional services businesses can do this by creating and leveraging offers and experiences that allow potential buyers to see, touch, and taste a bit of what you will provide for them as clients.

With a new sense of tangibility, you can promote your services more clearly and minimize the clients' risk (both perceived and actual) of engaging your services. Your clear depictions of the service tangibles will help your clients and prospects conceptualize, evaluate, and promote the offering internally.

How can you tell the difference between a potential client who has tasted your services and one who does not yet have a good sense of what you can offer them?

When you sit down at the table with a prospective client for the first time, you might encounter one of two possibilities:

Possibility #1: I've never heard of you. I don't know what you offer. I don't know why you're here. Now, what did you want to sell me?

Possibility #2: I've read two of your white papers, I saw you speak, and I regularly read your newsletter. I love your web site and your Assessment Methodology. I've been looking forward to speaking with you for several months now.

Of course, possibility #2 is what you want to hear. You can accomplish this through your firm's lead generation activities, *if you create and leverage offers and experiences* in your lead generation process.

> "If you don't have an engine that's going to fire up content and continue to crank out good stuff, then you've got a problem. I would implore firms to think about themselves less as a services marketing organization and more as a publisher around important themes and concepts. Just make sure those themes and concepts dovetail with your corporate strategy."
>
> —Paul Dunay, Global Director of Integrated Marketing, BearingPoint

COMMON OFFERS AND EXPERIENCES

- Consultation
- Sales call
- Entry service
- Seminar
- Teleseminar
- Podcast
- Webcast

- Speech
- Article
- White paper
- Case study
- Book
- Research

Why to Use Offers and Experiences

Offers and experiences are the best way to market actively in the lead generation process, for many reasons:

- **They provide a preview.** Offers and experiences give your prospects a chance to sample what it might actually be like to work with you. If you can provide value before they're your clients, they will easily be able to imagine what it will be like after they hire your firm.
- **They're easy for people to accept.** People will accept an offer of a white paper, a seminar, or an in-person dialogue about new research results much more readily than the too-often-used "Call us and become our client" offer.
- **They generate better response.** Marketing tactics using offers work better than those that don't. A recent ad in the *Harvard Business Review* for a major law firm touted the nature of the firm as offering "solutions" versus just "services." Many people saw that ad . . . and most likely did nothing. If the ad had focused on new research in intellectual property protection for technology companies that could be downloaded as a white paper, the ad might have been more successful. (Of course, when you start thinking like this, strict advertising becomes a much less attractive marketing option for most firms.)
- **They get attention, and get prospects to consider action.** Offers and experiences break through the noise and give prospects a decision to make. "New research—that sounds valuable. Do I want to take 15 minutes to hear the results?" The more valuable and interesting the offer, the more it breaks through the noise.
- **They allow you to approach prospects via thought leadership.** Through offers, you can introduce your valuable, genuine, and distinct points of view to prospects in nonthreatening, nonsales ways. Reading your white papers, hearing you speak, and meeting with you about a specific topic are all ways to hold a spot in the mind of the buyer while also demonstrating your expertise. If you want to gain clients and be viewed as a thought leader, creating and disseminating offers and experiences will do a lot to help you get there.

- **They can increase revenue opportunities with current and past clients.** Assume your firm offers a variety of services to 100 different clients. Perhaps 20 are using a particular service. If you're not actively marketing that service to the other 80 (assuming they're good targets for that service), they might not even know you offer the service. Since these 80 already know and trust you, they're much more likely than others to accept an offer you might make to them in your lead generation efforts and move into your pipeline.
- **Their impact improves over time.** Repeated, value-based offers over the long term will seduce clients with your value. There's no better lead than someone who has been following your work for years.
- **They generate contact information.** Acceptance of offers allows you to capture information that you can use appropriately for ongoing lead generation and lead nurturing.
- **They create both lead generation outcomes and relationship outcomes.** If you make an offer that truly has value for the prospect, you will generate leads *and* create relationships with people before you even meet them. You also strengthen the relationships you already have.

Much of professional service firm marketing is so focused on creating brand that it misses the point of the goal of brand—to build a perception about your firm for quality and value one by one with clients. Instead of branding by telling people that you're trustworthy and valuable, your marketing must *demonstrate* that you are trustworthy and valuable. Do that, and building the brand you so desire will take care of itself.

A LEAP OF FAITH

Buying professional services is a leap of faith. You can shorten that leap of faith with the stepping stones of offers and experiences that demonstrate your value.

19 | The Case for Sustained Lead Generation and Relationship Nurturing

The purpose of business is to create and keep a customer.

—Peter Drucker

Three truths:

1. In order to avoid the revenue roller coaster that plagues many professional services businesses, you need to *generate a steady stream of leads*.
2. For most professional services, *prospective clients do not make impulse buys*. Buying has to make it to the top of their to-do lists for any of your sales to happen.

3. As much as you (the seller) might like to shorten the sales cycle, *buying complex, important, trust-based services takes time.* The initial lead will culminate only if, when the buyer has a need that floats to the top of her to-do list (the elusive time of need), she thinks of you.

Unfortunately for service providers, it's nearly impossible to predict *when* this elusive time of need is going to arise for the buyer.

In the research report *Evaluating the Cost of Sales Calls in Business to Business Markets*,[1] the researchers found that it takes an average of 5.12 sales calls to close sales that exceed $35,000.[2] More than 75 percent of the 23,000-plus companies surveyed stated that a combination of direct and indirect marketing and sales efforts was necessary to get to the sale.

To most leaders of professional services firms, this will make immediate sense. Sales cycles are long. The competition works hard to blanket the best prospects with their messages. Many services are becoming viewed as commodities by buyers (even if they're not); and low-priced competitors make price competition more of a factor than ever before, which complicates prospects' buying cycles.

Why Sustained Lead Generation Is So Hard to Do, and Why It Matters

Professional services businesses fall down most in implementing and sustaining consistent lead generation efforts. The reasons for this tend to be internally driven:

- "Autonomous collective" decision making at professional services firms (i.e., everyone has to agree) makes decision making and action either go slowly or stop completely.

---

[1] Cahners Research, *Evaluating the Cost of Sales Calls in Business-to-Business Markets*, 2001 (23,341 businesses surveyed).

[2] For professional services, the appropriate context is to think about the annual value of a client (rather than the first sale), which often includes multiple, ongoing sales.

- Firms dig up the lead generation tree by the roots after two weeks to see if it's growing yet. (This is not a good way to grow a tree.)
- Firms don't put enough energy and resources into the process; and when they don't get the outcomes they (unreasonably) expect, they pull the plug on lead generation efforts too soon.
- Firms execute lead generation campaigns poorly. Then, when the efforts don't work, the company leaders pronounce, "We tried that, and it didn't work. It doesn't work." To us, this is like saying, "I baked a cake, and it didn't rise," and pronouncing that cakes don't rise. Cakes do rise, if you know how to bake.
- Firms assign billable resources to marketing and business development efforts. The people assigned either don't do them, don't do them well, do them well and then have to stop because they get billable, or get fired because they stop doing enough billable work.

Despite all these reasons that lead generation efforts fail, they can succeed. But they *must be sustained* to make them (1) work and (2) improve over time.

Let's assume that you begin lead generation activities, and you take the following actions:

- You offer value to your prospects, directly in your marketing and selling.
- You create and leverage offers and experiences.
- You use a targeted and integrated communication approach.

If you continue these actions for two months, you might get some short-term leads. But if you do it over the long term (and this is important), you'll get not only short-term leads, but also long-term leads and the brand effect you deserve.

"You talk to a lot of professional firms, and they only react once they're getting the squeeze. Then they want results quickly in a generally uncomfortable situation. If they had only done a baseline of ongoing marketing over the past five years, they wouldn't have the problems now that they're facing. You don't have to blow them away. A steady drip is far more effective than a bucket of water once every five years."

—Mike Sheehan, CEO, Hill Holliday

Consider the following example of a sustained one-to-one lead generation plan:

Week 1: Phone call and follow-up white paper.
Week 4: Custom e-mail with new research finding.
Week 8: Targeted direct mail campaign.
Week 11: E-mail with article on client's business or on a competitor.
Week 15: Phone call with invitation to seminar or speech.
Week 19: E-mail with offer to provide your view of a recent event.
Week 22: Targeted direct mail campaign highlighting recent client results you've achieved.
Week 26: Outbound phone call; prospect says, "Perfect timing. I was meaning to call you. Let's talk. . . ."

Not only can you use this process to create short-term leads, but you can also create affinity for your company, building your prospect's basis for trusting you through your offers and your value. With sustained messages like this, your prospects will want to work with you. What's most important is that when their elusive time of need becomes *now*, they'll remember you.

HELLO, I'M LAME

We truly enjoy speaking with salespeople when they call us. The enjoyment isn't always long-lived, though. Perhaps because we live and breathe selling every day, we are constantly disappointed with the lack of understanding from the sellers regarding how to connect with buyers on the phone.

One way sellers could make better connections is to have something worthwhile to tell us when they call. Recently Mike received a call from a sales representative with whom he has been working for quite some time. Our company has a particular need, and we might purchase something from this sales rep's company. We're just not sure when.

The call went something like this:

Sales rep: Hi, Mike, it's Dave Smith calling from Acme.
Mike: Hi, Dave. How goes it?
Sales rep: Going pretty well. And you?
Mike: Just ducky, thanks.
Sales rep: I'm just calling to follow up.
Mike: [*with silent voice*] Ugh. Can't you do any better than that? [*with out loud voice*] Thanks for calling, Dave. We're still in the same place as before. I'll get back to you when we've gotten further down the path of making a decision.
Sales rep: Great. Looking forward to speaking with you then.

In her well-written and practical book *Selling to Big Companies*,[3] Jill Konrath writes on Keeping the Campaign Alive, "To avoid sounding pathetic on follow-up calls, don't ever say something lame like, 'I'm just checking in.' These calls are as important as your initial one and require just as much planning."

We couldn't agree more. If you're going to call someone to "just follow up," don't. Call to offer some insight on new research your company just completed. Call to offer a discussion with one of your clients who just succeeded in conquering the issue that this prospect is facing. Call to see if you can take the prospect out for coffee when you're in town next week. Call to see if the appointment of a new president at the company is going to affect what they need, and offer to speak to them.

But don't call to "check in." As Jill says, it's lame.

---

[3]Jill Konrath, *Selling to Big Companies* (Chicago: Dearborn Trade Publishing, 2006).

Sustained Lead Generation Keeps You Top of Mind

Ask yourself the following two questions:

1. Think about 100 prospects for your services—not people you're currently speaking to, just people who are at the right organizations, at the right levels, who would buy from you. How many of them will proactively seek out services like yours *this month*?
2. *Over the next two years*, how many of these 100 prospects are likely to have the need for your services and proactively seek out providers in your area, even if they do it quietly or through their networks?

The answers to both questions vary by service specialty, but usually the answer to question #1 (seeking out services this month) is somewhere around "a few" to "a handful."

In contrast, the answer to question #2 (seeking out services over the next two years) is usually something like 20 to 45 prospects and can range up to 80 out of the 100 prospects.

How do you take these 100 prospects into a longer-term lead generation? At its simplest, you could:

- Get these prospects on a scrubbed target list.
- Send them direct mail and e-mail value-based offers regularly.
- Pleasantly, but rigorously, maintain value-based telephone contact with them.

Take these steps and add them to your overall marketing mix, and you are much more likely to be remembered by buyers at their elusive time of need. You're more likely to be one of the handful of service providers they bring in, and you may even be the one they are itching to work with because they've been reading your work and paying attention to your communications. And why wouldn't they feel this way, assuming the communications you've sent them have been value-based?

Nurture the Leads You Already Have

This brings us to the very important concept of *lead nurturing*, the process by which you keep people in your communication loop for those two years (or until they need your services).

According to a research report by BPM Forum, over 80 percent of generated leads are never followed up on or are dropped or mishandled.[4] Professional services businesses are particularly adept at neglecting the leads and business opportunities that they already have in-house, just waiting to be called.

And the negative results are staggering. An April 2003 article in *BtoB* magazine citing a Yankee Group research study found that, in a business-to-business environment, "An 11 percent reduction in dropped/lost leads, combined with a 1 percent improvement in lead-to-order conversion rate, increased annual gross profit by 136 percent."[5]

This may sound far-fetched, but we've run the numbers and seen similar phenomena with our clients—and they're right. Many professional services firms think they need more leads, when in fact they could see improved results just by better handling of and nurturing the leads they already have.

Here's what happens. You target your market. You create your list of suspects. You engage targeted, integrated, and direct value-based lead generation campaigns; and you create leads.

However, some of your leads are not hot now. Often, these leads are dropped completely from the pipeline and lost. (See Figure 19.1.)

Why do professional services firms let leads drop out of the pipeline? Maybe their database tracking is not standard across the board, and a contact simply did not show up in the right list. Maybe they got too busy with billable work to follow up. Maybe the leads that needed nurturing were too much work for partners and vice presidents. Maybe midlevel marketing people were not expected to follow up. They have to watch the web site . . . the brochures . . . the PR campaigns. Tracking actual leads is not in their purview.

---

[4] BPM Forum, *Gauging the Cost of What's Lost*, 2004.
[5] Craig Stephens, "Streamlining Sales," *BtoB* 88, no. 4 (2003): 7.

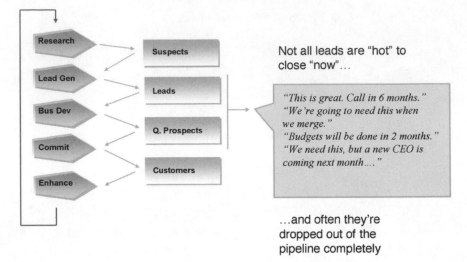

Figure 19.1   Pipeline Example 1

And so, for all these reasons and more, leads that may not be ready now can fall out of the sales pipeline.

According to a study done by Cahners Research, 89 percent of business-to-business buyers took more than 90 days to make purchases after they became a lead for a company.[6] What if the leads your own firm has lost were shepherded back into the pipeline so they could make it all the way to fruition? The result would look something like the diagram in Figure 19.2.

For many professionals, the concept of lead nurturing isn't a regular topic of conversation. Change the one word, and make the concept "relationship nurturing," and the picture begins to take shape. What are the best ways to maintain and deepen relationships? Things like regular interaction, giving versus receiving, and helping someone learn something new. That's all lead nurturing is, but it is systematic and focused on laying the foundation that will lead to business relationships based on value and trust by delivering said value consistently before the potential clients ever start working with you.

---

[6] Spyro Kourtis, "Sales or Marketing: Who Spilled the Leads?" *DM News*, May 3, 2004.

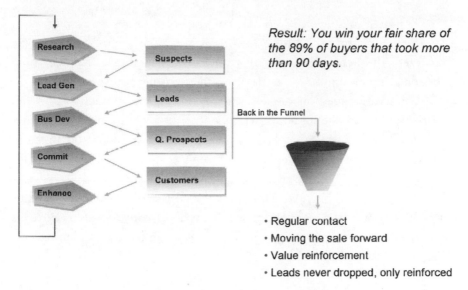

Figure 19.2   Pipeline Example 2

Marketing to Current Clients

Answer: More often than most think.

Question: How often should I send marketing messages to my current and recent clients?

In *How to Market Training and Information*, Don Schrello wrote:

Regardless of how often you contact your clients and prospects (those who have already . . . purchased something from you), you're probably not contacting them enough.

When I was mailing to my own customers four times a year I thought I would "wear out my welcome." Years later when I was mailing to my client list every five days (yes, that's right, over 70 times a year!) I was surprised to learn that each mailing was still profitable."[7]

---

[7] Don Schrello, *How to Market Training and Information*, 4th ed. (Schrello Direct Marketing, 1994)

Although these words were written years ago, they were reinforced in an article, "Getting the Most Out of All Your Customers."[8] This article analyzed, through fairly complex mathematical methods, the marketing spending of, among others, a major business-to-business service firm.

One major question the authors asked was: How much of a firm's marketing dollars should be spent on new client acquisition versus current client retention? While they had no silver bullet answer as to how much to spend on retention marketing, they did imply that it should be a significant portion of the marketing budget.

The article highlighted disconnect we all too often see: While firms should devote quite a bit of energy and focus here, many of the service firms we meet spend the goose egg, or close to it, on retention marketing.

Why Market to Current Clients

When conversations at service firms turn to marketing, new client acquisition tends to top the agenda. "How can we get more new clients?" service firm leaders routinely ask. Retention marketing never seems to come up.

But marketing to current clients should be front and center in any service revenue generation discussion. Consider:

- **The financial effects of retention.** While many service providers initially boast, "Oh, we have practically no client turnover," upon further examination, they do lose clients for one reason or another. If there's something you can do to increase the odds that a current client will stay with you, you should do it. It typically costs much more to acquire a new client than it does to retain an existing one. Spending on retention tends to have a very positive financial effect on your firm.

---

[8]Jacquelyn S. Thomas, Werner Reinartz, and V. Kumar, "Getting the Most Out of All Your Customers," *Harvard Business Review*, July 1, 2004.

- **Your "walletshare."** Most service firms have a variety of service offerings, but not all clients buy all offerings, nor do they buy them all from you. The service pie may actually be divided among you and many other firms. In the financial services industry, your firm's piece of the pie is called your "walletshare" of the client's total buy. When it comes to generating leads for services, the most likely respondents to a marketing campaign for new services are satisfied clients of existing services. But you can't get more walletshare if you don't let them know you have other services to offer.

Marketing can be a great resource to you if you'd like your current clients to remain your current clients and if you'd like to sell them more services than they're currently buying.

LEAD NURTURING AND RELATIONSHIP NURTURING—SAME THING

We recently conducted research for a client on how often his firm's past clients wish to be contacted by their professional service providers. Like most professionals, the client's hypothesis was that his past clients will simply call when they have more work. Like many professional service providers, his assumption was that to contact past clients too often would be an intrusion, an imposition, and, worst of all, unprofessional.

As a result, he was following the once-a-year (or less) approach to "staying in touch."

Our research findings, in keeping with what we have witnessed time and time again, were:

Service providers do not contact their current and past clients enough outside of the necessary tasks of working with them.

An actual conversation (names of client and firm are fictitious) with one of his past clients went something like this:

John Doerr: I am calling for Smith & Jones. Bill Smith did some work for you in the past, and I am looking to find out the best ways for him to communicate with his clients.

Client of my client: How is Bill? I remember the work he did for us. Oh, gee, it's been over a year now. How time flies. His approach was so much stronger than others. He was thoughtful, asked great questions, and actually changed what we were looking for. In the end, his suggestions made a huge difference for us.

John Doerr: Bill is doing great.

Client of my client: Good to hear that. You know, I had forgotten about how good his work was. Too bad you didn't call last week. I just awarded a major assignment that was right up Bill's alley. I am so busy right now—I have trouble remembering things from last week, let alone last year. The assignment came up, and I called who I met with most recently. They were in two weeks ago. Too bad for both of us, Bill probably would have been a great choice. Tell him to give me a call soon.

This was not Bill's only client who said this. Bill missed that potential assignment from his client (and now maybe future assignments with them as well, if the new provider is good). What could Bill have done better to stay in touch with his clients, staying top of mind, without being a pain in the neck? Relationship nurturing with ongoing communications.

What Marketing Can't Do

Let's be clear about a few things that marketing to current clients can't do:

- **Improve service quality and satisfaction:** Marketing doesn't materially affect how good your services are. If your retention rate is low because your service isn't up to par, you'll be disappointed with results from any retention marketing campaign.

■ **Make a service inherently more valuable to your clients:** You may provide one service to your current clients that they think is amazing. You want to sell them a new service; but this service, no matter how good the marketing is, buyers simply won't buy. A service may be behind the times or ahead of its time. It may be too difficult to buy or too difficult to understand. There may simply be no need. Marketing can affect demand creation; but the service itself needs to be inherently desirable, valuable, and competitive for marketing to be most successful.

"Marketers have so long to go in the sales cycle from awareness to consideration to purchase. Nine, twelve, sixteen months or longer. New media and content such as blogs, podcasts, RSS, social networking, online video, webcasts, white papers, and the like are really good for continuing that conversation and keeping the prospect warm.

If you were to just keep e-mailing someone over the course of nine or twelve months without these new media, you'd just end up bothering them."

—Paul Dunay, Global Director of Integrated Marketing, BearingPoint

What Marketing *Can* Do

Marketing to current clients can:

■ **Uncover ways to improve satisfaction:** Through your marketing you can solicit feedback from your clients. Whereas most people think of marketing as some form of direct solicitation for a service, the marketing itself can actually focus on improving client satisfaction through vehicles such as surveys. When you survey clients, you are communicating to them that you want to be as good as you can be. This is good branding for you, and the feedback you get can be invaluable to improve your services across the board and to fix satisfaction issues with current clients.

- **Keep mindshare (and walletshare) high for current services:** With your current clients, two things are always happening: (1) If you're not in front of your client, they're not thinking about you; they're focusing on the challenges of the day. (2) Your competitors are trying to get your clients to switch from you to them, or generally get the dollars in their wallets that your clients now send to yours. To make sure your clients continue to think about you, keep your messages in front of them when you, physically, are not.

- **Generate leads for new services:** If you have multiple services you want your clients to engage, one of the best ways to let clients know about them is to tell them, over and over, through marketing. The most likely buyers of new services are satisfied buyers of current services.

- **Reinforce the value of being your client:** Do you have private events available only to clients? Exclusive research? Special benefits of working with you? Whatever these are, it's within your power to consistently reinforce to clients why they want to keep working with you.

We understand why many service firms equate marketing with acquisition of new clients instead of retention and cross-selling of current clients. It's natural to want to add new clients to the fold. However, don't ignore the revenue growth and profit potential from your current client base.

They already like you, and you already know they buy.

Maybe you won the client last week. Maybe they've been with you for 10 years. Either way, make sure you're still marketing to them. How often? More often than you think.

20 | Targeting

"Like a poor marksman, you keep missing the target."

—Captain James T. Kirk

Target Your Best Prospects

Ask what's most important in the real estate business and you'll hear, "Location, location, location." Ask the same in marketing and lead generation and it's all about lists, lists, lists (or target, target, target). Although targeting is the least sexy of all marketing activities, spending time developing and managing your primary target lists will pay the biggest dividends in the end.

Targeting and segmentation are key early steps in any marketing effort and must be done with the utmost thought and rigor. Do you want to meet with someone who won't or can't buy your services? Do you want to spend time and money trying to generate relationships that go nowhere due to poor targeting?

As we know, you need leads if you want to sell anything; and most professional services firms can use direct, integrated tactics (such as mail, e-mail, or telephone calling) to market to them. We also know that marketing works best with strong value-proposition messaging and brand recognition.

Let's say you've got your strong value-propositon messaging in place, and you're gearing up to market directly to generate leads.

Without a target profile and target list, you won't make much progress. On the flip side, targeting in general, and clean target lists and database management in particular, can be the key to great success and a competitive advantage for your firm.

Let's say you've targeted prospects who:

- Work at the right level of the target organizations.
- Have the right titles.
- Control the budget or spending (decision makers).
- Can influence the sale (influencers and referral sources).
- Are in the right industry for you.
- Are at the right size companies.
- May have specific factors that make them good targets for you (e.g., a drug in the pipeline, certain kinds of technology, multinational operations, etc.).

Only after you've targeted your prospects can you create direct marketing and business development campaigns that position and brand you in the proper light. (Given your understanding from the preceding chapters of delivering value directly in your lead generation and of using offers and experiences to draw prospects into the seduction of your services, you can see how this might happen.)

Once you hold a strong position in the mind of your buyer, you have narrowed the trust gap and increased the likelihood that the buyer will accept an in-person meeting with you to discuss that company's current needs.

Achieving all these marketing outcomes depends first and foremost on your ability to create a clean, targeted prospect list of the potential client businesses and contacts that you think would be just right for your professional services.

The Boring Work of Targeting and Database Development

Cleaning up prospecting lists. Deciding, one by one, which companies out of these 30 or 300 or 3,000 we should target for lead generation. Finding out the names and the titles of the specific decision makers who would be the most likely buyers of our services. . . .

"I just don't have time to do things like this!"

Or

"Boring."

Or

"Just buy a list. Someone sells the right list for us, right?"

Or

"This menial work is beneath me. I should do more important things."

There are many excuses for why people don't spend the time and the diligence targeting possible buyers for their services one by one.

Let's look at the excuses (and, yes, they are excuses) listed here:

"I just don't have time to do things like this!" and **"Boring."** We've worked with many services firms over the years. When it comes to marketing, senior people at the firm meet again and again and again to talk about the web site graphic design, or the new logo, or the new brochure colors. They go through 12 design round edits when they should have gone through 3. Edits from the firm leaders come in volumes in terms of their markups and commentary (didn't they have anything better to do all weekend?), and they meet endlessly debating the final renditions. Design processes have a way of spiraling out of control.

We can't remember the last time we heard partners and marketers complaining about the endless meetings talking about delving more closely into their specific targets. That doesn't happen.

In terms of the list part being boring, so it is. Get over it.

"Just buy a list. Someone sells the right list for us, right?" Every once in a while, a list broker or association has just the right list for you. Typically, they don't. When it comes to list compilers (e.g., Dun & Bradstreet, Hoover's, InfoUSA, etc.), in our experience, the data isn't clean enough for decent lead generation without a lot of scrubbing of the lists. The mythical "perfect list" is usually just that: a myth.

"This menial work is beneath me. I should do more important things." Leaders at services firms spend plenty of time on brand identity design, including logos, web sites, taglines, and the like. Design plays an important role in marketing success, but the time leaders spend on design silliness is disproportionate to the success that good design can bring.

So how much time should you spend on targeting? In our research on *What's Working in Lead Generation*, we asked 731 leaders in professional services businesses a number of questions about their lead generation practices. Among the questions were these two:

1. Do you consider your company's overall ability to generate leads to be excellent, good, fair, or poor?
2. When it comes to lead generation, does your firm know:

   - The general profiles of your target companies?
   - The titles of decision makers at your target companies?
   - The specific names of the organizations that are your best targets?
   - The names of specific decision makers for your service areas at your best target companies?

How much time does your company spend on targeting? How would you answer these last four questions? Is this menial work still beneath you?

The chart shown in Figure 20.1 shows how other professional service firm leaders rated themselves. How do you compare?

Figure 20.1   Target Knowledge Ratings

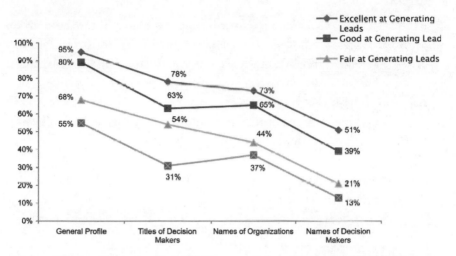

Figure 20.2 Companies' Ability to Generate Leads: Well-Known Companies are Better at Lead Generation

While the chart showing total responses is helpful to see the overall trend in professional services, looking at target market knowledge by the companies' self-reported ability to generate leads takes us a step further in underscoring just how important it is to know your target market well. (See Figure 20.2.)

Compare how much the self-reported excellent-at-lead-generation companies know about their targets versus how much the self-reported poor-at-lead-generation companies know.

There's a direct correlation—in our data and in our experience—between companies that know exactly who they target and how well they can generate leads.

Know Your Market

Many service firms fear being specific about their targeting. When they look at their current clients, they see a wide range of industries, sizes, geographic locations, and circumstances. They do not want to eliminate anyone from the target market since they can always think of a good client who may fall outside the target profile. (See Sample Target Profile on the next page.) But in marketing, if you are not targeting and marketing to someone, you cannot market to anyone. Your message, your offer, and your value will become spread too thin and sound too generic.

As you build a target list, you want to ask yourself the following questions:

- Who are the buyers of my services? What are the titles? Who makes the money decisions? Who makes the vetting decisions? Rank your answers according to who is the most important for you in the buying process.
- Who are the influencers? Who may recommend to my buyers about their service providers? These influencers may or may not be within the target.
- What revenue or workforce size is best for my type of service? Who is too big to buy? Who is too small to afford? Who is just right? Remember, you will have clients that fall outside this range for one reason or another, but who is the best fit?
- What geography should I target? East of the Mississippi? In an area I want to set up a new office? In my own backyard? Give yourself a good fighting chance for success.
- In which industries do I have a good track record? Clients like to know you have experience in their industries. Where do you have the best stories to tell?
- What is usually happening in your clients' companies before they buy from you? New management, a new acquisition, new laws— any change at all is usually good for a professional services firm. What are the triggering events that make a company a good prospect for you?
- What is important to your firm? You may be in a mode to take anyone who is available with cash, but more likely you have good prospects and less good ones. What kinds of marquee clients will add to your aura? Which clients can you grow with? Who do you want?

> "Successful business developers build their networks like a good minister builds a congregation—one believer at a time."
>
> —Kevin McMurdo, Chief Marketing Officer, Perkins Coie

SAMPLE TARGET PROFILE

Target Profile—What Do My Best Clients Look Like?

Buyers	CEO
	CFO
	Controllers
	Vice president—Finance
Influencers	Venture capitalists
	Bank vice presidents
Size	Post–IPO to $500 million
Geography	Within 50 miles of Boston (but not into Rhode Island)
Industries	High technology—software and hardware
Prospects' business situation	Growing firm; possibly shed by larger CPA firm; complex software situations; unhappy with most recent audit; new influx of capital
Your business considerations	Upgrade commercial clients; eventually can shed low-end, unprofitable clients
Number of targets	643 companies
	1425 individuals with appropriate titles in target 643 companies

Think of the very best clients you have (or the ones that you want). In the Target Profile Worksheet on the next page, fill in the specifics about whom you want to target. When you are finished, you will want to go to such sources as Hoover's, Info USA, Dun & Bradstreet, Jigsaw, SalesView, ZoomInfo, and so on, to fill in the specifics around the number of companies (and sometimes the individual people at those companies) that actually fall into your target profile.

TARGET PROFILE WORKSHEET

My Target Profile

Buyers
Influencers
Size
Geography
Industries
Prospects' business situation
Your business considerations
Number of targets

I Want Names

Once you have identified the profile of your targets, you need to start compiling names, addresses, phone numbers, e-mail addresses, and so on. You can begin by thinking of whom you already know who should be added to your current database (or list of names in your card file or contacts in your Outlook).

- Identify your key referrals, and make certain they are added to your database. They need to be reminded of the firm as much as any prospect.
- Categorize your referrals by type and possible practice reference.
- Build up your contact lists by thinking strategically about whom you know and who can and should be in the database.
- Establish a goal for every event you attend, and bring back new contacts for the database.
- Make sure all new contacts get into the database. Over time, this will fuel your marketing engine.
- Capture all lead sources. This needs to be drilled into everyone's mind. Only by capturing lead sources can you learn what is working

and where the best marketing return on investment (ROI) can be found.

- Leverage the entire firm to see who might have any kind of entry into the types of firms you are seeking.
- Use online resources, such as target company web sites, Spoke, Jigsaw, Twitter, and LinkedIn, to verify names, titles, phone numbers, and other essential targeting data.

Every marketing tactic, revenue growth plan, and branding campaign starts here. Without your targets clearly defined, your marketing efforts will inevitably fail to meet your expectations.

Now, imagine if this were possible:

- You have all the relevant data and details about your clients and top prospects in your database, and the data is constantly updated and clean so you can trust it.
- You just completed major research on trends in your industry. You write a white paper summarizing the trends. To get the white paper noticed, you run a marketing campaign via e-mail and direct mail to the people in your database to download this white paper.
- You run these campaigns directly out of your database. The database is your control center.
- Although you might send 500 or 5,000 e-mails or direct mail pieces, each of them has a unique URL landing page that the person can visit to download his or her own copy of your white paper.
- When the clients and prospects visit their unique URL landing page, their contact information is prefilled out on the Web response form, and the form itself is customized to their company and industry.
- They download the white paper. An automatic process sets up a task in your database for the "owner" of that client or prospect to follow up within a set period of time. The designated person at your firm is notified by an e-mail that he or she has follow-ups to make.
- When the designated person logs into the database to follow up, he or she can quickly scan a dossier of relevant company news, information

about the contact, and any other relevant information about your company's dealings with that person or company.

- A manager at your company can log onto a management dashboard to see how many white papers were downloaded; how the team is doing with follow-ups (and who may not be doing theirs); and what downloads have turned into real pipeline opportunities, new clients, and repeat business.
- As prospects become clients, critical data is stored (such as contracts); created (such as project plans and team assignments); and managed (such as time tracking, project tracking, expenses, and client satisfaction data) in one centralized, easy-to-view place.
- This information synchronizes seamlessly with all of your accounting information.
- This system is available anywhere you can get Internet access.

Imagine if this were all possible and within the reach of the typical professional services firm!

This is all core functionality of Salesforce.com.

Many professional services firms use Salesforce.com or one of the many other available database technologies such as Netsuite, Saleslogix, SugarCRM, ACT!, Oracle, RightNow, Microsoft CRM, OfficeAutopilot, and a host of others.

Most professional services firms own one of these systems or something much like it.

Many of them, however, take zero advantage of any of the database marketing and enterprise customer relationship management programs these technologies can help them run.

What does that mean? Opportunity for *you* to get ahead . . . if you can get done what other firms don't.

21

RAIN Selling

Whether you think you can or think you can't, you're right.

—Henry Ford

Up until now we have discussed the *marketing* of professional services. Although many professional services providers still use the terms *marketing* and *selling* interchangeably, we hope by now you have a good grasp of what marketing truly is, what it can do for you, and how to go about implementing successful marketing and lead generation efforts.

Let's assume your marketing efforts really start to pay off. You have RAMPed up your brand. You have seen a pickup in revenue per client. Just as important, you have started to generate new conversations that have taken you far beyond referrals. Now it is time to for you to start selling and make rain.

"THE DOG ATE MY ROLODEX"

At professional services firms, we know that marketing, selling, and delivery can be deeply intertwined. It would be so much easier to implement marketing if we didn't have to deal with those pesky client leaders (or if *we* weren't one of those pesky client leaders).

Alas, we do (or are). So we need to make it work.

First, let's get some of the most common excuses out of the way:

---

1. I'm booked for at least six weeks. I couldn't handle another deal if it landed on my desk.
2. My business development discussions, if I get into a good one, take an hour. I only have 45 minutes to make calls now, so I should wait until I have more time.
3. This isn't a good use of my time. Somebody else should source leads, and I should deliver work.
4. I'm not good at it, so what's the use? (And I sure can't tell anyone this, so I'll make up another reason.)
5. In my business, leads come only through referrals. Proactive outbound business development, even networking, doesn't work. Why bother?
6. I'm deathly afraid of selling.
7. If I reach out to prospects, I will sound like a used-car salesperson. Since I'm a professional, I can't set up that dynamic.
8. I know how to talk about what I do (I think). Yet, for some strange reason, the words never come out right.
9. I don't even know who to contact. I have the time and the will, but what do I do?
10. I hate selling.

Pick your poison: You're too young or too old. You're better in the mornings, and it's late in the day. If you get into a conversation, you will need to get your boss on the phone, and she's not around. The dog ate your Rolodex.

Regardless of your reason, the end result is the same: Another day goes by, and you don't work on business development.

Selling is often more challenging for professional services firms and providers. It's easy to understand why. First of all, full-time salespeople sell all day. They can go from rookie to retiree, and all they need to do is sell to be successful.

In contrast, professional service providers study the technical aspects of their craft for years. Then they work with clients all day, all the time, for years on end. This goes on until they find themselves up for partner, promoted to director, or off on their own. Then suddenly, they also need to develop business, or they might not have any clients to work with.

Whether they want to or they must, many professionals are driven toward making the transition from trusted advisor to rainmaker. So they look to the sales profession for tips on how to do it. Unfortunately, some of the tactics that salespeople may use to sell are counterproductive for aspiring rainmakers. Why? Because when most salespeople sell, they are selling either a product or a service delivered by someone else. Professionals who sell are typically selling something far more difficult: themselves and their colleagues.

Many professionals have yet to reconcile their "sales" role and their "trusted advisor" role. Thus professionals find themselves struggling with the following question:

Buyers inherently don't trust salespeople, but now I'm going to have to find and land clients for my firm and my services—in other words, sell. If I start off as the salesperson, how can I make the transition to trusted advisor, responsible for handling the most confidential and sensitive situations that arise?

Selling with Integrity

Oily. Smarmy. Phony. Mendacious. Two-faced. Right or wrong, these words are often associated with salespeople. None of us wants to be associated with these terms, nor do we want to engage in any selling tactics that will make these labels apply to us. We rarely see professionals engaging in tactics that will merit these labels, which is good. It is not, however, because they use the right tactics. More often than not it is because they avoid selling altogether.

Here's the good news: You can sell with high integrity and without snake oil tactics. You should never have to engage in any sales activity that makes you feel ethically uncomfortable.

Sell as You Serve

So many service providers think selling, by its nature, is a distasteful and less than ethical process, the sole purpose of which is to part people from their money for things they don't need. They believe that to be successful at selling, service providers must leave their values and everyday personalities at the door and adopt a sleazy persona and voice that would naturally say something like, "What's it gonna take to get you into this shiny red pre-owned sports car today, ma'am?"

Nothing is further from the truth. The best rainmakers bring clients and cash into their firms because they are no different when they sell their services than when they deliver their services.

They prepare.

They listen.

They solve problems.

They care about their clients' well-being and success.

They create new futures for their clients that the clients didn't know were possible. They are interpersonally sensitive. They can either push the limit or slow down when it is in the client's best interest. The best rainmakers meet mutually set expectations over and over again, building trust, relationships, and two-way confidence. The best rainmakers are ethical at all times.

> "In business development, the service is the sale. In the end, it's very much up to the lawyer and the lawyer's ability to work with the client and recognize that the sales process is ultimately the process of providing excellent service."
>
> —Kevin McMurdo, Chief Marketing Officer, Perkins Coie

In other words, the best rainmakers are simply great professional service providers. In effect, they are starting the process of being great service providers during the sales process *before clients officially engage their services*.

Sell to Need

Great service providers are masters at uncovering the goals and the challenges of their clients and prospects. Great rainmakers are no different. However, service providers often lack the tools to engage in the types of conversations that allow them to fully explore all of the client's needs.

Communicate the Value

Great service providers understand the value they provide to clients. They craft compelling solutions based on specific client needs and can *communicate that value* to the client clearly and articulately. When you can uncover, quantify, and communicate the impact of engaging your services, you are better able to articulate your true value to each client.

To facilitate the transition from trusted advisor to seller, we developed the concept of RAIN Selling^{SM} to help you plan your sales conversations in selling as you serve, selling to need, and communicating the value.

RAIN Selling^{SM} Basics

Since trial and error are the norm when it comes to learning how to be a rainmaker, the learning curve is long and steep and often filled with anxiety and pain. This leads us to ask the questions, "Is it possible to shorten the learning curve when it comes to selling professional services? Is it possible to make selling itself feel less 'salesy'? Can we increase the level of success of the seller?" The answers (as you may have guessed) are yes, yes, and yes. We at Wellesley Hills Group have worked not only to provide a process for selling professional services, but, to improve the process of learning to become a rainmaker.

RAIN is an acronym for *rapport, aspirations and afflictions, impact,* and *new reality*. The word RAIN, of course, is also a nod to the fact that this process is focused on *rainmakers*—the traditional name for those people who bring new clients and big fees into service firms.

Graphically, RAIN Selling looks like Figure 21.1.

Figure 21.1   RAIN Selling^SM: From Rapport to Commitment

R—*Rapport*

The ability to build rapport in sales conversations is an old concept that is more relevant and more important than ever.[1] At the same time, it's talked about less and less in sales training circles and dismissed as a ploy to make a surface-level connection to a potential client. Why is true rapport so important? Rapport sets the foundation of comfort for the rest of the conversation and for any future relationship. The word *rapport* also implies a real connection between people, not just a surface-level commonality.

Having a true connection to a potential client is so important in rainmaking because, all other things being equal, buyers tend to buy from service providers that they like as much as they buy from those who can meet their needs the best. Yes, there should be a strong focus on creating and presenting a compelling value proposition, but rapport is an often overlooked factor that can tip the scale in favor of one service provider over another.

---

[1] See Chapter 9 section "Emotional Resonance," p. 115.

A—Aspirations and Afflictions

The "A" in RAIN Selling stands for aspirations as well as afflictions. Many sales discussion methodologies suggest that to sell products and services as solutions to needs, you must first uncover the problems and/or pain of the potential client. We suggest that uncovering problems and pain (afflictions) is only half the story.

When clients buy professional services, they are typically thinking as much about aspirations (where they want to go) as they are about afflictions (problems or pain). If you think about asking questions in the negative context, you will find yourself always positing, "What's not happening for you?" or the trite "What keeps you up at night?"

> "The best rainmakers are just those who are most passionate about what they do. They believe more than everyone else that what they do matters, and they're good at, and not shy about, articulating that."
>
> —Mike Sheehan, CEO, Hill Holliday

WHERE DO ASPIRATIONS FIT IN?

Imagine you are a partner at a diversified accounting, financial, and business advisory firm. You have a meeting scheduled with the owner of a medium-sized business because he is not happy with the tax services he has been receiving from his CPA firm.

Through a series of questions, you have uncovered several problems this business owner has had with his current accounting firm, including missed deadlines, impersonal service, and a suspicion that the firm isn't keeping fully up to date on the latest tax regulations. He's nervous that any one of these three issues may come back to haunt him if he doesn't change firms.

Because you know your firm specializes in his industry and because of your dedication to exceptional client service, you know you can stack up well against his current firm and have a good shot at winning the business. You ask him what his greatest problems are. You get a straight answer about his afflictions, and now you know how you can help. You continue the conversation, proposing next steps on how to move forward with a potential new relationship.

You feel fairly confident in how you managed the sales conversation and believe that a new client will be in your future.

You are just about to say good-bye when he says, "I'm meeting my company's attorney for lunch. You two don't know each other. Want to join us?" Not wanting to pass up an opportunity to further the relationship (and because he eats at expensive French restaurants), you are happy to oblige.

You get to lunch, exchange pleasantries all around, and sit down to eat. A few minutes into the conversation, the lawyer asks your potential client, "So what's going on at your company lately?"

Other questions follow, such as, "What do you want to get done in the next year or so? . . . What are your stretch goals for the businesses? . . . What do you think you need to do to get these things done? . . . What don't you know yet that you need to find out?"

These questions are focused on future seeking (aspirations), not problem solving (afflictions).

They open an entire new range of possibilities. You are amazed by some of your potential client's answers. The client has opened up, going on for good chunks of time about the major initiatives at his company, and some initiatives he has not yet even launched.

As you listen, you realize there are at least three areas within these strategic initiatives for which your expertise is a perfect fit and your firm can greatly help him. One such initiative—valuing a niche company he's thinking about acquiring—is your personal expertise and passion! And the fees in these areas are usually three times as large as what you just talked about in your meeting with the prospect an hour before.

You might get good answers. But if you also think of questions in the positive context, you will find yourself asking "Where do you want to go?" and "What are the possibilities?" By asking questions in a positive light, you will find that, instead of just negating problems or filling a need, you can paint a vision of a new reality (more on this later) for the clients that takes them past problem solving and into new possibilities and innovation.

I—Impact

After you uncover the potential client's aspirations and afflictions, the question then becomes "So what?" If the afflictions don't get solved, what will or won't happen? Will they get worse? How do they affect the bottom line of the client's company, division, or department?

If your aspirations don't become reality, so what? In a business-to-business scenario, these questions might sound like, "Will your competition get ahead of you if you don't innovate? Will you lose market share if you aren't aggressive in your strategy?"

The exact "so what?" questions will vary depending on the situation, but your ability to quantify and paint the "so what?" picture is the foundation for just how important engaging your services is to the prospective buyer. This is of paramount importance to you because, as we have discussed previously, when it comes to selling professional services, your competition is often the *indifference of your client*, not another organization or service provider. So creating urgency for buying your services hinges on how well you help your client answer the "so what?" questions.

> "It really gets down to the people at your firm and their skill in asking the right questions to uncover what the prospective clients' issues are and to see if you can help them."
>
> —Ed Russ, Chief Marketing, Grant Thornton

BALANCING ADVOCACY AND INQUIRY

Willy: I don't know why—I can't stop myself—I talk too much. A man oughta come in with a few words. One thing about Charley. He's a man of few words, and they respect him.
Linda: You don't talk too much, you're just lively.

—Arthur Miller, *Death of a Salesman*

We all have sympathy for poor Willy Loman in *Death of a Salesman*. He knew he talked too much; but he couldn't figure out why and he couldn't stop talking too much, even though he wanted to be like Charley—a man of few words—who was respected by all.

When business developers talk too much, they generate too few clients. So why do those of us trying to develop business constantly find ourselves in a similar position? Perhaps because, like Willy Loman, we do not understand why we talk too much.

While many people do indeed talk too much during the business development process, on the other side of the spectrum others learn somewhere along the line that good business developers ask great questions. They then take the advice to an extreme and ask question after question, offering no advice and making the people on the other side feel like they're getting the third degree. So instead of talking too much, they're asking too many questions.

The key to talking and questioning each in the right amount comes in balancing advocacy (giving advice, talking) and inquiry (asking questions, finding out more, and letting the client have the airtime).

In RAIN, you now know the "A" stands for *aspirations* and *afflictions* and the "I" stands for *impact*. The "A" and the "I" do double duty, though, helping us to remember *advocacy* and *inquiry*.

"To your point about balancing advocacy and inquiry, when I first started with Accenture, a technology partner and I had a meeting to win a job with the CEO of the bank that is now JPMorgan Chase. We had 60 minutes. My teammate wanted 60 slides. No gaps. Solid content, solid talking. I wanted no more than five slides. We needed a conversation if we wanted to make a connection."

–Mike May, Professor at Babson College, former Co-Vice Chair of KPMG, and former Global Managing Partner of the strategy business for Accenture

N—New Reality

One of the greatest difficulties in rainmaking is helping potential clients to understand exactly what they get when they work with you and then communicating this benefit to other people involved in the buying decision. At the end of a well-managed sales process, your job is to create a new reality that will be the best for your client, given the client's specific aspirations and afflictions and the impact of doing (or not doing) something about them.

This process can start even before you have engaged your complete needs discovery and solution-crafting process. Ask prospects what they want the world to look like once your work is done. Broad questions that start them envisioning the future are a good way to get the creative juices flowing.

- At the end of this engagement, what will success look like?
- After working with us for six months, what do you see happening?
- What is your current service provider delivering in terms of creating the changes you need? Where are they falling short?
- What do you want to have happen as a result of our work together?
- What would a *Wall Street Journal* article say about you (your company, your group) three years from now?

Don't be surprised if the prospect's first answer to these questions is, "I don't know." More than likely she also will say, "That's a good question." If this happens, do not jump right in. Silence will indicate you expect an answer, and with some thought she will give you one. Prompt her if need be.

As much as possible, you should present this new reality in both qualitative (descriptive) terms and quantitative (financial measurement or other numerically based) terms.

Applying RAIN

Like any good conceptual model, RAIN Selling goes a lot deeper than how it looks on its face. The power of RAIN Selling is that you can apply it right away and have it make a difference. Good models, while having deep intrinsic value, are also easy to understand and apply.

Thus, the best way to get you started is to simply remember what the acronym RAIN stands for. Selling professional services (i.e., rainmaking) requires that you connect with a potential client (rapport), because professional services buyers often choose who they like the best; that you get a sense of where you can make a difference, either by solving their problems (afflictions) or by helping them innovate and grow (aspirations); that you help everyone involved in the buying process to understand the "so what?" (impact) of moving forward; and that you make tangible how the world will be different by painting a picture of a better future (new reality).

22 | Networking, Relationships, Trust, and Value

For it is mutual trust, even more than mutual interest, that holds human associations together. Our friends seldom profit us, but they make us feel safe.

—H. L. Mencken

Life Before BlackBerry . . .

Years ago, heading out of the office for a leisurely three-hour, three-martini lunch with professional colleagues wasn't so out of the ordinary. With no Internet, no e-mail, no cell phones, no fax machines, no BlackBerry, no video conferences, no webinars, and less complexity in our work lives, this kind of meeting not only was common, it was necessary.

In those days, especially since marketing for professional services was virtually unheard-of (or, in some cases, illegal), the core way to build a client base was by constructing a professional network comprised of either potential clients or potential referral sources. It was relatively easy to network in the old days, as there were significantly fewer distractions. You knew where to go, you met colleagues there, and you began business relationships, which, for better or worse, may have included gin, just a touch of dry vermouth, and a few olives.

Fast-forward to today. We have:

- Hundreds more professional networking options with conferences, associations, trade shows, seminars, technology-based meetings, technology communications methods, and the like.
- Greater awareness of both our markets and our competition. This increases our potential for professional networking because we can identify new people to meet, but it intimidates us because we feel like small fish in a much more competitive large pond.
- Many more demands on our time. We're expected to produce more, work longer hours, and contribute more to our offices than ever before and with fewer resources. It seems so long ago that everyone had a secretary (before the term *administrative assistant* even made sense to anyone) to answer phones, file, and manage calendars.
- Seemingly less emphasis placed on relationships and networking because we can now, of course, find just the professional we need by typing a few key terms into Google. Who needs to go meet people?
- Less practice interacting with people. Conversations that used to happen face-to-face, even on the same floor in the same office, happen over instant messaging or e-mail.

So we have less time to go out and interact, less time to maintain relationships if we start them, and more ability to find people and services quickly anyway. Why bother with the pain of networking at all?

The Outcome of Networking

It might seem to some like professional networking is a thing of the past, a dinosaur, a convention of slower times when relationships were more important than the ability to move fast and be flexible. As we struggle to produce deliverables on time, keep our teams and our tasks on track, or bill more hours, networking is often the first item that falls off the to-do list.

Given the reasons just listed, why bother building relationships? It takes a lot of time, you never know what results (if any) it will produce, and it is hard work for the majority of us who are not hardwired to be networkers and relationship builders.

Well, business evolves, but some things stay the same. Relationships are still the number one thing that separates the crème of the rainmaking crop from the also-rans.

In our interviews when researching *Professional Services Marketing* with top professional service leaders, we asked each leader two questions:

1. What is the key for those people who make the transition from top practitioner to rainmaker?
2. What is the key to making the transition from rainmaker to super-rainmaker, those stars that outperform the rest many times over?

The answer from all: relationships.

Paul Dunay, Global Director of Integrated Marketing at Bearing-Point, says:

I think if I have to sum it up in one word, it would be *relationships*—the ability to create them and keep them, and working their networks accordingly. The guys I know who are pulling in the tens of millions of dollars or the high upper-single-digit millions are masterful at starting, keeping, and extending those relationships.

When they become a rainmaker extraordinaire they take that up a notch. Their clients will take them around the C-suite at a Fortune 500 company and introduce them around. Ask them why their clients do this, and they say something like, "Because he's a businessperson and believes in what we do, believes in our brand promise. And he's a close friend." The top rainmakers create a relationship out of a deep trust and become a trusted advisor. The other people can't.

It's All about the Relationship

Networking is a means to an end, not an end in itself. That end is building and sustaining *relationships* with people. The word *networking* may bring to mind thoughts of busy bars with rapid-fire business card exchanges, insincere glad-handing, and constant elevator pitching. This isn't what we're talking about. When we refer to networking, we're talking about creating authentic and honest relationships. By focusing on how we can help others to succeed and prosper, we contribute to their success as well as our own. But first things first: We have to meet people of similar minds and similar business interests who will be good connections.

Are you familiar with the open-source computer operating system Ubuntu or the rallying cry of the Boston Celtics basketball team— "*Ubuntu, ubuntu, ubuntu!*"?[1] Derived from the African Bantu language, the word *ubuntu* roughly translates as "I am what I am because of what we are together." Whether you are a member of a sports team, a community group, or a business, the concept of *ubuntu* applies. It is a humanistic philosophy in which we achieve our potential through others by being unselfish, generous, and trustworthy. (See Figure 22.1.)

Networking

↓

Relationships

↓

Referrals

↓

New Business

Figure 22.1   Networking

---

[1] Author's note: "Go Celtics!"

The authentic relationship-based approach to networking is one that even the most introverted professional services practitioner can adopt and feel good about. *Ubuntu.*

Referrals top the list of how buyers find professional services providers. As we discussed in Chapter 1 (see Figure 1.1), in *How Clients Buy* we asked buyers of professional services how they initially identify potential service providers. Their top two answers were referrals and referrals:

1. Referrals from colleagues—79 percent of buyers are somewhat or very likely to find service providers this way.
2. Referrals from other service providers—75 percent of buyers are somewhat or very likely to find service providers this way.

Through networking and sustaining relationships, you are able to increase the likelihood of generating these valuable referrals.

What Is Networking?

If networking is so important, why do so many people avoid doing it? Many professional services providers simply fail to understand what networking is or the benefits it brings. We like the *American Heritage Dictionary* definition:

> **network** (*verb*): To interact or engage in informal communication with others for mutual assistance or support.[2]

Key to this definition is the concept of *mutual* benefit. Use this as your touchstone to remain focused on the positive (and effective) elements of networking.

---

[2] *The American Heritage Dictionary of the English Language*, 4th ed. (Boston: Houghton Mifflin, 2000).

WHAT NETWORKING IS AND IS NOT

Networking *is:*

- Building relationships *before* you need them—or laying the groundwork to produce good results.
- Building relationships with people you can help and who can also help you—it's as much about what you give as it is about what you get.
- Teaching people what you need from them and what they can expect to get from you in return—in other words, keeping the lines of communication open both ways.
- Trusting that if you put energy into your relationships, you will receive something in return—which means *not* keeping a precise scorecard.

Networking *is not:*

- Something you do *to* someone.
- Going to conferences and collecting a lot of business cards.
- Manipulating people to get them to work with you.

If you go into the process thinking that networking is just collecting business cards or reeling in favors, you'll be disappointed. Networking in its simplest form is first about giving, not about getting. (The more you give, though, the more you do get in return.)

Trust and the Building Blocks of Winning New Clients

To demonstrate how trust and networking work together, we will let John Doerr's early childhood memory serve as a trigger:

"Some of my most pleasant memories as a child are of playing with wood building blocks. Once I mastered the basics of stacking one block on top of another, my goal was always to build as high as I possibly could. Being the quick learner that I am, I soon discovered that the stronger the foundation, the higher each stage of my skyscraper could be. Sacrificing width for height (I had only so many blocks) would result in skyscraper collapse."

The same building-block rules apply to selling services: The stronger and broader the foundation of the relationship, the higher and sturdier your business development success. The question then becomes, "How do we build this foundation?" Especially, "how do we *begin* to build it with a prospect we meet for the first time?"

The building blocks of a strong service relationship are trust, need, solution, and value.

- **Trust:** Trust *begins* with the initial rapport (think RAIN Selling) that we develop with each person. We need a certain amount of rapport just to get a conversation started. As prospects begin to feel that we indeed are competent and professional, they will start to let us into their world. At this point, we can begin to uncover their needs.
- **Need:** It is with this block that we find out what kinds of needs our prospect might have in our general area of expertise. Often these needs exhibit themselves as pain or afflictions. But they can also be goals or aspirations for a brighter future. In either case, our job is to uncover as much need as we can in order to develop a solution.
- **Solution:** Once we have engaged in the conversation (or conversations) to uncover needs, we now can craft a solution. It is not a question of offering all the services we have available, but of offering only those that connect with the scope of the articulated needs. (This seems rather obvious; but, amazingly, many service providers cannot resist the urge to mention everything they offer, even though the prospect has shown zero interest in the additional services.) In order for our solution to be considered, we must then make the value tangible.
- **Value:** By engaging us to perform our services, what specific value will the client gain? This value can be articulated in dollars, in

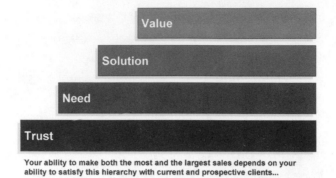

Your ability to make both the most and the largest sales depends on your
ability to satisfy this hierarchy with current and prospective clients...

Figure 22.2   Service Relationship Hierarchy

efficiencies, in quicker resolution of their problem, and in many
other ways. No matter what method you use, by being specific and
clear about your solution, you will make it easier for the prospect to
buy from you.

When we stack our blocks one on top of the other, we create and move
up the Service Relationship Hierarchy, shown in Figure 22.2.

> "What do you need to succeed at rainmaking? Interpersonal skills and
> analytics, in that order. I have hired thousands of people in my
> 30-some-year career. I've hired Rhodes scholars. I've hired brilliant
> geniuses. I even hired one guy who put his IQ on his resume. Why? I
> don't know. All of that is not a proxy for being successful in terms of
> getting in front of a client, making an impact, and making a sale. It's all
> around developing trust."
>
> —Mike May, Professor at Babson College, former Co-Vice Chair of KPMG, and former
> Global Managing Partner of the strategy business for Accenture

Each step of the hierarchy needs to be broader than the one above it in
order for you to be successful in selling your services.

- You certainly want to explain to the fullest how your solution offers maximum value. If you can't articulate the full value, you may not sell the full solution.
- You won't excel if you offer solutions beyond the stated and uncovered needs of the prospect. Clients won't (and shouldn't) buy superfluous services. You will probably even hinder the level of trust you've built.
- A certain extent of trust is necessary to simply begin to uncover needs. If prospects doubt you or suspect your motives, they won't typically be forthcoming with their real problems and goals.

Let's take a look at how the concept of the Service Relationship Hierarchy might appear in practice.

Consider this scenario:

You're a management consultant and you work with large businesses on strategy and innovation. You've had initial discussions with a new prospect. During conversations, you uncovered a number of needs for which you would be the perfect service provider. In fact, you have been so good at uncovering needs, this could be one of the biggest clients you have ever landed.

Even though you haven't had what you feel is enough interaction with the prospect, the needs are so clear and compelling that you craft your proposal (outlining your incredible solution) and construct a strong case for the value that your solution will provide. In total, the proposal is for $225,000 –a huge win for you, especially for a first project with a client.

You send the prospect the proposal and . . . voilà . . . you do *not* get the job. You are certain of the prospect's needs. You are confident of your solution and the value it will add. What happened?

> "What makes a good rainmaker? The ability to put yourself in the other person's shoes."
>
> —Ed Russ, Chief Marketing, Grant Thornton

When you think about it, you already know the answer. You were right about the needs, solution, and value. But you were also right about this being such a *big* win so early in the relationship. In essence, you were providing too much too early for such a new relationship. You had asked to be the trusted advisor to the tune of a $225,000 commitment at a point when you were just building an initial amount of trust with the prospect.

You were at this stage in the relationship: You had developed a fair amount of trust, but the uncovered needs and the proposed solution were far beyond the trust level you had established. You had not yet built a proper foundation to support the solution you had presented.

When the prospect received your proposal, the entire relationship toppled over, resulting in no $225,000 sale and maybe no further relationship with that prospect (see Figure 22.3).

Now consider an alternative:

- The need set is the same: $225,000 in services will be just right.
- You realize the client isn't ready to drop this much money on you to start, so you break the project into phases so you can prove the concept and prove that you are a top-notch and dependable service provider.
- Phase 1 is for $35,000—much more palatable for a new relationship.
- You close the deal and then succeed with flying colors in your delivery of Phase 1.

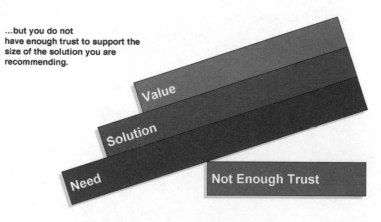

Figure 22.3   Losing the Sale!

After showing that you are reliable and competent by delivering a successful Phase 1, your trust looks like this:

The need is still the same (or possibly even greater now that you know the client so much better by performing Phase 1). However, you have now built the necessary trust in the process of delivering on your promise. This is the time to propose the solution and the value to meet the entire need your client has articulated.

As much fun as it is seeing wooden blocks collapse as a child, the collapse of a service relationship we are working so hard to build is no fun at all.

Think of the how you can build each relationship with your building blocks of trust, need, solution, and value. Your success in making both the most and the largest sales will grow as you develop your ability to satisfy the Service Relationship Hierarchy with current and prospective clients.

Yes, the pace of our work and personal lives leaves us with difficult challenges for building meaningful connections through our professional networks and relationships. But, as with most things, the more difficult a task, the fewer people will do it. This creates an opportunity for great success and career growth for those who make the effort to build a network filled with rich, rewarding, trusting relationships.

23 | Selling with Hustle, Passion, and Intensity

Take time to deliberate; but when the time for action arrives, stop thinking and go in.

—Napoleon Bonaparte

In our work with professional services providers over the years, we have seen more professionals intend to sell than we have seen *actually* sell. They talk about how they are going to make the transition to rainmaker and build their own practices or how they are going to achieve phenomenal, top-line revenue growth for their service firms through more focused business development efforts. They read books and attend seminars. They make plans to sell. They talk a good game.

Then many do nothing. Oh, they can justify their inaction: They were busy with other things. Perhaps worse than the nothing-doers are the people who shuffle papers or do *next* to nothing. These toe-dipper-inners deceive themselves by saying, "I did my practice growth work today!" even if their action was listless, untargeted, and unproductive.

If you really want to bring in some clients and some dollars, you've got to "stop thinking and go in"! With hustle. With passion. With intensity. (HPI, folks.) And your HPI needs to go on for hours on end. For days on end. For months on end.

If you don't, then you'll never know if you could have succeeded.

The ideas in this chapter were originally published as an article in a RainToday.com e-book, *The One Piece of Advice You Can't Sell Without*.

In the Introduction to *The One Piece of Advice You Can't Sell Without*, we commented:

"The concept is simple. We've read a lot of advice about selling professional services, and there are a lot of people who claim to know it all. But when you boil it all down, what's *really* important? What do you *need* to know? To answer this question, we asked 11 experts in selling professional services: *What is the one piece of advice you simply cannot sell without?*"

At the time we said, "We don't know, however, the nature of their contributions, as our editorial team has kept the submissions under lock and key. We are going to guess, though, that you might see good advice about building trust and relationships, communicating and selling the value of the solution versus the price of the service, listening, focusing on the best buyers, helping others to succeed, and a host of other topics."

We did get all this advice. It's all good advice. Take any one of these pieces of good advice away and your chances for success will be greatly diminished. Yet we contend that hustle, passion, and intensity supersede them all.

It was said by the Roman dramatist Seneca that "luck is when preparation meets opportunity." Everything just mentioned is about *preparation*. If you aren't trustworthy, you don't deserve the sale. If you don't sell the value, buyers will buy on price (or buy from someone else). If you don't focus on the best buyers and have a good business development plan, then you will spend all your time trying to sell to people who won't or can't buy. If you don't listen, you'll fall apart in so many ways that you won't know what hit you.

But if you don't stop thinking and go in, if you don't create *opportunities*, then you won't even have the chance to succeed (or fail) with all of your preparation.

SHOOT YOUR SHOTS, KNOCK 'EM STIFF

Another story from Mike's youth . . .

Starting when I was 12 and through my teens, I used to caddy and work in the bag room at Salem Country Club, a very nice private golf course in lovely Peabody, Massachusetts (go Tanners!).

There was this one member, a certain Mr. MacTavish (name changed to protect the guilty), who would come in seething about his round of golf. He was a former club champion and somewhere around a 2 handicap. He used to throw his clubs at us to clean them as he complained to his friends about that shot he missed on the 17th. "If I got up and down from the bunker, I would have had a good round. Damn lip on the bunker made me go from par to double bogey. Grrrrr . . . "

The man might have scored under par on 17 of the 18 holes, but he seemed about as happy as my dog at bath time, because he missed a shot. Of course, regardless of his mood, he didn't tip (MacTavish, not the dog).

Then there was Dr. Vontzalides (actual name used to praise the praiseworthy). He'd invariably come back from a round of golf in a good mood. "Did you see that shot I had on the 11th? Never knocked it so stiff from 175 yards before in my life." Of course Dr. Vontzalides was a terrible golfer—constant golf lessons notwithstanding—and might have scored 120 on the round if not for all his mulligans (for you nongolfers, a *mulligan* is a polite way of saying he took an uncounted do-over). And he always had two bucks for the kid.

Last week I was speaking with a professional at a major accounting firm. After nearly a decade in the profession, she is just now beginning to get started with business development and revenue generation. I told her the Dr. Vontzalides story for two reasons:

1. She was beating herself up for everything she tried that didn't seem to work.
2. She was playing only one hole at a time.

Right now her ability to succeed in business development is about as good as Dr. Vontzalides' ability to succeed on the course. She's new at it. She's going to have a lot of misses. Unlike accounting, where many accountants get virtually everything right every day, business development is fraught with dead ends and lost deals. It's just how it goes, and she needed to stop taking it so personally.

If she played 18 holes, new at this as she is, she'd knock it stiff to the pin from 175 here and there. However, she was playing only one hole at a time. I suggested to her that instead of making two phone calls over a two-day period, she should make 20 and send 20 e-mails, then join the board of a group she's already involved with and plan an event, contact 10 associations with a proposal for a speech at an upcoming event, and send five lunch invitations to business contacts she already has.

If she adds more activity, she'll give herself more chances of succeeding, while at the same time improving her skills with all the practice.

Then she can celebrate when fortune favors her with success, and forget about all the shots that didn't pan out (yet).

"People are reluctant to make that first call, but they shouldn't be. It's amazing how you don't get hurt if someone says, 'No.' They don't break your nose."

—Mike Sheehan, CEO, Hill Holliday

Kareem Abdul-Jabbar is the National Basketball Association's all-time scoring leader with 38,387 points. He hit 15,837 field goals in his career. He also missed 12,470. That's a 56 percent field goal percentage. (For those who don't know basketball, that's pretty darn good.) When he got the ball, he sure was *prepared*. Then again, he figured out a way to create 28,307 *opportunities* for himself.

How did he do that? He played 57,446 minutes in his career, almost 3,000 minutes more than anyone else. He was *in the game!*

Basketball is fun, though, you say? Selling not so much? Don't get us wrong—we understand why some service providers are squeamish about selling. They don't understand what it means to be in professional sales. They have competing priorities for their time. They're not sure if they have the skills to succeed. They're afraid of having sales conversations. They're afraid of failure. They're afraid of success. They're afraid!

If selling is truly a priority for you, and yet you're not taking the actions you need to sell, here's our best advice.

YOUR CHALLENGES TO SELLING WITH HPI

Challenge	Advice
You don't feel you have the best selling skills.	Read. Get training. Get a coach. Get practice. Then stop making excuses, use the skills that you have, and get in the game. Regardless of how much practice you've had, it is time for some game experience.
You are afraid of failure.	Talk to Tony Robbins. Find your inner strength. See what Stuart Smalley has to say this week. Then stop making excuses and get in the game. You're going to fail here and there, perhaps more often than you succeed. That's the nature of the beast.
You have too many competing priorities for your time. You don't have the hours available to	Change your priorities. Stop making excuses and get in the game.

(Continued)

Challenge	Advice
make calls, generate leads, write and speak, and so on.	
You are taking the actions; but in your heart of hearts, you know you're just going through the motions of marketing and selling. You're not really getting it done.	Stop making excuses and get in the game. Or get out of the game and do something else. There should be no halfway *in your head.* Commit, or don't.
You think selling is distasteful.	Do you believe that when people use your services, they're better for it? Do you believe that more people should be using your services versus other people's because they get more value with you? Selling is the process of bringing your value to more people. Now that we have that all cleared up, stop making excuses and get in the game.

If you get in the game and do the work with HPI, you'll likely figure out the *preparation* topics noted earlier. You'll find the right people to help you figure out your value and articulate it. You'll learn how to lead sales conversations with methodologies such as RAIN Selling. You'll figure out how to build trust the right way. (*Hint:* Start by being trustworthy and delivering on your promises.)

If you don't get passionate about business development, if you don't approach revenue growth and new client acquisition with HPI, you might just find yourself heavy on preparation (even if it might not feel that way) and light on opportunity.

It's been said that people will judge you by your actions, not your intentions. You may have a heart of gold—but so does a hard-boiled egg. Don't *intend* to sell. Sell!

Question: What is the one piece of advice you can't sell without?
Answer: Hustle, passion, and intensity (HPI). Everything else has a way of falling into place after that.

Now imagine if your entire team, your practice, and your firm were to engage this selling piece of advice for generating new clients with HPI. As Arlo Guthrie might put it, "They'd call it a movement."[1] Just think how much more successful your marketing efforts would become.

---

[1] See "Alice's Restaurant Massacree" by Arlo Guthrie (1967).

About Wellesley Hills Group

Recently named to *Inc.* magazine's list of the fastest growing firms in the United States, Wellesley Hills Group is a management consulting, marketing, and business development firm dedicated to helping professional services companies increase revenue, prices, and profits. Wellesley Hills Group helps clients in three core areas:

1. **Strategy and brand development:** Service firms are often at a loss for how to grow. They don't know what strategies or tactics will work; and when they do work, they often don't know how to make them most effective. We understand the distinct challenges of growing, branding, and managing a service business. Our core strategy and brand development services include helping our clients develop strategies for growth, craft marketing and business development plans, and research their clients and their markets.

2. **Marketing and lead generation:** Lead generation for business-to-business services is different from that for most other industries. We understand the unique dynamics of service businesses and know what tactics will be most effective to help you generate the leads, the revenue, the relationships, and the brand you need to grow. Our core services include helping our clients generate and nurture leads with our Services in Demand^{SM} program; craft and execute brands and core marketing messages; build and execute web site and Internet

321

marketing strategies; and become thought leaders through thought leadership development, marketing, and public relations (PR).

3. **Sales training and performance improvement:** Making the transition from service provider to rainmaker, balancing your responsibility between delivering services and selling services, and creating a culture of business development at your service firm are all challenging tasks. We work with leaders, professionals, business developers, and marketers to help them create a business development culture while giving them and their team the sales skills and tools they need to succeed. Professional services firms turn to our Rainmaker Development Program^{SM} to help their professionals develop the skills and get the coaching and support they need to become leaders in new business and client development.

Wellesley Hills Group is committed to providing the freshest insight, research, and ideas to professional services leaders, business developers, and marketers through publishing articles, white papers, the *Services Marketing Blog* and *Newsletter,* and research. The Wellesley Hills Group publishes RainToday.com, the premier site for marketing and sales for professional services.

To learn more about Wellesley Hills Group, visit www.whillsgroup .com.

About RainToday.com

Published by Wellesley Hills Group, RainToday.com is the premier online source for insight, advice, and tools for growing your service business. RainToday.com's offerings include:

- **Annual Membership** to RainToday.com that brings you the freshest insights, tools, and advice to help you grow your service business.
- **Free newsletter** with articles by well-respected marketing, sales, and service business experts such as Mike Schultz, John Doerr, Patrick McKenna, Michael McLaughlin, Jill Konrath, Andrew Sobel, Bruce W. Marcus, and Charles Green on core topics in selling and marketing professional services.
- **Best practice and benchmark research,** such as *What's Working in Lead Generation, How Clients Buy*, and *Fees and Pricing Benchmark Report* by analysts and experts at RainToday.com.
- **Case studies** on what's working in marketing and selling professional services.
- **Interviews** with world-renowned services marketers, rainmakers, and firm leaders.
- **Premium content, templates, and tools** designed specifically for helping services providers to grow their firms.
- **Podcast series** on marketing and selling professional services.

- **Webinars, seminars, conferences, and events** for rainmakers and marketers.

RainToday.com Membership

Membership brings you insights, tools, and advice to help you grow your service business. With annual membership you have unlimited access to exclusive members-only premium content, how-to guides and tools, article archives, and webinars. Learn more: www.RainToday.com/Membership .cfm.

Rainmaker Report—Free Weekly Newsletter

Rainmaker Report, RainToday.com's free weekly newsletter, provides proven tactics to market and sell professional services from rainmakers, firm leaders, and your fellow services marketers worldwide. Visit www.raintoday.com to subscribe.

RainToday.com Research

The RainToday.com Research team produces best practices and benchmarking research to help marketers, sellers, and leaders of professional services firms grow their business. The RainToday.com Research team delivers custom market and client research studies for individual organizations.

For a complete list of available research titles, visit www.raintoday.com/ RTStore.cfm.

About the Authors

Mike Schultz, Publisher, RainToday.com

Mike Schultz is Co-President of the Wellesley Hills Group and consults with professional services firms worldwide. As its publisher, Mike is responsible for leading RainToday.com, the world's foremost content publication on growth strategy, marketing, and selling for professional services firms.

Mike is an engaging and thought-provoking speaker, delivering dozens of keynote talks each year in-house for clients and at leading industry conferences. He has also written over a hundred articles, research reports, and other publications in the areas of marketing and selling for professional services.

An avid fly fisherman, golfer, and skier, Mike holds an MBA in marketing and entrepreneurship from Babson College. Mike actively teaches Seirenkai karate and jujitsu, holding the ranks of third-degree black belt and sensei.

John Doerr, Co-President, Wellesley Hills Group

John Doerr's extensive career in professional services has included senior executive management, business development and marketing, and product and service development. As Co-President of the Wellesley Hills Group, he works closely with clients to develop marketing and growth strategies that produce measurable and sustainable results.

John also provides executive and business development coaching for lawyers, accountants, and consultants. He speaks on the subject of professional development marketing and selling for clients and conferences throughout the world.

John's international experience includes a stint in Brussels, Belgium, where he was president of Management Centre Europe, the largest pan-European management development and training services firm in Europe. In addition, he has consulted and spoken at numerous events in Europe, including a three-year run as chair of Management Centre Turkiye's Human Resources Conferences in Istanbul.

John holds an MBA, magna cum laude, from the Graduate School of Management at Boston University, and an AB, summa cum laude, Phi Beta Kappa, from Boston College.

Index

A.G. Edwards, 173
Abdul-Jabbar, Kareem, 316–317
Accenture, xxi, 94, 125, 117
　advertising, 231
　brand, 98
　market messaging, 184–190
　value proposition strength, 131
Accessibility, 168
Accounting:
　brand attributes and, 124
　pricing structure, 55
　revenues and fees, 13
ACT!, 288
Advertising, 230–232
　revenues and fees, 13
All Marketers Are Liars, 144
Amplification effect, 145–147
Analysis, marketing planning and, 26–27
Andersen Consulting, 125
Appreciation, thought leadership and, 206
Architectural Digest, 138
Architecture:
　pricing structure, 55
　revenues and fees, 13
Articles, 234–236, 262
Assets, 143–144
　amplification effect, 145–147
　barriers to brand and revenue, 147–149
　building an army of brand advocates,
　　149–150
　client market and research, 144–145
　innovation opportunities, 147
Assignment, performance culture and, 87–88
Assumptions:
　marketing planning and, 26–27
　outcomes, 41–44
　playing with, 44–46
Audits, marketing and revenue, 23, 24–25
Aurelius, Marcus, 139
Awareness:
　top-of-mind, 102, 108
　unaided vs. aided, 102

Bain, value proposition strength and, 131
Bank of America, 173
Bank of New York Mellon, 173
BANT (budget, authority, need, time frame),
　252–253

BearingPoint, value proposition strength and,
　131
Beckhart, Richard, 204
Belafonte, Harry, 79
Bell, Alexander Graham, 39
Benchmark Report on Fees and Pricing in Professional
　Services, xx
Bennis, Warren, 204
BHAG (big, hairy, audacious goal), 21
Billable hour, death of, 56
Blink, xxi
Bonaparte, Napoleon, 313
Books, 238–241, 262
Boston Business Journal, 156–158
Boston Celtics, 304
Boston Consulting Group (BCG), value proposition
　strength and, 131
Boston Private, 173
BPM Forum, 271
Brainstorming, marketing planning and,
　25–26
Brand:
　advocates and skeptics, 93–94
　attributes, 121–122
　　Bain's advantage, 132–134
　　building blocks, 134–138
　　Everon and, 128–129
　　strength of value proposition, 123–128
　building, 177–178
　　how to think about, 179–184
　client perspectives, 102–104
　company value, 100
　competition, 99
　defining, 100–102
　establishing and strengthening, 12–13
　facilitating repeat business, 99
　fee maximization, 62–63
　　premium fees, 98–99
　foundation of value proposition messaging,
　　112–119
　generating leads, 96–98
　perceptions vs. misconceptions, 106
　promise statement, 133, 180
　sales effectiveness, 95–96
　Service Brand Strategy Model, 151
　top talent, 8
　reach and reputation, 62–63
　what buyers want to know, 106–112

327

Brand RAMP (recognize, articulate, memorize, prefer), 153–156
  articles, 234–235
  articulate, 158–159
  direct mail, 216, 218
  impact on lead generation, 254
  increasing number of leads, 48
    qualified leads, 49
  memorize, 159–161
  prefer, 161–162
  public speaking, 244
  recognize, 156–158
  seminars, 241
  trade shows, 227
  writing books, 239
Brown Brothers Harriman, 173
BtoB, 271
Budget Planning Tool, 30
The Business Impact of Publishing a Book, xx, 207–208, 239
Business management, 168
BusinessWeek, 234
Buzzword bingo, 75

Cahners Advertising Research Report (CARR), 153
Cahners Research, 272
Capabilities:
  articulation of, 102
  delivering, 140
Capture mechanisms, 48
Carson, Johnny, 108
Case study, 262
Category, Law of, 171–172
CBS Evening News, 233
Charles Schwab, 173
CIMS Business Influencer Study, 10
Circadian Technologies, 181
Citigroup, 173
Citizens Bank, 173
Clichés, 74–75
Collaboration, graphic design and, 192
Commitment:
  vs. compliance, 34
  marketing planning, 28–29
Communication:
  brand, 101
  value, 293
  See also specific types of communication
Competencies, delivering, 141–143
Competition, 69–70, 76
  brand, 99
  fee maximization and focus on, 66
  mistakes
    clichés, 74–75
    client indifference, 75
    competitive differentiation, 71
    crowded markets, 72–74
    excessive research, 70
    ignoring marketing advice, 71–72
    market and service offering reluctance, 70
    shift focus to clients, 74
    unique methodology, 71
Compliance, cautions about, 34
Conferences, moving beyond, 5–6. *See also specific types*

Consequences:
  intellectual capital, 201
  performance culture, 84–86
Construction, pricing structure, 55
Consultation, 262
  pricing structure, 55
  revenues and fees, 13
Cooch, Michael, 128
Cost saving analysis, 158
Credibility, 116. *See also* Substantiation, ability and
Cross-selling, 12
Crowded markets, 72
Czerniawska, Fiona, 197

Database population, 48
Davenport, Tom, 200
Death of a Salesman, 298
Deep dive messaging, 180, 189
Defensibility, intellectual capital and, 201–202
Deliver, 212, 215
Delivery, fee maximization and, 64–65
Dell, 73
Demand:
  Metrics of Services in Demand, 41, 42, 45
  Services in Demand, 11, 133, 321
Differentiation:
  Bain, 132
  brand, 103, 113, 116
  increasing number of leads, 48
Dilbert, 95
Direct mail, 216, 218–219
Disclosure, fee maximization and, 65–66
Distinction:
  attributes of, 137
  differentiation and overall, 132
  intellectual capital, 200–203
Doerr, John, 306–307
Doubt. *See* FUD (fear, uncertainty, and doubt)
Drucker, Peter:
  intellectual capital, 202
  measurable outcomes of marketing, 1, 15
  sustained lead generation, 265
  thought leadership, 196, 204
Drucker Foundation, 199
Dun & Bradstreet, 281, 285
Dunay, Paul:
  amplification effect, 147
  building an army of brand advocates, 149
  differentiation, 166
  intellectual capital, 201
  lead generation, 262
  networking, 303
  sustained lead generation, 277

Eastern Bank, 173
Edward Jones, 173
Einstein, Albert, 27
Eisenhower, Dwight, 17
Elegance, intellectual capital and, 202
Elevator pitch, 133, 180, 183
E-mail, 221–223
Emerson, Ralph Waldo, 177, 193
Engineering:
  pricing structure, 55
  revenues and fees, 13

Entry service, 262
Environment, execution and, 36
Ernst & Young, 181
Evaluating the Cost of Sales Calls in Business to Business Markets,
 259, 260
Everon Technology Services, 128–129
 taglines, 182
Expectations, performance culture and, 81—82, 83
Experience, attributes of, 138
Experts, need for, 34–35

Facebook, 225
Fear. *See* FUD (fear, uncertainty, and doubt)
FedEx, 181
Feedback, performance culture and, 81–82, 83
Fees:
 brands generating premium, 98
 contingent, 60–61
 fixed, 58–59
  vs. value-based pricing, 59–60
 hourly and daily, 55–58
 maximizing, 61–67
 Median Hourly Billing Rates, 98
Fees and Pricing Benchmark Reports, 13, 96
Fidelity Investments, 173
Fiduciary Trust International, 173
Financial services:
 advisory firms and Law of Opposite, 171
 revenues and fees, 13
Fit, 168
Ford, Henry, 289
FUD (fear, uncertainty, and doubt), brand and,
 12–13, 15

Gallup Consulting, 81
Gates, Bill, 196
"Getting the Most Out of All Your Customers," 274
Ghostwriting, 236
Gladwell, Malcolm, xxi
GlaxoSmithKline, 73
Glenn, Mary, 210
Goals, marketing plan and firm, 22–23
Godin, Seth, 144, 196
Goethe, Johann Wolfgang von, 195
Goldman Sachs, 173
Goldsmith, Marshall, 199, 204
Google:
 brand messaging, 106
 SEO, 246
 weighting, 234
Graphic design, 190–194
 identity, collateral presentations and, 229
Gross, T. Scott, 172
Growth rate, improving per retained client, 50
Guthrie, Arlo, 319

Hagen, Walter, 17
Harter, Jim, 81
Harvard Business Review, 128, 175, 233, 234, 263, 274
Heinz, H.J., 121, 137
Hemingway, Ernest, 105
Heskett, James, 175
Hesselbein, Frances, 204
Holland and Hart, 182
Hoover's, 281, 285

How Clients Buy. 2009 Benchmark Report on Professional Services
 Marketing and Selling from the Client Perspective, xviii, 3,
 75
How Important Is the Reputation of a Brand Name?, 153
How to Market Training and Information, 243, 273
HP, 73
HPI (hustle, passion, intensity), selling with, 313–319
Hustle:
 competition, 75
 selling with, 313–319

IBM, 13
Identity, 179, 180
Impact, 168
Implementation, marketing planning, 29–30
Impressions, Brand RAMP and, 160–161
Incentives, performance culture and, 84–86
Industry practices, 180
InfoUSA, 281, 285
Integrity, 291–293
Intellectual capital:
 assets, 143
 exposure of, 197–199
 quality of, 197–199, 200–203
Intensity, selling with, 313–319
Internet marketing, value proposition and, 130
IT consultants, Law of Opposite and, 171

Janeway, Katherine, 94
Jigsaw, 285, 287
John Hancock, 173
Johnson, Spencer, 202
Jones, Bobby, 17
JPMorgan, 173

Kellogg's Eggo Waffles, 181
Knowledge, performance culture and, 86–87
Kotler, Philip, 174

Law firms:
 Law of Opposite, 171
 pricing structure, 55
 revenues and fees, 13
Lead generation:
 characteristics of a qualified, 252–253
 conversion to clients, 49–50
 converting potential buyers into clients, 249–251
 demonstrating value, 258–260
 engine and fee maximization, 63
 expectations, 252–253
  brand RAMP, 254
  long-term leads, 254
  short-term leads, 253
 increasing, 48–49
  qualified, 49
 intangibility of services and, 260–262
 seven rules for, 254–255
 sustained, 265–266
  being remembered through, 270
  current clients, marketing to, 273–276
  difficulty and importance of, 266–269
  limitations and possibilities, 276–278
  nurturing preexisting leads, 271–273
 tactics, 211–216, 217
 using offers and experiences, 262, 263–264

Leavitt, Theodore, 163
Legg Mason, 173
LinkedIn, 225, 287
Loyalty Rules, 175

Macfarlane, Willie, 17
MacMillan, Ian, 128
Marketing audits. *See* Audits, marketing and revenue
Marketing and Sales Funnel Analysis Tool, 30–31
Market share, being the leader in, 174–175
May, Mike, xxi, 94
    assets, 144
    RAIN Selling, 299
    strength of value proposition, 125
    substantiation, 117
    trust, 308
McGraw-Hill Publishing Company, 93, 95, 96, 210
McMurdo, Kevin, xxi
    billable hours, 57
    brand and communication, 101
    coalition of willing, 91
    marketing communication, 126
    performance culture, 82
    RAIN Selling, 292
    targeting, 285
    thought leadership, 197
    visibility in targeted markets, 46
    web sites, 110
    winning new clients, 9
Median Hourly Billing Rates. *See* Fees, Median Hourly
        Billing Rates
Memorization, brand and, 102
Mencken, H.L., 301
Mercedes-Benz, 181
Merck, 73
Merrill Lynch, 173
Messaging, market, 177–178
    cascade, 184–190
    graphic design, 190–194
Methology, unique, 71
Metrics of Services in Demand. *See* Demand, Metrics of
        Services in Demand
Microsoft CRM, 288
Miller, Arthur, 298
Mind-set, thought leader, 203–204
Monitor Group, value proposition strength and, 131
Monopolies:
    characteristics of, 72–73
    competition and, 72
Monty Python and the Holy Grail, 90
Morgan Stanley, 173
Motivation:
    performance culture, 88–89
    thought leader, 203–204
Mover advantage, first, 172–173
MSN, 246

National Basketball Association, 316
Netsuite, 288
Networking, 223–225
    defined, 305–306
    outcome of, 302–303
    social, 225–226
Nike, 181
Northwestern University, 163–164

Ockham's Razor, 193
OfficeAutopilot, 288
Oligopoly, competition and, 72, 73
One-pager, 180
The One Piece of Advice You Can't Sell Without, 314
Opposite, Law of, 170–171
Oppositioning, 116
Oracle, 288
Outcomes, measurable, 1–2
    affinity with workforce, 2, 6, 9–11
    making assumptions about, 41–44
    new buyers
        engaging conversations with, 2–7
        winning, 7–11

Packaging, service, 11
PaineWebber, 173
Passion, selling with, 313–319
Performance readiness, lack of, 80–89
Personalization, 179, 180
Peters, Tom, 196
Pipeline opportunity, brand and, 108, 109
Planning, marketing, 17–18
    cautions about
        building from top down, 34
        changes, failing to plan for, 36–37
        execution, not prioritizing, 36
        expertise, ignoring tactical, 34–35
        inspiration, limiting sources of, 35
        marketing committees, 37–38
    preceding business plan, 18–21
    process, 21
        alignment with goals, 22–23
        analysis and assumptions, 26–27
        brainstorming, 25–26
        final plan and adoption, 28–29
        implementation, 29–30
        marketing and revenue audit, 23–25
        straw man plan, 27–28
    tools, 30–31
Plaxo, 225
Podcast, 262
Porter, Michael, 196
Positioning:
    brand, 109–110, 111–112, 113
    key components of, 185–186
    marketing messages cascade, 178–189
Preferences:
    brand, 103
    performance culture, 88–89
Presentation:
    identity, collateral, 228–230
    intellectual capital, 202
PricewaterhouseCoopers, 35
Pricing:
    basic landscape of structure, 53–61, 67–68
    maximization, 54–55
    value-based, 59
        employment of, 66–67
    See also Fees
Professional services firm, wasted spending on, 39–41
Professional Services Marketing, 303
Prudence, 168
Prudential Financial, 173
Prusak, Larry, 200

Publicity, 232–234
Public relations, revenues and fees, 13
Purchase intent, brand and, 108, 109
"Putting the Service–Profit Chain to Work,"
    175

RAIN Selling, 289–291
    applying, 300
    basics of, 293–294
        advocacy and inquiry, 298
        aspirations and afflictions, 295–297
        impact, 297
        new reality, 299–300
        rapport, 294
    HPI and, 318
    integrity and, 291–293
RainToday.com:
    brand, 97
    changing times, 3
    overview, 323–324
    substantiation, 117–118
RAMP (recognize, articulate, memorize, prefer).
        See Brand RAMP
RBC Dain Rauscher, 173
Realism, intellectual capital and, 202
Reality, disconnection with, 89–91
Referrals, 48
    moving beyond, 2–3
Reicheld, Fred, 175
Relationship management, 168, 304–305
Relevance, intellectual capital and, 201
Reliability, 168
Repeat business:
    brand, 99
    moving beyond, 2–3
Reputation, reach, 97
Research, 35, 168, 262. *See also specific methods*
Resonance:
    emotional and performance
        Bain, 132
        brand, 103, 113–115
        taglines, 181, 183
    increasing number of leads, 48
Resources, performance culture and, 82, 84
Retention, financial effects, 274
Return on investment (ROI):
    brand, 95
    graphic design, 191
    Marketing and Sales Funnel Analysis Tool for,
        31
    performance resonance, 114
    targeting, 287
    wasted spending, 40
Revenue:
    being the leader in, 174–175
    increasing per client, 50
    retention, 42–43
    increasing, 50
    seven levers to increase, 47–50
    See also Fees; Pricing
Revenue audits. *See* Audits, market and revenue
Ries, Al, 170, 172, 173
Ries, Laura, 172, 173
RightNow, 288
Rogers, Martha, 206–207

Russ, Ed, 258
    Brand RAMP, 162
    RAIN Selling, 297
    relationships, 309
Russ, Edmond, xxi

Sales call, 262
Saleslogix, 288
SalesView, 285
Salience, intellectual capital and, 200–201
Sarbanes–Oxley, 134
Satisfaction, fee maximization and client, 64, 65
Scarcity, perception of, 132
Schrello, Don, 243, 273
Schultz, Mike, 115
Schulz, Charles, 211
Search engine advertising (SEA), 246–248
Search engine optimization (SEO), 246–248
Selden, Larry, 128
Selection, performance culture and, 87, 88
Seminars, 5–6, 241–244, 262
Seneca, 314
Service Brand Strategy Model. *See* Brand, Service Brand
        Strategy Model
Service-level agreements (SLAs), fixed-fee pricing and,
        58
Service lines, 180
The Service Profit Chain, xx
Service Relationship Hierarchy, 308, 309, 311
Services in Demand. *See* Demand, Services in Demand
Services Insider Blog, 322
Sheehan, Mike, xxi
    changing times, 6
    confronting barriers to brand and revenue, 148
    HPI and, 316
    marketing planning and, 25–26
    RAIN Selling and, 295
    selection and assignment, 88
    sustained lead generation and, 268
    taglines, 181
Similarity, attributes of, 136–137
Skills, performance culture and, 86–87
Smith, Steve, 5
Smith, Thomas, 160–161
Southwest Airlines, 181
Sovereign Bank, 173
Speaking, 244–246, 262
    rates, 206–207
Spoke, 225, 287
Stewart, Potter, 202
Stockdale, James, 139
Strategic business unit (SBU), implementing a
        marketing plan and, 29
Strategy consultants, Law of Opposite and, 171
Straw man, 27, 28
Substantiation:
    ability, 116–117, 133
    brand, 103, 110–112, 113
    increasing number of leads, 48
    marketing messages cascade, 180, 183–190
SugarCRM, 288

Tagline, 180–182
    common themes for, 183
Talent, brand and, 100

Targeting:
  best prospects, 279–280
  contact information, 286–288
  database development, 280–283
  market knowledge, 283–284
  number and quality, 47–48
  sample profile, 285–286
  visibility and, 46
TD Banknorth, 173
TD Waterhouse, 173
Teaching, 168
Telephone, 219–221
Teleseminars, 243–244, 262
Thin slicing, xxi
Thoreau, Henry David, 53, 170
Thought leadership, 195–197
  expectations, 204–208
  keys to, 197–199
  mind-set and motivation, 203–204
  pillars of, 200–203
  research results, 208–210
Timex, 181
Tools, performance culture and, 82, 84
Toyota, 73
Trade shows, 226–228
  increasing number of leads, 48
Trout, Jack, 170
Trust:
  building through marketing, 10
  transferred, 3, 5
  winning new clients with, 306–311
Twitter, 225, 287

U.S. Open, 17
Uncertainty. See FUD (fear, uncertainty, and doubt)
Uniqueness, 163–165
  client wants, 166–169
  competition, 71
  selling propositions (USPs), 164–165
    labels, 165–166
University of Chicago, 164
URL landing page, 287
USAA, 175

Value:
  fee maximization and focus on, 67–68

proposition
  communicating a strong, 12
  defined, 111
  delivery, 109, 122
  foundation of developing, 112–119
  increasing number of leads and, 48
  research, 141–142
  strength, 122–134
  in selling, 63–64
Value-based pricing. See Pricing, value-based
Vanity exercises, 40
Viewpoint, brand and, 103
VW, 73

Wainwright Bank, 173
Walletshare, 275
Wall Street Journal, 22–23, 43, 233, 234, 299
Wanamaker, John, 156
Webcast, 262
Webinars, 243–244
Web sites:
  increasing number of leads, 48
  substantiation and brand messaging, 110
Weiss, Alan, 238
Welch, Jack, 174
Wellesley Hills Group:
  brand, 97, 98
  changing times, 3
  fee maximization and value focus, 68
  overview, 321–322
  performance culture, 79
  substantiation, 117–118
Wendy's, 231
What's the Big Idea: Creating and Capitalizing on the Best Management Thinking, 200
What's Working in Lead Generation, xx, 62, 79, 97, 212, 237, 282
White papers, 236–238, 262
Will, lack of, 91–92
Williams, Robin, 85
Woods, Tiger, 188, 231
Word ownership, 173–174

Yahoo!, 246
Yellow Pages, 72

ZoomInfo, 285